The Smithsonian Guides to Natural America
THE PACIFIC NORTHWEST

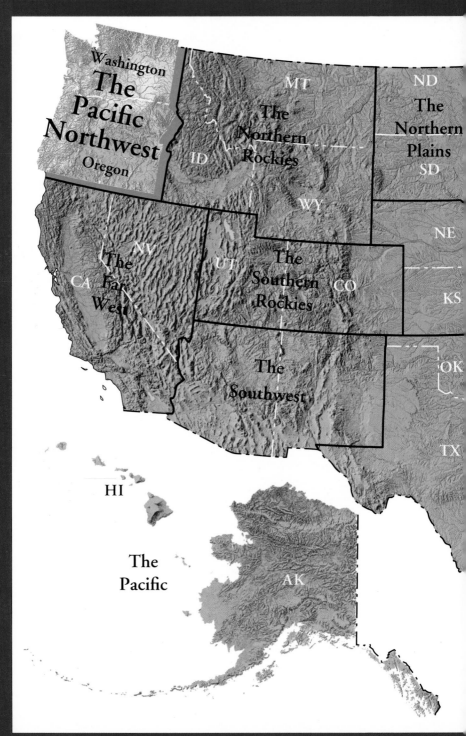

MN

WI

MI

The
Great
Lakes

IA

The
Heartland

IL

IN

OH

MO

Central
Appalachia

KY

WV

The
Atlantic
Coast

VA

NC

TN

The
South
Central
States

AR

MS

AL

GA

The
Southeast

SC

LA

FL

Northern
New
England

ME

VT

NH

NY

The
Mid-Atlantic
States

MA
CT RI

Southern
New
England

PA

NJ

DE

MD

THE PACIFIC NORTHWEST
WASHINGTON- OREGON

THE SMITHSONIAN GUIDES TO NATURAL AMERICA

THE PACIFIC NORTHWEST

WASHINGTON AND OREGON

TEXT
Daniel Jack Chasan

PHOTOGRAPHY
Tim Thompson

PREFACE
Thomas E. Lovejoy

SMITHSONIAN BOOKS • WASHINGTON, D.C.
RANDOM HOUSE • NEW YORK, N.Y.

Front cover: Mount Shuksan, North Cascades National Park, Washington
Half-title page: Great horned owl
Frontispiece: Summer wildflowers, Gifford Pinchot National Forest, Washington
Back cover: Harbor seal; Ecola State Park, Washington; great horned owl

THE SMITHSONIAN INSTITUTION
SECRETARY I. Michael Heyman
COUNSELOR TO THE SECRETARY FOR
BIODIVERSITY AND ENVIRONMENTAL AFFAIRS Thomas E. Lovejoy
DIRECTOR, SMITHSONIAN PRESS/SMITHSONIAN PRODUCTIONS Daniel H. Goodwin
EDITOR, SMITHSONIAN BOOKS Alexis Doster III

THE SMITHSONIAN GUIDES TO NATURAL AMERICA
SERIES EDITOR Sandra Wilmot
MANAGING EDITOR Ellen Scordato
PHOTO EDITOR Mary Jenkins
ART DIRECTOR Mervyn Clay
ASSISTANT PHOTO EDITOR Ferris Cook
ASSISTANT PHOTO EDITOR Rebecca Williams
EDITORIAL ASSISTANT Seth Ginsberg
COPY EDITORS Helen Dunn, Karen Hammonds
FACT CHECKER Jean Cotterell
PRODUCTION DIRECTOR Katherine Rosenbloom

Library of Congress Cataloging-in-Publication Data
Chasan, Daniel Jack
  The Smithsonian guides to natural America. The Pacific Northwest—
Washington and Oregon/text, Daniel Jack Chasan; photography, Tim
Thompson; preface, Thomas E. Lovejoy.
    p. cm.
  Includes bibliographical references (p. 254) and index.
  ISBN 0-679-76313-9 (pbk.)
  1. Natural history—Washington (State)—Guidebooks. 2. Natural
history—Oregon—Guidebooks. 3. Washington (State)—Guidebooks.
4. Oregon—Guidebooks. I. Thompson, Tim. II. Title
QH105.W2C48 1995   95-1485
508.795—dc20   CIP

Manufactured in the United States of America
98765432

How to Use This Book

The SMITHSONIAN GUIDES TO NATURAL AMERICA explore and celebrate the preserved and protected natural areas of this country that are open for the public to use and enjoy. From world-famous national parks to tiny local preserves, the places featured in these guides offer a splendid panoply of this nation's natural wonders.

Divided by state and region, this book offers suggested itineraries for travelers, briefly describing the high points of each preserve, refuge, park or wilderness area along the way. Each site was chosen for a specific reason: Some are noted for their botanical, zoological, or geological significance, others simply for their exceptional scenic beauty.

Information pertaining to the area as a whole can be found in the introductory sections to the book and to each chapter. In addition, specialized maps at the beginning of each book and chapter highlight an area's geography and geological features as well as pinpoint the specific locales that the author describes.

For quick reference, places of interest are set in **boldface** type; those set in **boldface** followed by the symbol ❖ are listed in the Site Guide at the back of the book. (This feature begins on page 259, just before the index.) Here noteworthy sites are listed alphabetically by state, and each entry provides practical information that visitors need: telephone numbers, mailing addresses, and specific services available.

Addresses and telephone numbers of national, state, and local agencies and organizations are also listed. Also in appendices are a glossary of pertinent scientific terms and designations used to describe natural areas; the author's recommendations for further reading (both nonfiction and fiction); and a list of sources that can aid travelers planning a guided visit.

The words and images of these guides are meant to help both the active naturalist and the armchair traveler to appreciate more fully the environmental diversity and natural splendor of this country. To ensure a successful visit, always contact a site in advance to obtain detailed maps, updated information on hours and fees, and current weather conditions. Many areas maintain a fragile ecological balance. Remember that their continued vitality depends in part on responsible visitors who tread the land lightly.

C O N T E N T S

PART II OREGON

PREFACE

The Pacific Northwest region of natural America lived in my fantasies from early childhood. Vivid *National Geographic* photographs of Washington State's Olympic rain forest, festooned with garlands of moss, cast upon me a verdant spell like a veritable Brigadoon. Decades would pass before I finally was to hike in this temperate equivalent of the tropical forests where I spend so much time, and find, indeed, that the photographs had not deceived.

Winds and the lay of ocean currents contribute the moisture for the biological paradise of the western slope of the Cascades. The price to be paid for this treasure is fewer sunny days than cloudy, but the lush vegetation brought by the rain makes this seem a small price to pay.

Today these forests have become an environmental caricature in which the jobs of workers in the timber industry seem to have been pitted against the northern spotted owl, a phantom that floats on ghostly quiet wings. The story, of course, is more complex than that and really involves the myriad plant and animal species of the old-growth forest and an old-growth timber supply rapidly headed to exhaustion. I can but hope that the bitterness will wane, and more and more people will experience the exuberant biology that reached out to me in those photographs.

Concerns about conservation have a long history in the Pacific Northwest. Theodore Roosevelt, perhaps our greatest conservation president, did much to protect the natural wealth of Oregon and Washington, including establishing a national monument on the Olympic Peninsula to protect a species of deer that ultimately became known as Roosevelt elk. Later, Franklin Delano Roosevelt built on that effort, and, in 1938,

PRECEDING PAGES: *With a mist still softening the coastal sea stacks and rocky headlands, the sky above Oregon's Cannon Beach clears after a storm.*

Congress created Olympic National Park. Other preserves of the Northwest read like a who's who of the history of American conservation: Camp Muir, Gifford Pinchot National Forest, and the William O. Douglas and Henry M. Jackson wilderness areas.

This region of natural America also features spectacular coasts and abundant marine life: Puget Sound and a myriad of islands; a molluscan cornucopia that includes the awesome geoduck; dramatic sea stacks; tidal pools brimming with life; and too-big-to-be-true starfish in designer colors. It is a place for marking the annual passage of gray whales as they make their way south to now protected calving grounds in Baja California and for watching a pod of toothy killer whales cavort in sparkling seas. At Grays Harbor, Washington, shorebirds form spectacular congregations at this key migration stopover.

On clear days, the Cascades preside with grandeur over all of this, with their snow-covered peaks and slumbering volcanoes: Mounts Rainier, Hood, Baker, St. Helens, plus Adams, Jefferson, and Washington. It is particularly appropriate that Jefferson is among them, for it was this gentleman-scholar president who had the vision to send the Lewis and Clark expedition across unknown wilderness to this part of the continent. There was no Smithsonian. Had there been, Jefferson would probably have become its secretary after leaving 1600 Pennsylvania Avenue. In any case, specimens from this expedition with labels in the handwriting of the great explorers themselves were deposited in America's oldest museum, the Academy of Natural Sciences of Philadelphia, where they remain to this very day. In the streams of the Cascades, now as then, the American dipper or water ouzel, a peculiar bird, is as much at home walking along the stream bottom as perching on a rock.

Farther east, beyond the Cascades themselves, lies drier country, where erosion lays bare such prominent treasures as the fossil tree remains at Ginkgo Petrified Forest State Park. The country's drainage is to the west, through the Columbia River

Gorge and, ultimately, to the sea. The Columbia and other rivers were once the scene of spectacular migrations of salmon upstream to their spawning grounds. Pacific salmon runs now represent an enormous conservation challenge, having been reduced dramatically by hydroelectric projects, habitat degradation from forestry practices, and heavy fishing pressure at sea. Salmon ladders help adults make it upstream past the barriers of dams, but the altered flow of the river hinders young fingerlings as they attempt to follow their primal urge seaward. To the south of the Columbia, Oregon packs in its own natural wonders: the Coast Range; Crater Lake, the deepest in the United States; the spectacular Oregon Dunes, humbling in their immensity; and the Big Obsidian Flow.

The Pacific Northwest offers important signs of hope for the future of natural America. The slopes of Mount St. Helens reveal nature's ability to recover after massive change, in this case the result of natural phenomena. The history of Lake Washington, in Seattle, reflects man-made environmental change first for ill and then, more recently, for the good. It demonstrates that scientific knowledge can enable a concerned citizenry to recognize, understand, and reverse a trend of degradation.

So don't wait, like I did, for a chance to savor this part of natural America. Pack your bags, and let Dan Chasan's text lead you to the multiple and unique wonders of the Pacific Northwest. You will also find, like I did, that pictures can't conceivably suffice.

—Thomas E. Lovejoy
Counselor to the Secretary for
Biodiversity and Environmental Affairs,
SMITHSONIAN INSTITUTION

LEFT: *In the valleys of Washington's Olympic Peninsula, old-growth hemlock and Sitka spruce rise like the piers of a Gothic cathedral. Moss and ferns, watered by storms and fog, cover the forest floor.*

INTRODUCTION

FURTHER READING: OREGON AND WASHINGTON

ALT, DAVID D., AND DONALD W. HYNDMAN. *Roadside Geology of Oregon.* Missoula, MT: Mountain Press, 1978. A good addition to any glove compartment, this geologic highway guide for the nonscientist is part of a useful series for anyone interested in the shape of the land. Volume also available for Washington State from the same publisher.

KITTREDGE, WILLIAM. *Owning It All.* St. Paul, MN: Graywolf Press, 1988. The author's reminiscences of growing up on a ranch in Oregon's Warner Valley in the 1930s and 1940s.

LA TOURRETTE, JOE. *Washington Wildlife Viewing Guide.* Helena, MT: Falcon Press, 1992. A survey of wildlife viewing sites in Washington. Illustrated with color maps and photos.

MATHEWS, DANIEL. *Cascade-Olympic Natural History: A Trailside Reference.* Portland, OR: Raven Editions, 1988. A well-organized, single-volume guide to the plants, animals, and geology of the Cascade and Olympic mountain ranges (illustrated with color photographs and drawings).

MCPHEE, JOHN. *Encounters with the Archdruid.* New York: Farrar, Straus and Giroux, 1971. A classic of environmental conservation writing, in which the philosophical divide over ecological consumption and conservation is explored through characters who meet on journeys into three wilderness areas, including Washington's Glacial Peak Wilderness.

Oregon Atlas and Gazetteer. 1st ed. Freeport, ME: DeLorme, 1991. Highly detailed road maps. Includes much practical recreation and touring information, including campgrounds, bicycle routes, wildlife areas, terrain, elevations, museums, and historic sites.

WALLACE, DAVID RAINS. *The Klamath Knot.* San Francisco: Sierra Club Books, 1983. A thoughtful book on the natural history of the Klamath Mountains that sheds light on the relationship between natural science and the human imagination.

Washington Atlas and Gazetteer. Freeport, ME: DeLorme, 1988. Highly detailed road maps and recreation information for the state of Washington in a format similar to the Oregon version described above.

Western Forests. The Audubon Society Nature Guides. New York: Knopf, 1985. An in-depth field guide, illustrated with color photographs, to the trees, wildflowers, birds, mammals, and insects of North America's western forests, including those of Washington and Oregon.

YUSKAVITCH, JAMES A. *Oregon Wildlife Viewing Guide.* Helena, MT: Falcon Press, 1994. A survey of wildlife viewing sites in Washington. Illustrated with color maps and photos.

GLOSSARY

alpine pertaining to mountain zones of extremely high elevation

andesite volcanic rock composed primarily of the mineral feldspar

basalt dark, dense rock cooled and hardened from a lava flow; sometimes columnar in structure

bog wetland, formed in glacial kettle holes; acidic nature produces large quantities of peat moss

butte tall, steep-sided tower of rock formed from an eroded plateau

caldera crater with a diameter many times that of the vent formed by collapse of a volcano's center

Channeled Scabland area of southeastern Washington scoured by massive glacial floods that created complex channel systems while stripping soil off the countryside and ripping up basalt beneath

cinder cone cone-shaped hill formed from accumulation of charred lava around the volcano vent

cirque large, bowl-shaped depression in a mountain hollowed out by glacial movement

conifer cone-bearing tree of the pine family; usually evergreen

coulee deep ravine, usually dry, worn away by running water

delta alluvial deposit, often triangular, that forms at river mouths

endemic originating in and restricted to one particular environment

estuary region of interaction between ocean water and the end of a river, where tidal action and river flow mix fresh and salt water

fault break in the earth's outermost layer, or crust, along which rock may move against rock

fjord narrow inlet of the sea between cliffs or steep slopes

natural dike vertical sheet of rock formed when molten rock cools on its way to the earth's surface

petroglyph carving on rock, especially one made by prehistoric people

pictograph prehistoric painting or drawing on rock created with natural pigments applied with animal-hair brushes

rain shadow area of dry land on the side of a mountain facing away from the moisture-laden winds blowing inland from the ocean

rapids broken, fast-flowing water that tumbles around boulders; classified from I to VI according to increasing difficulty of watercraft navigation

rhyolite fine-grained volcanic rock rich in the mineral silica

tectonic referring to changes in the earth's crust, the forces involved, and the resulting formations

tephra volcanic debris ejected during an eruption

timberline boundary that marks the upper limit of forest growth on a mountain or in high latitudes; beyond the boundary, temperatures are too cold to support tree growth

tuff volcanic rock consisting of small volcanic debris

tundra treeless region of arctic, subarctic, or alpine regions dominated by lichens, mosses, and low-growing vascular plants

wetland area of land covered or saturated with groundwater; includes swamps, marshes, and bogs

LAND MANAGEMENT RESOURCES

*The following public and private organizations are among the important admin-
istrators of the preserved and protected areas described in this volume. Brief expla-
nations of the various legal and legislative designations of these areas follow.*

MANAGING ORGANIZATIONS

Bureau of Land Management (BLM) Department of the Interior

Administers nearly half of all federal lands, some 272 million acres, predominantly
in the western states. Resources are managed for multiple uses: recreation, grazing, logging, mining, fish and wildlife, and watershed and wilderness preservation.

National Park Service (NPS) Department of the Interior

Regulates the use of national parks, monuments, and preserves. Resources are
managed to preserve and protect landscape, natural and historic artifacts, and
wildlife. Also administers historic and national landmarks, national seashores,
wild and scenic rivers, and the national trail system.

The Nature Conservancy (TNC) Private organization

International nonprofit organization that owns the largest private system of nature sanctuaries in the world, some 1,300 preserves. Aims to preserve significant
and diverse plants, animals, and natural communities. Some areas are managed
by other private or public conservation groups, some by the Conservancy itself.

Oregon Department of Fish and Wildlife

Conserves and enhances state fish and wildlife resources. Maintains fish hatcheries and wildlife management areas, regulates hunting and fishing licenses, and
protects state's endangered species.

Oregon Parks and Recreation Department

Manages 250 state parks, scenic and wild rivers, all beaches, and nonfederal
nature trails.

U.S. Fish and Wildlife Service (USFWS) Department of the Interior

Principal federal agency responsible for conserving, protecting, and enhancing
the country's fish and wildlife and their habitats. Manages national wildlife
refuges and fish hatcheries as well as programs for migratory birds and endangered and threatened species

U.S. Forest Service (USFS) Department of Agriculture

Administers more than 190 million acres in the national forests and national
grasslands and is responsible for the management of their resources.
Determines how best to combine commercial uses such as grazing, mining,
and logging with conservation needs.

Washington State Department of Fish and Wildlife

Responsible for preservation, protection, and management of all wildlife areas
within Washington. Maintains state hunting and fishing areas and licenses.

Washington State Parks and Recreation Commission

Administers and maintains state parks and recreation areas. Also responsible for
seashore conservation projects, water and boating regulation, and natural and
historic landmark preservation.

DESIGNATIONS

National Backcountry Byway

Dirt or gravel road designated for its scenic, geologic, or historic attributes. Mainly for sightseeing and recreation via automobile. Managed by BLM.

National Conservation Area

Area set aside by Congress to protect specific environments. Rules for use of land are less restrictive than those in wilderness areas. Managed by BLM.

National Estuarine Research Reserve

Established to ensure a stable environment for research through long-term protection of fragile estuarine areas. Managed by National Oceanic and Atmospheric Administration.

National Forest

Large acreage managed for the use of forests, watersheds, wildlife, and recreation by the public or private sectors. Managed by USFS.

National Historic Site

Land area, building, or object preserved for its national historic importance. Managed by NPS.

National Monument

Nationally significant landmark, structure, object, or area of scientific or historic significance. Managed by NPS.

National Park

Spacious primitive or wilderness area with scenery and natural wonders so outstanding it has been preserved by the federal government. Managed by NPS.

National Recreation Area

Site established to conserve and develop for recreational purposes an area of national scenic, natural, or historic interest. Power boats, dirt and mountain bikes, and ORVs allowed with restrictions. Managed by NPS.

National Scenic Area

Land protected and enhanced under the National Scenic Area Act for its natural beauty or its cultural and recreational resources. Managed by USFS.

National Wildlife Refuge

Public land set aside for wild animals; protects migratory waterfowl, endangered and threatened species, and native plants. Managed by USFWS.

Wild and Scenic River System

National program set up to preserve selected rivers in their natural free-flowing condition; stretches are classified as wild, scenic, or recreational, depending on the degree of development on the river, shoreline, or adjacent lands. Management shared by BLM, NPS, and USFWS.

Wilderness Area

Area with particular ecological, geological, scientific, scenic, or historic value that has been set aside in its natural condition to be preserved as wild land; limited recreational use is permitted. Managed by BLM and NPS.

Wildlife Management Area

Natural area owned, protected and maintained by the state for recreation. Aside from seasonal restrictions, hunting, fishing, and public access are allowed. Managed by individual states.

NATURE TRAVEL

The following is a selection of national and local organizations that sponsor nature-related travel activities from extended tours to day trips and ecology workshops.

NATIONAL

National Audubon Society
700 Broadway
New York, NY 10003
(212) 979-3000
Offers a wide range of ecological field studies, tours, and cruises throughout the United States.

National Wildlife Federation
1400 16th St. NW
Washington, D.C. 20036
(703) 790-4363
Offers training in environmental education for all ages, wildlife camp and teen adventures, conservation summits involving nature walks, field trips, and classes.

The Nature Conservancy
1815 North Lynn St.
Arlington, VA 22209
(703) 841-5300
Offers a variety of excursions from regional and state offices. May include hiking, backpacking, canoeing, horseback riding. Contact above number to locate state offices.

Sierra Club Outings
730 Polk St.
San Francisco, CA 94109
(415) 923-5630
Offers tours of different lengths for all ages throughout the United States. Outings may include backpacking, hiking, biking, skiing, and water excursions.

Smithsonian Study Tours and Seminars
1100 Jefferson Dr. SW
MRC 702
Washington, D.C. 20560
(202) 357-4700
Offers extended tours, cruises, research expeditions, and seminars throughout the United States.

REGIONAL

The Mazamas
909 Northwest 19th Ave.
Portland, OR 97209
(503) 227-2345
An outdoors club offering courses and tours in mountain and glacier climbing, skiing, white-water rafting, and hiking. Areas of activity include the Columbia River Gorge, the Cascades, Mt. Hood, and the Oregon coast. Call or write for schedules and brochures.

The Mountaineers
300 Third Ave. West
Seattle, WA 98119
(206) 284-6310
An outdoors club that offers courses and tours in mountain climbing, hiking and backpacking, kayaking, alpine scrambling, and sailing. Activities take place mostly in western Washington, including the Cascades and the Olympics.

Oregon Tourism Division
775 Summer St. NE
Salem, OR 97310
(800) 547-7842
Publishes and distributes annual tourist guidebooks containing information on transportation, recreation, and accommodations. Can direct travelers to local chambers of commerce.

Washington State Tourism
Tourism Division
General Administration Bldg., AX-13
Olympia, WA 98504
(800) 544-1800
(206) 586-2088
Offers free annual vacation planning guides. Operators can answer specific questions regarding transportation, accommodations, and recreation.

How To Use This Site Guide

The following site information guide will assist you in planning your tour of the natural areas of Oregon and Washington. Sites set in **boldface** and followed by the symbol ❖ in the text are here organized alphabetically by state. Each entry is followed by the mailing address (sometimes different from the street address) and phone number of the immediate managing office, plus brief notes and a list of facilities and activities available. (A key appears on each page.)

Information on hours of operation, seasonal closings, and fees is not listed, as these vary from season to season and year to year. Please also bear in mind that responsibility for the management of some sites may change. Call well in advance to obtain maps, brochures, and pertinent, up-to-date information that will help you plan your adventures in the Pacific Northwest.

Each site entry in the guide includes the address and phone number of its immediate managing agency. Many of these sites are under the stewardship of a forest or park ranger or supervised from a small nearby office. Hence, in many cases, these sites will be difficult to contact directly, and it is preferable to call the managing agency.

The following umbrella organizations can provide general information for individual natural sites, as well as the area as a whole:

OREGON AND WASHINGTON
Bureau of Land Management
P.O. Box 2965
Portland, OR 97208
(503) 952-6001

U.S. Fish and Wildlife Service
911 NE 11th Ave.
Portland, OR 97232
(503) 231-6124

OREGON
National Park Service
c/o Crater Lake National Park
P.O. Box 7
Crater Lake, OR 97604
(503) 594-2211

Oregon Department of Fish and Wildlife
P.O. Box 59
Portland, OR 97207
(503) 229-5410

Oregon Parks and Recreation Department
1115 Commercial St., NE
Salem, OR 97310
(503) 378-6305

U.S. Forest Service
c/o Nature of the Northwest Information Center
800 NE Oregon St., Rm. 177
Portland, OR 97232
(503) 872-2750

WASHINGTON
National Park Service
c/o Olympic National Park
600 E. Park Ave.
Port Angeles, WA 98362
(360) 452-4501/0330

The Nature Conservancy of Washington
217 Pine St., Ste. 1100
Seattle, WA 98101
(206) 343-4344

Washington State Parks and Recreation Commission
7150 Cleanwater Lane, KY-11
Olympia, WA 98504
(206) 902-8509

OREGON

ANKENY NATIONAL WILDLIFE REFUGE
U.S. Fish and Wildlife Service
26208 Finley Refuge Rd.
Corvallis, OR 97333
(503) 757-7236
   Limited winter access   **BW, H, I, MT**

BADGER CREEK WILDERNESS
Mount Hood National Forest
Barlow Ranger District
PO Box 67
Dufor, OR 97021
(503) 467-2291   **C, F, H, HR, MT**

BANDON MARSH NATIONAL WILDLIFE REFUGE
U.S. Fish and Wildlife Service
Oregon Coastal Refuges Headquarters
2030 S. Marine Science Dr.
Newport, OR 97365-5296   **BW, F**

BANDON STATE PARK
c/o Bullards Beach State Park
PO Box 569
Bandon, OR 97411
(503) 347-2209
   Day-use only; beach fire regulations;
   whale watching late December and
   early May   **BW, F, H, HR, I, MB, MT, PA**

BASKETT SLOUGH NATIONAL WILDLIFE REFUGE
U.S. Fish and Wildlife Service
26208 Finley Refuge Rd.
Corvallis, OR 97333
(503) 757-723
   Limited winter entry   **BW, H, I, MT**

BEAR VALLEY NATIONAL WILDLIFE REFUGE
U.S. Fish and Wildlife Service
Route 1, Box 74
Tulelake, CA 96134
(916) 667-2231
   No entry; view from adjacent roads; winter eagle fly-out January–March   **BW**

BLACK CANYON WILDERNESS
Ochoco National Forest
PO Box 490
Prineville, OR 97754
(503) 447-6247
      BW, C, F, H, HR, MT, XC

BONNEVILLE LOCK AND DAM
U.S. Army Corps of Engineers
PO Box 2946, Portland, OR 97208-2946
(503) 374-8820
   BW, F, GS, H, I, MT, PA, RA, T, TG

BOULDER CREEK WILDERNESS
Umpqua National Forest
Diamond Lake Ranger District
PO Box 1008
Roseburg, OR 97470
(503) 672-6601   **BW, C, H, HR, MT**

BRIDAL VEIL FALLS STATE PARK
Oregon Parks and Recreation Dept.
c/o Columbia Gorge State Park
Corbett, OR 97019
(503) 695- 2261   **BW, H, MT, PA, T**

BRIDGE CREEK WILDERNESS
Ochoco National Forest
PO Box 490
Prineville, OR 97754
(503) 447-6247   **BW, C, H**

BULLARDS BEACH STATE PARK
Oregon Parks and Recreation Dept.
PO Box 569, Bandon, OR 97411
(503) 347-2209; (800) 547-7842
   Includes Bullards Beach Horse Camp
   and Coquille River Light House
   BT, BW, C, F, H, HR, L, MT, PA, RA, T

BULL OF THE WOODS WILDERNESS
U.S. Forest Service
Estacada Ranger District
595 Industrial Way
Estacada, OR 97023
(503) 630-6861
   Includes old abandoned mine; spotted
   owls; scenic lookout   **F, H, MT, S**

CAPE ARAGO STATE PARK
Oregon Parks and Recreation Dept.
10965 Cape Arago Hwy.
Coos Bay, OR 97420
(503) 888-4902
   Day-use only   **BW, F, H, MT, PA, T**

CAPE BLANCO STATE PARK
Oregon Parks and Recreation Dept.
PO Box 1345, Port Orford, OR 97465
(503) 332-6774
   Permits required for metal detector use
   and firewood removal
   BT, BW, C, F, H, HR, MT, PA, T

BT Bike Trails	**CK** Canoeing, Kayaking	**F** Fishing	**HR** Horseback Riding
BW Bird-watching		**GS** Gift Shop	
C Camping	**DS** Downhill Skiing	**H** Hiking	**I** Information Center

CAPE KIWANDA STATE PARK
c/o Cape Lookout State Park
13000 Whiskey Creek Rd. W
Tillamook, OR 97141
(503) 842-4981
  Permit required for beach access   **BW, F**

CAPE LOOKOUT STATE PARK
Oregon Parks and Recreation Dept.
13000 Whiskey Creek Rd. W
Tillamook, OR 97141
(503) 842-4981   **BW, C, H, I, MT, PA, RA, T**

**CAPE MEARES NATIONAL
WILDLIFE REFUGE**
U.S. Fish and Wildlife Service
Oregon Coastal Refuges Headquarters
2030 S. Marine Science Dr.
Newport, OR 97365-5296
(503) 867-4550
  Limited public access; known for nature
  studies photography; birds can be
  viewed from state park   **BW, MT**

CAPE MEARES STATE PARK
c/o Cape Lookout State Park
13000 Whiskey Creek Rd. W
Tillamook, OR 97141
(503) 842-4981
            BW, GS, H, I, MT, PA, T, TG

**CARL G. WASHBURNE
MEMORIAL STATE PARK**
Oregon Parks and Recreation Dept.
93111 Route 101 N
Florence, OR 97439
(503) 997-3851
  No charge for beach access; license not
  required for clamming
            BW, C, F, H, MT, PA, T

**COLD SPRINGS NATIONAL
WILDLIFE REFUGE**
U.S. Fish and Wildlife Service
PO Box 700, Umatilla, OR 97882
(503) 922-3232
Day-use only   **BW, F**

**COLUMBIA RIVER GORGE
NATIONAL SCENIC AREA**
U.S. Forest Service, 902 Wasco Ave., Ste. 200
Hood River, OR 97031
(503) 386-2333
  Includes Horsetail Falls and Multnomah
  Falls   **BT, BW, C, CK, F, GS, H, I,
            MB, MT, PA, RA, RC, S, T**

COLUMBIA WILDERNESS
Mount Hood National Forest
Columbia Gorge Ranger District
2955 N.W. Division St.
Gresham, OR 97030
(503) 695-2276
  Self-issue permit required, available at
  trailhead   **BW, C, F, H, HR, MT**

CRANE PRAIRIE RESERVOIR
Deschutes National Forest
Bend Ranger District
1230 N.E. 3rd St., Suite A-262
Bend, OR 97701
(503) 388-5664
            BW, C, CK, F, PA, RA, S, T

CRATER LAKE NATIONAL PARK
National Park Service
PO Box 7, Crater Lake, OR 97604
(503) 594-2211
  Includes Wizard Island and Mount Scott
            **BW, C, F, GS, H, HR, I,
            L, MT, PA, RA, T, TG, XC**

CUMMINS CREEK WILDERNESS
Siuslaw National Forest
Waldport Ranger District
1049 S.W. Pacific Hwy., PO Box 400
Waldport, OR 97394
(503) 563-3211
  Visitor information center at Cape
  Perpetua   **BW, C, H, I, MT**

DARLINGTONIA STATE WAYSIDE
c/o Honeyman State Park
84505 Route 101 S
Florence, OR 97439-8405
(503) 997-3851   **H, MT, PA**

DEAN CREEK ELK VIEWING AREA
Bureau of Land Management
Coos Bay District
1300 Airport Lane
North Bend, OR 97459
(503) 756-0100; (503) 271-1704
  Best times to view elk early morning
  and before dusk   **BW, F, GS, I, T**

DESCHUTES NATIONAL FOREST
U.S. Forest Service
1645 Route 20
East Bend, OR 97701
(503) 388-2715
      **BT, BW, C, CK, DS, F, H, HR, I, L, MB,
            MT, PA, RA, RC, S, T, TG, XC**

L	Lodging	**PA**	Picnic Areas
MB	Mountain Biking	**RA**	Ranger-led Activities
MT	Marked Trails		

RC	Rock Climbing	**TG**	Tours, Guides
S	Swimming	**XC**	Cross-country Skiing
T	Toilets		

DEVIL'S ELBOW STATE PARK
c/o Honeyman State Park
84505 Route 101 S
Florence, OR 97439
(503) 997-3851
Includes Heceta Head Lighthouse; day-use only; parking fee; beach access
BW, F, H, MT, PA, T

DIAMOND PEAK WILDERNESS
U.S. Forest Service
Rigdon Ranger District
49098 Salmon Creek Rd.
Oakridge, OR 97463
(503) 782-2283
Voluntary registration at trailhead
BW, C, F, H, HR, MT, RC, S, XC

DRIFT CREEK WILDERNESS
Siuslaw National Forest
Waldport Ranger District
PO Box 400, Waldport, OR 97394
(503) 563-3211
Kayaking in rapids; no canoes
BW, C, H, MT

EAGLE RIDGE PARK
Klamath County Public Works
Parks Division
3735 Shasta Way
Klamath Falls, OR 97603
(503) 883-4696   **BW, C, CK, F, H, PA, T**

ELK RIVER
Siskiyou National Forest
Powers Ranger District
Powers, OR 97466
(503) 471-6516   **C, F, H, PA, S**

FERN RIDGE WILDLIFE AREA
Oregon Dept. of Fish and Wildlife
26969 Cantrell Rd.
Eugene, OR 97402
(503) 935-2591
Seasonal restrictions on 3 units to protect wintering waterfowl; call or write for maps and bird checklist
BW, H, MT, PA

FOREST PARK
City of Portland, Bureau of Parks
and Recreation
1120 S.W. 5th Ave., Rm. 1302
Portland, OR 97204
(503) 823-2223
Day-use only
BT, BW, H, HR, MT, PA, T

FORT ROCK STATE PARK
c/o Tumalo State Park
62976 O.B. Riley Rd.
Bend, OR 97701
(503) 388-6211; (503) 388-6055
BW, H, PA, T

GEARHART MOUNTAIN WILDERNESS
Fremont National Forest
Bly Ranger District
PO Box 25, Bly, OR 97622
(503) 353-2427
BW, C, F, H, MT, PA, XC

GOLDEN AND SILVER FALLS STATE PARK
Oregon Parks and Recreation Dept.
10965 Cape Arago Hwy.
Coos Bay, OR 97420
(503) 888-4902
Day-use only   **BW, H, MT, PA,**

GRASSY KNOB WILDERNESS
Siskiyou National Forest
Powers Ranger District
200 N.E. Greenfield Rd.
Grants Pass, OR 97526-0242
(503) 471-6500; (503) 439-3011
BW, F, H

HART MOUNTAIN NATIONAL ANTELOPE REFUGE
U.S. Fish and Wildlife Service
18 South G St., PO Box 111
Lakeview, OR 97630
(503) 947-3315
Backcountry permit required for camping
BW, C, F, H, HR, I, PA, T, XC

HELLS CANYON NATIONAL RECREATION AREA
U.S. Forest Service
88401 Route 22
Enterprise, OR 97828
(503) 426-4978; (503) 426-5546
No campfires within ¼ mile of Snake River   **BT, BW, C, CK, DS, F, GS, H, HR, I, MB, MT, PA, RC, S, T, TG, XC**

HELLS CANYON WILDERNESS
Wallowa-Whitman National Forest
PO Box 907
Baker City, OR 97814
(503) 523-1205
Rafting; no permits required; self-registration requested
BW, C, F, H, HR, MT, S, XC

BT	Bike Trails	**CK**	Canoeing, Kayaking	**F**	Fishing	**HR**	Horseback Riding
BW	Bird-watching			**GS**	Gift Shop		
C	Camping	**DS**	Downhill Skiing	**H**	Hiking	**I**	Information Center

HIGH DESERT MUSEUM
59800 S. Route 97
Bend, OR 97702
(503) 382-4754
  Admission charge; allow 2-3 hours
                    BW, GS, I, MT, PA, T, TG

HUMBUG MOUNTAIN STATE PARK
Oregon Parks and Recreation Dept.
PO Box 1345, Port Orford, OR 97465
(503) 332-6774
  Permit required for metal detector use
  and firewood removal
                    BW, C, F, H, MT, PA, T

ILLINOIS RIVER
Siskiyou National Forest
Illinois Valley Ranger District
26568 Redwood Hwy.
Cave Junction, OR 97523
(503) 592-2166
        BW, C, CK, F, H, HR, MB, MT, PA, S, T

**JOHN DAY FOSSIL BEDS
NATIONAL MONUMENT**
National Park Service
420 W. Main St.
John Day, OR 97845
(503) 987-2333 (visitor center)
(503) 987-2334 (for hearing impaired)
  Stay off fossil exposures; rattlesnake precautions
        BW, F, GS, H, HR, I, MT, PA, RA, T, TG

JOHN DAY RIVER
Bureau of Land Management
PO Box 550, Prineville, OR 97754
(503) 447-4115
                BW, C, CK, F, H, PA, S, T, TG

KALMIOPSIS WILDERNESS
Siskiyou National Forest
Chetco Ranger District
200 N.E. Greenfield Rd.
Grants Pass, OR 97526-0242
(503) 471-6500; (503) 469-2196
                    BW, C, F, H, HR, I, MT, S

**KLAMATH MARSH NATIONAL WILDLIFE
REFUGE**
U.S. Fish and Wildlife Service
HC 63, Box 303
Chiloquin, OR 97624
(503) 783-3380
  Day-use only
                BT, BW, CK, F, MT, PA, XC

KLAMATH WILDLIFE MANAGEMENT AREA
Oregon Dept. of Fish and Wildlife
1800 Miller Island Rd. W
Klamath Falls, OR 97603
(503) 883-5734   **BW, MT, PA, T**

LADD MARSH WILDLIFE AREA
Oregon Dept. of Fish and Wildlife
107 20th St.
La Grande, OR 97850
(503) 963-2138
  Primarily a wildlife production area;
  year-round access limited to 3/4 mile nature trail   **BW, H, MT**

LAKE OWYHEE STATE PARK
Oregon Parks and Recreation Dept.
PO 247, Adrian, OR 97901
(503) 339-2331
  Camping mid-April–October; hilly, rocky
  terrain; scenic viewpoints; 4 boat ramps
                    BW, C, CK, F, PA, T

**LEWIS AND CLARK NATIONAL
WILDLIFE REFUGE**
U.S. Fish and Wildlife Service
PO Box 566
Cathlamet, WA 98612
(206) 795-3915
  Day-use only; 1 marked canoe trail; in-
  formation center at boat launches
                                CK, I

LOEB STATE PARK
c/o Harris Beach State Park
1655 Route 101, Brookings, OR 97415
(503) 469-2021
                BW, C, F, H, MT, PA, S, T

LOST FOREST RESEARCH NATURAL AREA
Bureau of Land Management
PO Box 151, Lakeview, OR 97630
(503) 947-2177
  Rough roads, high-clearance vehicle rec-
  ommended   **BW, C, H, MB**

**LOWER DESCHUTES NATIONAL
BACKCOUNTRY BYWAY**
Bureau of Land Management
PO Box 550
Prineville, OR 97754
(503) 447-4115
  White-water rafting   **C, F, PA, S, T**

**LOWER KLAMATH NATIONAL
WILDLIFE REFUGE**
U.S. Fish and Wildlife Service

L	Lodging	**PA**	Picnic Areas	**RC**	Rock Climbing	**TG**	Tours, Guides
MB	Mountain Biking	**RA**	Ranger-led Activities	**S**	Swimming	**XC**	Cross-country Skiing
MT	Marked Trails			**T**	Toilets		

Route 1, Box 74
Tulelake, CA 96134
(916) 667-2231
    Marked automobile trails   **BW, MT**

MALHEUR NATIONAL FOREST
U.S. Forest Service
139 N.E. Dayton St.
John Day, OR 97845
(503) 575-1731
    Includes the Malheur and the North
    Fork Malheur wild and scenic rivers
        BT, BW, C, CK, F, GS, H, HR,
        L, MB, MT, PA, S, T, TG, XC

MALHEUR NATIONAL WILDLIFE REFUGE
U.S. Fish and Wildlife Service
HC 72, Box 245
Princeton, OR 97721
(503) 493-2612
    Permit for research required 2 weeks in
    advance   **BW, F, GS, I, MT, PA, T, TG**

**MCKAY CREEK NATIONAL
WILDLIFE REFUGE**
U.S. Fish and Wildlife Service
PO Box 700, Umatilla, OR 97882
(503) 922-3232
    Day-use only   **BW, F, T**

MENAGERIE WILDERNESS
Willamette National Forest
Sweet Home Ranger District
3225 Route 20, Sweet Home, OR 97386
(503) 367-5168   **BW, C, H, MT, RC**

MIDDLE SANTIAM WILDERNESS
Willamette National Forest
Sweet Home Ranger District
3225 Route 20, Sweet Home, OR 97386
(503) 367-5168
                BW, C, F, H, HR, MT, RC, S

MILL CREEK WILDERNESS
Ochoco National Forest
PO Box 490, Prineville, OR 97754
(503) 447-6247   **BW, C, F, H, HR, MT, S**

MOLALLA RIVER STATE PARK
Oregon Parks and Recreation Dept.
c/o Champoeg State Park
7679 Champoeg Rd. NE
St. Paul, OR 97137
(503) 633-8170
    Day-use only; boat launch
            BW, CK, F, H, MT, PA, T

MONUMENT ROCK WILDERNESS
U.S. Forest Service
Prairie City Ranger District
PO Box 337, Prairie City, OR 97869
(503) 575-1731   **BW, C, F, H, HR, MT, XC**

MOUNTAIN LAKES WILDERNESS
Winema National Forest
Klamath Ranger District
1936 California Ave.
Klamath Falls, OR 97601
(503) 885-3400   **BW, F, H, HR, MT**

MOUNT HOOD NATIONAL FOREST
U.S. Forest Service
2955 N.W. Division St.
Gresham, OR 97030
(503) 666-0771; (503) 666-0704
            BW, C, CK, DS, F, GS, H, HR,
            I, L, MB, MT, PA, RA, RC, S, T, XC

MOUNT HOOD WILDERNESS
Mount Hood National Forest
2955 N.W. Division St.
Gresham, OR 97030
(503) 352-6002 (Hood River Ranger
District)
(503) 666-0704 (Zigzag Ranger District)
    Self-issue permit required, available at trail-
    head   **BW, C, F, H, HR, MT, RC, XC**

MOUNT JEFFERSON WILDERNESS
U.S. Forest Service
Detroit Ranger Station
HC 73, Box 320
Mill City, OR 97360
(503) 854-3366
    Mandatory entry permits; check with
    ranger station
            BW, C, F, H, HR, MT, RC, S, XC

MOUNT THIELSEN WILDERNESS
U.S. Forest Service
Chenault Ranger District
PO Box 1008, Roseburg, OR 97470
(503) 365-7001; (503) 883-6714
    Group numbers limited in pristine sec-
    tions; register at trailhead
            BW, C, F, H, HR, MT, PA, RC, XC

MOUNT WASHINGTON WILDERNESS
U.S. Forest Service
McKenzie Ranger District
Route 126, McKenzie Bridge, OR 97413
(503) 822-3381
    Mandatory entry permits; check with

BT	Bike Trails	**CK**	Canoeing, Kayaking	**F**	Fishing	**HR**	Horseback Riding
BW	Bird-watching			**GS**	Gift Shop		
C	Camping	**DS**	Downhill Skiing	**H**	Hiking	**I**	Information Center

ranger station
BW, C, F, H, HR, MT, RC, S, XC

NEHALEM BAY STATE PARK
Oregon Parks and Recreation Dept.
9500 Sandpiper Lane
Nehalem, OR 97131
(503) 368-5154 (summer)
(503) 368-5943 (off-season)
BT, BW, C, H, HR, I, MT, PA, T

NEWBERRY NATIONAL VOLCANIC MONUMENT
Deschutes National Forest
Bend-Fort Rock Ranger District
1230 N.E. 3rd St., Bend, OR 97701
(503) 593-2421; (503) 388-5664
Monument open year-round; visitor center open May–October; check in at station and use trail map
BT, BW, C, CK, F, GS, H, HR, I, L, MT, PA, RA, S, T, TG, XC

NORTH FORK JOHN DAY RIVER
Umatilla National Forest
North Fork John Day River Ranger District
PO Box 158
Ukiah, OR 97880
(503) 427-3231
Barbless hooks required; check for other fishing regulations
BW, C, CK, F, H, HR, MT, PA, T

NORTH FORK JOHN DAY WILDERNESS
Umatilla National Forest
North Fork John Day Ranger District
PO Box 158
Ukiah, OR 97880
(503) 427-3231
Some areas closed to fishing or have special fishing restrictions as to species and tackle **C, F, H, HR**

NORTH FORK UMATILLA WILDERNESS
Umatilla National Forest
Walla Walla Ranger District
1415 W. Rose, Walla Walla, OR 99362
(509) 522-6290
BW, C, F, H, HR, MT, PA, T

OCEANSIDE STATE WAYSIDE
Oregon Parks and Recreation Dept.
c/o Cape Lookout State Park
13000 Whiskey Creek Rd. W
Tillamook, OR 97141
(503) 842-4981 **BW, H, T**

OCHOCO NATIONAL FOREST
U.S. Forest Service
PO Box 490, Prineville, OR 97754
(503) 447-9538
BW, C, F, H, HR, MB, PA, XC

OREGON CAVES NATIONAL MONUMENT
National Park Service
19000 Caves Hwy.
Caves Junction, OR 97523
(503) 592-2100
BW, GS, H, I, L, MT, PA, RA, T, TG

OREGON DUNES NATIONAL RECREATION AREA
Siuslaw National Forest
855 Highway Ave., Reedsport, OR 97467
(503) 271-3611; (503) 271-3614
(for hearing impaired)
ORV permit required; kite flying area
BW, C, CK, F, GS, H, HR, I, MT, PA, RA, S, T, TG

OSWALD WEST STATE PARK
c/o Nehalem Bay State Park
9500 Sandpiper Lane
Nehalem, OR 97131
(503) 368-5154 (summer)
(503) 368-5943 (off-season)
Open mid-March–October
BW, C, H, MT, PA, T

OXBOW PARK
Metro Regional Parks and Greenspaces
600 N.E. Grand Ave.
Portland, OR 97262
(503) 663- 4708; (503) 797-1850
No pets allowed
BT, BW, C, CK, F, H, HR, I, MB, MT, PS, RA, S, T, TG

PACIFIC CREST NATIONAL SCENIC TRAIL
U.S. Forest Service, Pacific N.W. Region 6
Recreation Information
333 S.W. 1st Ave.,
Portland, OR 97208
(503) 549-3551
Call for maps **BW, H**

RED BUTTES WILDERNESS
Rogue River National Forest
PO Box 520, Medford, OR 97501
(503) 858-2200; (503) 899-1812
Groups limited to 8 people, 12 head of stock; grazing restriction for stock until
August 1 **BW, C, F, H, HR, MT, S, XC**

L	Lodging	**PA**	Picnic Areas	**RC**	Rock Climbing	**TG**	Tours, Guides
MB	Mountain Biking	**RA**	Ranger-led Activities	**S**	Swimming	**XC**	Cross-country Skiing
MT	Marked Trails			**T**	Toilets		

ROCK CREEK WILDERNESS
U.S. Forest Service
Waldport Ranger District
PO Box 400
Waldport, OR 97394
(503) 563-3211
  Very wild area; no trails   **BW,C, H**

ROGUE RIVER
Bureau of Land Management
3040 Biddle Rd.
Medford, OR 97504
(503) 479-3735 (Rand visitor center, permits)
(503) 770-2200 (BLM)
  Permits required to float wild section
  May–October   **BW, C, K, F, H, I, L, S**

ROGUE RIVER NATIONAL FOREST
U.S. Forest Service
2819 Dahlia, Klamath Falls, OR 07601
(503) 883-6714   **BW, C, CK, DS, F, H, HR, MB, I, MT, PA, S, T, XC**

ROGUE-UMPQUA DIVIDE WILDERNESS
U.S. Forest Service
Piller Ranger District
PO Box 1008
Roseburg, OR 97470
(503) 672-6601   **BW, C, F, H, HR, MT**

SADDLE MOUNTAIN STATE PARK
c/o Fort Stevens State Park
Ridge Road
Hammond, OR 97121
(503) 861-1671
  Known for wildflowers
    BW, C, H, MT, PA, T

SALMON HUCKLEBERRY WILDERNESS
Mount Hood National Forest
70220 E. Route 26
Zigzag, OR 97049
(503) 622-5741
  Registration required at trailhead
    BW, C, F, H, MT, S, T

SAUVIE ISLAND WILDLIFE AREA
Oregon Dept. of Fish and Wildlife
18330 N.W. Sauvie Island Road
Portland, OR 97231
(503) 621-3488
Parking permit required; no permit required
for drive through   **BW, CK, F, H, S, T**

SHORE ACRES
Oregon Parks and Recreation Dept.

10965 Cape Arago Hwy.
Coos Bay, OR 97420
(503) 888-3732; (503) 888-4902
    BW, F, GS, H, I, MT, PA, RA, S, T, TG

SILVER FALLS STATE PARK
Oregon Parks and Recreation Dept.
20024 Silver Falls Hwy.
Sublimity, OR 97385
(800) 452-5687; (503) 873-8681
  Wheelchair accessible; park user fee
  March–September, waived if camping;
  no dogs on trails
    BT, BW, C, F, GS, H, HR, I, L, MT, PA, S, T

SISKIYOU NATIONAL FOREST
U.S. Forest Service
200 N.E. Greenfield Rd.
Grants Pass, OR 97526-0242
(503) 471-6500; (503) 471-6516
  Permits required to remove anything
  from forest
    BT, BW, C, F, GS, H, HR, I, L, MB, MT, PA, RA, S, T, XC

SKY LAKES WILDERNESS
U.S. Forest Service
1936 California Ave.
Klamath Falls, OR 97601
(503) 885-3400   **BW, F, H, HR, MT**

SMITH ROCK STATE PARK
Oregon Parks and Recreation Dept.
9241 N.E. Crooked River Dr.
Terrebonne, OR 97760
(503) 548-7501
  Bivouac area for climbers, hikers, and
  campers; rest of park day-use only
    BW, C, H, HR, MT, PA, RC, T, XC

SOUTH SLOUGH NATIONAL ESTUARINE RESEARCH RESERVE
State of Oregon, Division of State Lands
PO Box 5417
Charleston, OR 97420
(503) 888-5558
  Some trails for physically disabled
    BW, CK, GS, H, I, MT, PA, T, TG

STEENS MOUNTAIN
Bureau of Land Management
HC 74, 12533
Route 20 W
Hines, OR 97738
(503) 573-4400
  Visitor center at Frenchglen; most of

BT	Bike Trails	**CK**	Canoeing, Kayaking	**F**	Fishing	**HR**	Horseback Riding
BW	Bird-watching			**GS**	Gift Shop		
C	Camping	**DS**	Downhill Skiing	**H**	Hiking	**I**	Information Center

area closed to ORVs

BW, C, F, H, HR, I, MB, PA, T

STRAWBERRY MOUNTAIN WILDERNESS
Malheur National Forest
Prairie City Ranger District
PO Box 337
Prairie City, OR 97869
(503) 575-1731   **BW, C, F, H, HR, MT**

SUCCOR CREEK STATE PARK
Oregon Parks and Recreation Dept.
PO Box 247
Adrian, OR 97901
(503) 339-2331
No potable water

BW, C, H, HR, PA, RC, T

SUMMER LAKE WILDLIFE AREA
Oregon Dept. of Fish and Wildlife
36981 Route 31
Summer Lake, OR 97640
(503) 943-3152
Group tours by advance arrangement

BW, C, CK, F, H, HR, PA, S, T, TG

SUNSET BAY
Oregon Parks and Recreation Dept.
10965 Cape Arago Hwy.
Coos Bay, OR 97420
(503) 888-4902
Day-use only

BW, C, CK, F, H, MT, PA, S, T

THREE ARCH ROCKS
NATIONAL WILDLIFE REFUGE
U.S. Fish and Wildlife Service
Oregon Coastal Refuges
2127 S.E. OSU Drive
Newport, OR 97365
(503) 867-4550   **BW**

THREE SISTERS WILDERNESS
Eastern portion
Willamette National Forest
211 E. 7th Ave.
Eugene, OR 97401
(503) 465-642
Western portion
Deschutes National Forest
1645 Route 20E
Bend, OR 97701
(503) 388-2715
Permits required; call office for current
regulations

BW, C, F, H, HR, MT, RC, XC

TRYON CREEK STATE PARK
Oregon Parks and Recreation Dept.
11321 S.W. Terwilliger Blvd.
Portland, OR 97219
(503) 653-3166; (503) 636-4398
Wheelchair accessible facilities

BT, BW, H, HR, GS, I, MT, RA, T, TG

UMATILLA NATIONAL WILDLIFE REFUGE
U.S. Fish and Wildlife Service
PO Box 700
Umatilla, OR 97882
(503) 922-3232   **BW, F, MT, T**

UMPQUA NATIONAL FOREST
U.S. Forest Service
PO Box 1008, Roseburg, OR 97470
(503) 672-6601

BT, BW, C, CK, F, H, HR,
I, L, MB, MT, PA, RA, S, T, XC

UPPER KLAMATH
NATIONAL WILDLIFE REFUGE
U.S. Fish and Wildlife Service
Route 1, Box 74
Tulelake, CA 96134
(916) 667-2231   **BW, CK, F**

WALDO LAKE WILDERNESS
Willamette National Forest
46375 Route 58
Oakridge, OR 97492
(503) 782-2291

BW, C, F, H, HR, MT, RC, S, XC

WALLOWA LAKE STATE PARK
Oregon Parks and Recreation Dept.
72214 Marina Lane
Joseph, OR 97846
(503) 432-4185   **BW, C, F, GS, PA, RA, S, T**

WALLOWA-WHITMAN NATIONAL FOREST
PO Box 907
Baker City, OR 97814
(503) 523-6391
Includes Eagle Cap Wilderness

BT, BW, C, CK, DS, F, GS, H, HR,
I, L, MB, MT, PA, S, T, TG, XC

WENAHA-TUCANNON WILDERNESS
Umatilla National Forest
Pomeroy Ranger District
Route 1, Box 53-F
Pomeroy, WA 99347
(509) 843-1891

BW, C, F, H, HR, MT

L	Lodging	**PA**	Picnic Areas	**RC** Rock Climbing	**TG** Tours, Guides
MB	Mountain Biking	**RA**	Ranger-led	**S** Swimming	**XC** Cross-country
MT	Marked Trails		Activities	**T** Toilets	Skiing

WENAHA WILDLIFE MANAGEMENT AREA
Oregon Dept. of Fish and Wildlife
85060 Grande Ronde Rd.
Enterprise, OR 97828
(503) 828-7721; (503) 276-2344
Plan ahead, lodging in area sparse
BW, C, CK, F, H, HR, MT, PA, XC

WILD ROGUE WILDERNESS
Siskiyou National Forest
200 N.E. Greenfield Rd.
Grants Pass, OR 97526-0242
(503) 471-6500; (503) 247-6651
BW, F, H, I, MT, S

WILLAMETTE NATIONAL FOREST
U.S. Forest Service
PO Box 10607, Eugene, OR 97440
(503) 465-6521
BT, BW, C, CK, DS, F, GS, H, HR, I, L, MB, MT, PA, RC, S, T, XC

WILLIAM FINLEY NATIONAL WILDLIFE REFUGE
U.S. Fish and Wildlife Service
26208 Finley Refuge Rd.
Corvallis, OR 97333
(503) 757-7236
Entry limited during winter
BW, F, H, I, MT, T

WINEMA NATIONAL FOREST
U.S. Forest Service
2819 Dahlia St., Klamath Falls, OR 97601
(503) 883-6714
Includes portion of Pacific Crest
National Scenic Trail
BT, BW, C, CK, F, GS, H, HR, I, L, MB, MT, PA, RA, S, T, XC

YAQUINA HEAD OUTSTANDING NATURAL AREA
Bureau of Land Management
PO Box 936, Newport, OR 97365
(503) 265-2863
Foul weather gear usually needed
BW, H, I, RA, T

WASHINGTON

ALPINE LAKES WILDERNESS
U.S. Forest Service
Leavenworth Ranger District
600 Sherbourne
Leavenworth, WA 98826
(509) 782-1413
Cle Elum Ranger District

803 W. 2nd St.
Cle Elum, WA 98922
(509) 674-4411
Fee for Enchantments area and permit
required; definite campfire restrictions
BW, C, F, H, HR, I, MT, RC, S, TG, XC

ASAHEL CURTIS NATURE TRAIL
Mt. Baker–Snoqualmie National Forest
North Bend Ranger District
42404 S.E. North Bend Way
North Bend, WA 98045
(206) 888-1421
No motorized vehicles **BW, C, H, MT, PA**

BEACON ROCK STATE PARK
Wash. State Parks and Recreation Commission
PO Box 42650
Olympia, WA 98504-2650
(509) 427-8265; (360) 902-8563
9,500 ft. of freshwater shoreline; boat
launch
BW, C, F, H, HR, MB, MT, PA, RC, T

BLAKE ISLAND STATE PARK
Wash. State Parks and Recreation Commission
PO Box 277
Manchester, WA 98353
(360) 731-0770
Densely wooded island; accessible by
boat only **BW, C, CK, F, H, MT, PA, T**

BOGACHIEL STATE PARK
Wash. State Parks and Recreation
Commission
HC 80, Box 500
Forks, WA 98331
(360) 374-6356 **C, H, PA**

BOULDER RIVER WILDERNESS
Mt. Baker–Snoqualmie National Forest
Darrington Ranger District
1405 Emmens St.
Darrington, WA 98241
(360) 436-1155
BW, C, F, H, HR, MT, RC, XC

BROTHERS WILDERNESS
Olympic National Forest
Hood Canal Ranger District
PO Box 68, Hoodsport, WA 98548
(360) 877-5254 **BW, C, CK, F, GS, H, HR, I, MT, PA, S, T, XC**

BUCKHORN WILDERNESS
Olympic National Forest

BT	Bike Trails	**CK**	Canoeing, Kayaking	**F**	Fishing	**HR**	Horseback Riding
BW	Bird-watching			**GS**	Gift Shop		
C	Camping	**DS**	Downhill Skiing	**H**	Hiking	**I**	Information Center

Quilcene Ranger District
PO Box 280
Quilcene, WA 98376
(360) 765-3368
                        BW, C, CK, F, H, HR, MT, S, XC

CAMP WILLIAM T. WOOTEN STATE PARK
Wash. State Parks and Recreation
Commission
Route 1, Box 33, Pomeroy, WA 99347
(509) 843-3708
     Environmental learning center for groups
     by prearrangement   **H, I, MT, S, T**

CEDAR RIVER WATERSHED
City of Seattle Water Department
19901 Cedar Falls Rd. SE
North Bend, WA 98045
(206) 233-1515
     Restricted access; educational tours for
     groups by prearrangement   **BW, I, TG**

CLEARWATER WILDERNESS AREA
Mount Baker–Snoqualmie National Forest
White River Ranger Station
857 Roosevelt Ave. E
Enumclaw, WA 98022
(360) 825-6585   **H**

COLONEL BOB WILDERNESS
Olympic National Forest
Quinault Ranger District
PO Box 9, Quinault, WA 98575
(360) 288-2525   **C, H, HR, MT**

COLUMBIA NATIONAL WILDLIFE REFUGE
U.S. Fish and Wildlife Service
PO Drawer F, Othello, WA 99344-0227
(509) 488-2668   **BW, C, CK, F, MT, PA, T**

**COLUMBIA RIVER GORGE NATIONAL
SCENIC AREA**
U.S. Forest Service
902 Wasco Ave., Hood River, OR 97031
(503) 386-2333
                   **BT, BW, C, CK, F, GS, H, I,
                   MB, MT, PA, RA, RC, S, T**

COLVILLE NATIONAL FOREST
U.S. Forest Service
765 S. Main St., Colville, WA 99114
(509) 684-3711
     August and September—extreme fire
     precautions
            **BT, BW, C, CK, DS, F, GS, H, HR, I,
            MB, MT, PA, RA, RC, S, T, TG, XC**

**CONBOY LAKE NATIONAL WILDLIFE
REFUGE**
100 Wildlife Refuge Rd.
PO Box 5
Glenwood, WA 98619
(509) 364-3410   **BW, F, MT, RA, T, XC**

**COULEE DAM
NATIONAL RECREATION AREA**
National Park Service
1008 Crest Dr.
Coulee Dam, WA 99116
(509) 633-9441
Includes Dry Falls
            BW, C, CK, F, I, MT, PA, RA, S, T, TG

CRAWFORD STATE PARK
Wash. State Parks and Recreation
Commission
c/o Mount Spokane State Park
26107 Mount Spokane Park Dr.
Mead, WA 99021
(509) 456-4169
     Includes Gardner Cave; open summers
     only   **BW, C, H, TG**

DAMON POINT STATE PARK
Wash. State Parks and Recreation Commission
7150 Cleanwater Lane
PO Box 42650
Olympia, WA 98504-2650
(360) 289-3553   **BW, F, H, PA, T**

DECEPTION PASS STATE PARK
Wash. State Parks and Recreation Commission
5175 N. Route 20
Oak Harbor, WA 98277
(360) 675-2417 **BW, C, CK, F, H, MT, PA, S**

**DISHMAN HILLS NATURAL RESOURCE
CONSERVATION AREA**
Dishman Hills Association
10820 E. Maxwell
Spokane, WA 99206-4894
(509) 926-7949
     Park and walk in   **BW, C, H**

DUNGENESS NATIONAL WILDLIFE REFUGE
U.S. Fish and Wildlife Service
Washington Coastal Refuges
33 South Barr Rd.
Port Angeles, WA 98362
(360) 457-8451
     Entrance fee or current federal duck
     stamp; camping at adjacent county park
                        BW, CK, F, H, MT, PA, T

L	Lodging	**PA**	Picnic Areas	**RC**	Rock Climbing	**TG**	Tours, Guides
MB	Mountain Biking	**RA**	Ranger-led Activities	**S**	Swimming	**XC**	Cross-country Skiing
MT	Marked Trails			**T**	Toilets		

269

FEDERATION FOREST STATE PARK
Wash. State Parks and
Recreation Commission
49201 Enunclaw/Chinook Pass Rd.
Enumclaw, WA 98022
(360) 663-2207
Day-use only
BW, CK, F, H, I, MT, PA, T, TG, XC

**FLUME CREEK MOUNTAIN GOAT
VIEWING AREA**
Colville National Forest
Sullivan Lake Ranger District
Metaline Falls, WA 99153
(509) 446-2681
C, CK, F, H, I, MT, PA, S, T

FOULWEATHER BLUFF PRESERVE
The Nature Conservancy of Washington
217 Pine St., Ste. 1100
Seattle, WA 98101
(206) 343-4344
No fires; no pets; stay on trails or beach;
no natural materials to be removed from
area **BW, H, MT**

GIFFORD PINCHOT NATIONAL FOREST
U.S. Forest Service
6926 E. 4th Plain Blvd.
Vancouver, WA 98660
(360) 750-5000
Permits, available at trailheads, required
for 7 wilderness areas; permit in advance required to climb Mt. St. Helens
in summer
**BT, BW, C, CK, DS, F, H, HR,
I, L, MB, MT, PA, RC, S, T, XC**

GINKGO PETRIFIED FOREST STATE PARK
Wash. State Parks and Recreation
Commission
PO Box 42650
Olympia, WA 98504-2650
(509) 856-2700; (360) 902-8563
Includes Wanapum Recreation Area;
27,000 ft. of freshwater shoreline on reser-
voir **BW, C, F, GS, H, I, MT, PA, S, T**

GLACIER PEAK WILDERNESS
U.S. Forest Service
Lake Wenatchee Ranger District
22976 Route 207
Leavenworth, WA 98826
(509) 763-3103
Chelan Ranger District
PO Box 189
Chelan, WA 98816

(509) 682-2576
BW, C, F, H, HR, MT, RC, XC

GLACIER VIEW WILDERNESS
Gifford Pinchot National Forest
Packwood Ranger District
13068 Route 12, Packwood, WA 98361
(360) 494-5515 **C, F, H**

GOAT ROCKS WILDERNESS
U.S. Forest Service
Naches Ranger District
10061 Route 12, Naches, WA 98937
(509) 653-2205
Self-issue permits; campfire restrictions
BW, C, CK, F, H, HR, MT, RC, S, TG, XC

GRANDE RONDE RIVER CANYON
Bureau of Land Management
Baker Resource Area
PO Box 987, Baker City, OR 97814
(503) 523-1256
BW, C, CK, F, H, I, RA, RC, S

**GRAYS HARBOR NATIONAL
WILDLIFE REFUGE**
U.S. Fish and Wildlife Service
c/o Nisqually NWR
100 Brown Farm Rd.
Olympia, WA 98516
(360) 753-9467
Very limited access; shorebirds can be
viewed in mid-April **BW**

GRIFFITHS-PRIDAY STATE PARK
Wash. State Parks and Recreation
Commission
c/o Ocean City State Park
148 Route 115, Hoquiam, WA 98550
(360) 289-3553
Day-use only; reservable kitchen shelter
BW, CK, G, H, MT, PA, T

HANFORD NUCLEAR RESERVATION
U.S. Department of Energy
PO Box 550, Richland, WA 99352
(509) 376-7501
Not open to the general public except
by special arrangement **I, TG**

HENRY M. JACKSON WILDERNESS
U.S. Forest Service
Lake Wenatchee Ranger District
22976 Route 207
Leavenworth, WA 98826
(509) 763-3103

BT	Bike Trails	**CK**	Canoeing, Kayaking	**F**	Fishing	**HR**	Horseback Riding
BW	Bird-watching			**GS**	Gift Shop		
C	Camping	**DS**	Downhill Skiing	**H**	Hiking	**I**	Information Center

Campfire restrictions around high alpine lakes

BW, C, CK, F, H, HR, MT, RC, S, TG, XC

HOH RAINFOREST VISITOR CENTER

Olympic National Park
18113 Upper Hoh Rd.
Forks, WA 98331
(360) 374-6925

BW, C, F, H, I, MT, PA, RA, T

HOPE ISLAND STATE PARK

Wash. State Parks and Recreation Commission
c/o Deception Pass State Park
5175 N. Route 20, Oak Harbor, WA 98277
(360) 675-2417

Undeveloped area; beach access

BW, F, PA

HURRICANE RIDGE VISITOR CENTER

Olympic National Park
600 E. Park Ave., Port Angeles, WA 98362
(360) 452-0330

BW, DS, GS, H, I, MT, PA, RA, T, XC

INDIAN HEAVEN WILDERNESS

Gifford Pinchot National Forest
Mount Adams Ranger District
2455 Route 141, Trout Lake, WA 98650
(509) 395-2501

Permits required   **BW, C, F, H, HR, MT**

JULIA BUTLER HANSEN NATIONAL WILDLIFE REFUGE FOR THE COLUMBIAN WHITE-TAILED DEER

U.S. Fish and Wildlife Service
PO Box 566, Cathlamet, WA 98612
(360) 795-3915   **BW, H**

JUNIPER DUNES WILDERNESS AREA

Bureau Of Land Management
1103 North Fancher,
Spokane, WA 99212-1275
(509) 536-1200

No legal access; call office

BW, C, H, HR

LAKE CHELAN NATIONAL RECREATION AREA

National Park Service
2105 Route 20, Sedro, Woolley, WA 98284
(360) 856-5700

No natural materials or cultural artifacts may be removed from area

**BW, C, F, GS, H, HR, I, L, MT
PA, RA, RC, S, T, TG, XC**

LAKE CHELAN–SAWTOOTH WILDERNESS

U.S. Forest Service
Twisp Ranger District
502 Glover St., Twisp, WA 98856
(509) 997-2131

Outfitter guided trips; no permits necessary

BW, C, F, H, HR, MT

LARRABEE STATE PARK

Wash. State Parks and Recreation Commission
245 Chuckanut Dr.
Bellingham, WA 98226
(360) 676-2093

Beach access; boat launch

BW, C, CK, F, H, MT, PA, T

LEADBETTER POINT STATE PARK

Wash. State Parks and
Recreation Commission
c/o Fort Canby, PO Box 488
Ilwaco, WA 98624
(360) 642-3078

No cars   **BW, H, MT, T**

LEWIS AND CLARK STATE PARK

Wash. State Parks and
Recreation Commission
4583 Jackson Hwy.
Winlock, WA 98596
(360) 864-2643   **C, F, H, HR, MT, PA, T**

LIME KILN POINT STATE PARK

Wash. State Parks and
Recreation Commission
Northwest Region
PO Box 487
Burlington, WA 98233
(360) 755-9231

Includes Lime Kiln Point Lighthouse;
day-use only; stay on trails   **BW, H**

LITTLE PEND OREILLE NATIONAL WILDLIFE REFUGE

U.S. Fish and Wildlife Service
1310 Bear Creek Rd.
Colville, WA 99114
(509) 684-8384

4WD vehicle recommended

BW, C, CK, F, H, HR, MB, T, XC

McNARY NATIONAL WILDLIFE REFUGE

U.S. Fish and
Wildlife Service
PO Box 544
Burbank, WA 99323
(509) 547-4942   **BW, H, MT**

L	Lodging	**PA**	Picnic Areas	**RC**	Rock Climbing	**TG**	Tours, Guides
MB	Mountain Biking	**RA**	Ranger-led	**S**	Swimming	**XC**	Cross-country
MT	Marked Trails		Activities	**T**	Toilets		Skiing

MORAN STATE PARK
Wash. State Parks and
Recreation Commission
Star Route, Box 22
East Sound, WA 98245
(360) 376-2326
No motor boating; lodging for groups at
Environmental Learning Center
BW, C, CK, F, H, L, PA, S, T

MOUNT ADAMS WILDERNESS
Gifford Pinchot National Forest
Mount Adams Ranger District
2455 Route 141
Trout Lake, WA 98650
(509) 395-2501
Permits required   **BW, C, F, H, HR, MT**

**MOUNT BAKER NATIONAL
RECREATION AREA**
Mt. Baker-Snoqualmie National Forest
Mt. Baker Ranger District,2105 Route 20
Sedro Woolley, WA 98284
(360) 856-5700; (360) 599-2714
BW, C, F, H, HR, MB, MT, PA, XC

**MOUNT BAKER–SNOQUALMIE
NATIONAL FOREST**
U.S. Forest Service, 21905 64th Ave. W
Mountlake Terrace,
WA 98043-2278
(206) 744-3200
**BW, C, CK, DS, F, H, HR,
I, MB, MT, PA, RC, S, T, XC**

MOUNT BAKER WILDERNESS
Mt. Baker-Snoqualmie National Forest
Mt. Baker Ranger District
2105 Route 20,
Sedro Woolley, WA 98284
(360) 856-5700
No permits; group size limits
BW, C, F, H, HR, MT, RC, XC

MOUNT RAINIER NATIONAL PARK
National Park Service
Tahoma Woods, Star Route
Ashford, WA 98304
(360) 569-2211
No gas available in park; backcountry
permits required for overnight camping
**BT, BW, C, F, GS, H, HR,
L, MT, PA, RA, RC, T, TG, XC**

MOUNT SI
Wash. State Department of Natural Resources

PO Box 68, Enumclaw, WA 98022
(360) 825-1631
Keep animals on leash; no fires
BW, H, MT, PA, T

MOUNT SKOKOMISH WILDERNESS
Olympic National Forest
Hood Canal Ranger District
PO Box 68, Hoodsport, WA 98548
(360) 877-5254
No fires above 3500 ft. elevation

MOUNT SPOKANE STATE PARK
Wash. State Parks and Recreation Commission
N. 26107 Mount Spokane Park Dr.
Mead, WA 99021
(509) 456-4169
Views of 3 states from Vista House; per-
mit for parking required in winter
**BT, BW, C, DS, H, HR, I,
MT, MB, PA, RA, T, TG, XC**

**MOUNT ST. HELENS NATIONAL VOLCANIC
MONUMENT**
U.S. Forest Service
42218 N.E. Yale Bridge Rd.
Amboy, WA, 98601
(360) 750-3900; (360) 750-3902 (TDD)
Includes Mount St. Helens and
Coldwater Ridge visitor centers
**BT, BW, C, CK, F, GS, H, HR,
I, MB, MT, PA, RA, T, XC**

NISQUALLY NATIONAL WILDLIFE REFUGE
U.S. Fish and Wildlife Service
100 Brown Farm Rd.
Olympia, WA 98516
(360) 753-9467
No pets allowed   **BW, H, I, MT, T**

NOISY-DIOBSUD WILDERNESS
Mt. Baker-Snoqualmie National Forest
Mt. Baker Ranger District
2105 Route 20, Sedro Woolley, WA 98284
(360) 856-5700
Mountain and glacier climbing
BW, C, F, H, MT, XC

NORSE PEAK WILDERNESS
U.S. Forest Service
Naches Ranger District
10061 Route 12
Naches, WA 98937
(509) 653-2205
Self-issue permits
BW, C, CK, F, H, HR, MT, RC, S, TG, XC

BT	Bike Trails	**CK**	Canoeing, Kayaking	**F**	Fishing	**HR**	Horseback Riding
BW	Bird-watching			**GS**	Gift Shop		
C	Camping	**DS**	Downhill Skiing	**H**	Hiking	**I**	Information Center

NORTH CASCADES NATIONAL PARK
National Park Service
2105 Route 20, Sedro Woolley, WA 98284
(360) 856-5700
  No natural materials or cultural artifacts
  may be removed from area
          BW, C, CK, F, GS, H, I, L,
          MT, PA, RA, RC, T, TG, XC

NORTHERN PUGET SOUND STATE PARKS
Wash. State Parks and
Recreation Commission
Northwest Region
PO Box 487
Burlington, WA 98233
(360) 755-9231
  Includes Blind, Clark, Doe, James,
  Jones, Matia, Patos, Posey, Turn, and
  Sucia Island state parks; accessible only
  by boat; some have pit or vault toilets
               BW, C, F, H

NORTHWEST TREK
Metropolitan Park District of Tacoma
11610 Trek Dr. E, Eatonville, WA 98328
(360) 832-6117; (800) 433 TREK (recording in WA & OR only)
        GS, H, I, MT, PA, T, TG

OKANOGAN NATIONAL FOREST
U.S. Forest Service
1240 S. Second Ave.
Okanogan, WA 98840
(509) 826-3275
  Includes North Cascades Scenic
  Highway, Slate Peak, and portions of
  the Pacific Crest Trail
      BT, BW, C, DS, F, GS, H, HR, I,
      MB, MT, PA, RA, RC, T, TG, XC

OLYMPIC NATIONAL PARK
National Park Service
600 E. Park Ave.
Port Angeles, WA 98362
(360) 452-4501
  See park ranger for fishing and clamming regulations
      BT, BW, C, CK, DS, F, GS, H, HR,
      I, L, MB, MT, PA, RA, S, T, XC

OLYMPIC WILDLIFE AREA
Wash. Dept. of Fish and Wildlife
48 Devonshire Rd.
Montesano, WA 98563-9618
(360) 249-6522
  Conservation permit required; call office
            BW, CK, F, H, T

PACIFIC CREST NATIONAL SCENIC TRAIL
U.S. Forest Service, Pacific N.W. Region 6
Recreation Information
333 S.W. 1st Ave., Portland, OR 97208
(503) 326-2877
  Call for maps   **BW, H**

PALOUSE FALLS STATE PARK
Wash. State Parks and Recreation
Commission
c/o Central Ferry State Park
Route 3, Box 99, Pomeroy, WA 99347
(509) 549-3551   **BW, C, H, MT, PA**

PASAYTEN WILDERNESS
Okanogan National Forest
Methow Valley Ranger District
PO Box 579, Winthrop, WA 98862
(509) 996-2266
  No permits; group size limits
        BW, C, F, H, HR, MT, XC

POINT DEFIANCE PARK
Metropolitan Park District of Tacoma
5400 N. Pearl
Tacoma, WA 98407
(206) 591-5337
  Includes zoo and aquarium
       BT, BW, F, GS, H, I, MT, T

PROTECTION ISLAND
NATIONAL WILDLIFE REFUGE
U.S. Fish and Wildlife Service
Washington Coastal Refuges
33 South Barr Rd.
Port Angeles, WA 98362
(360) 457-8451
  Accessible only by boat; closed to the public; bird-watching 200 yards offshore   **BW**

ROCKPORT STATE PARK
Wash. State Parks and Recreation Commission
5051 Route 20
Concrete, WA 98237
(360) 676-2093
  Closed in winter; boat launch
          BW, C, H, MT, PA, T

ROSS LAKE NATIONAL RECREATION AREA
North Cascades
National Park
2105 Route 20
Sedro Woolley, WA 98284
(360) 856-5700
  No natural materials or cultural artifacts
  may be removed from area
         BW, C, CK, F, H, HR,

L	Lodging	**PA**	Picnic Areas	**RC**	Rock Climbing	**TG**	Tours, Guides
MB	Mountain Biking	**RA**	Ranger-led	**S**	Swimming	**XC**	Cross-country
MT	Marked Trails		Activities	**T**	Toilets		Skiing

273

SALMO-PRIEST WILDERNESS
U.S. Forest Service
Sullivan Lake Ranger District
12641 Sullivan Lake Rd.
Metaline Falls, WA 99153
(509) 446-2681; (208) 443-2512
Voluntary sign-in; no permits; bear precautions **BW, C, F, H, HR, MT**

**SAN JUAN ISLAND
NATIONAL HISTORICAL PARK**
National Park Service
PO Box 429,
Friday Harbor, WA 98250
(360) 378-2240
Day-use only **BW, F, GS, H,
I, MT, PA, RA, T**

**SAN JUAN ISLANDS NATIONAL
WILDLIFE REFUGE**
U.S. Fish and Wildlife Service
c/o Nisqually NWR
100 Brown Farm Rd.
Olympia, WA 98516
(360) 753-9467
Camping at Matia and Turn only **BW, C**

SCHMITZ PARK
Seattle Dept. of Parks and Recreation
100 Dexter Ave. N
Seattle, WA 98109
(206) 684-8021 **BW, H, MT**

SEWARD PARK
Seattle Dept. of Parks and Recreation
100 Dexter Ave. N
Seattle, WA 98109
(206) 684-8021
Bald eagles reside here; beach access;
no mountain bikes allowed
BT, BW, F, H, MT, PA, T, TG

**SKAGIT RIVER BALD EAGLE
NATURAL AREA**
The Nature Conservancy of Washington
217 Pine St., Ste. 1100
Seattle, WA 98101
(206) 343-4344
Avoid disturbing eagles; do not beach
boats; call office for boating regulations
BW

SKAGIT WILDLIFE AREA
Wash. Dept. of Fish and Wildlife
16018 Mill Creek Blvd.
Mill Creek, WA 98012
(206) 775-1311

Conservation permit required
BW, CK, F, H, I, MT, S, T

SNAKE LAKE NATURE CENTER
Metropolitan Park District of Tacoma
1919 S. Tyler, Tacoma, WA 98405
(206) 591-6439
BW, GS, H, I, MT, PA, RA, T, TG

STONEROSE INTERPRETIVE CENTER
15 North Kean St., PO Box 987
Republic, WA 99166
(509) 775-2295
Donation requested; some restrictions
on fossil hunting **GS, I, PA, T, TG**

SUN LAKES STATE PARK
Wash. State Parks and
Recreation Commission
34875 Park Lake Rd., NE
Coulee City, WA 99115
(509) 632-5583;
(509) 632-5214 (vs. center, summer)
open all year; boat launch
**BT, BW, C, CK, F, GS,
H, I, L, MB, PA, S, T,**

TATOOSH WILDERNESS
Gifford Pinchot National Forest
Packwood Ranger District
13068 Route 12
Packwood, WA 98361
(360) 494-5515 **C, F, H, HR**

**TOPPENISH NATIONAL
WILDLIFE REFUGE**
U.S. Fish and Wildlife Service
21 Pumphouse Rd.
Toppenish, WA 98948
(509) 865-2405
No vehicles **BW, H, I, MT, PA, T**

TRAPPER CREEK WILDERNESS
Gifford Pinchot National Forest
Mount Adams Ranger District
2455 Route 141,
Trout Lake, WA 98650
(509) 395-2501
Permits required
BW, C, F, H, HR, MT, TG, XC

TURNBULL NATIONAL WILDLIFE REFUGE
U.S. Fish and Wildlife Service
S. 26010 Smith Rd.
Cheney, WA 99004
(509) 235-4723
Day-use only **BT, BW, H, I, MT, T, XC**

BT	Bike Trails	**CK**	Canoeing, Kayaking	**F**	Fishing	**HR**	Horseback Riding
BW	Bird-watching			**GS**	Gift Shop		
C	Camping	**DS**	Downhill Skiing	**H**	Hiking	**I**	Information Center

UMATILLA NATIONAL FOREST
U.S. Forest Service
2517 S.W. Hailey Ave.
Pendleton, OR 97801
(503) 278-3716   **BT, BW, C, CK, DS, F, H
HR, I, MB, MT, PA, S, T, XC**

UMATILLA NATIONAL WILDLIFE REFUGE
U.S. Fish and Wildlife Service
PO Box 700, Umatilla, OR 97882
(503) 922-3232   **BW, F, MT, T**

WALLACE FALLS STATE PARK
Wash. State Parks and
Recreation Commission
PO Box 230, Goldbar, WA 98251
(360) 793-0420
Camping; tents only
BW, C, F, H, MB, MT, PA, T

WENAHA-TUCANNON WILDERNESS
Umatilla National Forest
Pomeroy Ranger District
Route 1, Box 53-F
Pomeroy, WA 99347
(509) 843-1891   **BW, C, F, H, HR, MT**

WENATCHEE NATIONAL FOREST
U.S. Forest Service
PO Box 811, Wenatchee, WA 98807
(509) 662-4335
Eight wilderness areas; permits required
**BT, BW, C, CK, DS, F, H, HR, I,
MB, MT, PA, RA, RC, S, T, TG, XC**

WILLAPA NATIONAL WILDLIFE REFUGE
U.S. Fish and Wildlife Service
HC 01, Box 910
Ilwaco, WA 98624
(360) 484-3482   **BW, C, CK, H, T**

WILLIAM O. DOUGLAS WILDERNESS
U.S. Forest Service
Naches Ranger District
10061 Route 12
Naches, WA 98937
(509) 662-4335 (Wenatchee N.F.)
(360) 750-5000 (Gifford Pinchot N.F.)
BW, C, F, H, HR, MT, RC, S, XC

**YAKIMA RIVER CANYON
RECREATION AREA**
Bureau of Land Management
915 N. Walla Walla Ave.
Wenatchee, WA 98801
(509) 665-2100
Nesting raptors; rafting
BW, C, CK, F, H, HR, PA, RC, S, T

YELLOW ISLAND PRESERVE
The Nature Conservancy of Washington
217 Pine St., Ste. 1100
Seattle, WA 98101
(206) 343-4344
Day-use only; groups of 6 or more get
permission first; no food allowed
BW, CK, H, MT

L Lodging	**PA** Picnic Areas	**RC** Rock Climbing	**TG** Tours, Guides
MB Mountain Biking	**RA** Ranger-led	**S** Swimming	**XC** Cross-country
MT Marked Trails	Activities	**T** Toilets	Skiing

275

INDEX

ABOVE: *While her car and driver wait, Mrs. D. L. Reaburn adds the finishing touches to her view of Mount Rainier National Park in 1918.*

CREDITS

All photography by Tim Thompson except for the following:

i: John Shaw, Colorado Springs, CO
iv: Tom and Pat Leeson, Vancouver, WA
viii, right: Pat O'Hara, Port Angeles, WA
x-xi: David Muench, Santa Barbara, CA
xiv: Charles Mauzy, Seattle, WA
xvi–1: Steve Terrill, Portland, OR
11: John Hendrickson, Clipper Mills, CA
14: James O. Holloway, Portland, OR
15: Tom and Pat Leeson, Vancouver, WA
16–17: Steve Terrill, Portland, OR
19: Museum of History and Industry, Historical Society of Seattle and King County, Seattle, WA (Neg. #83.10 7394)
21: John Marshall, Peshastin, WA
22: Royal Ontario Museum, Toronto, Canada (ROM #912.1.78)
26–27: Pat O'Hara, Port Angeles, WA
32–33: Tom and Pat Leeson, Vancouver, WA
36–37: John Marshall, Peshastin, WA
42: John Shaw, Colorado Springs, CO
47, top: John Hendrickson, Clipper Mills, CA
47, bot: Bates Littlehales, Arlington, VA
50, left: Charles Krebs, Issaquah, WA
50, right: Tom and Pat Leeson, Vancouver, WA
51: John Marshall, Peshastin, WA
54–55: Charles Gurche, Spokane, WA
56–57: Susan Drinker, Snow Mass Village, CO
67, 68–69, 71: Tom and Pat Leeson, Vancouver, WA
72: Charles Gurche, Spokane, WA
76: Tom and Pat Leeson, Vancouver, WA
80–81: Pat O'Hara, Port Angeles, WA
84, left: Jim Dutcher, Sun Valley, ID
84, right: Erwin and Peggy Bauer, Livingston, MT
87: Tom and Pat Leeson, Vancouver, WA
89, 97: Thomas D. Mangelsen/Images of Nature, Jackson, WY
102: Washington State Historical Society, Tacoma, WA
103, 106: Pat O'Hara, Port Angeles, WA
110: Roger Werth/Woodfin Camp & Associates, New York, NY

112: Tom and Pat Leeson, Vancouver, WA
118–119: James O. Holloway, Portland, OR
120: Art Wolfe, Seattle, WA
121: Tom and Pat Leeson, Vancouver, WA
126, 127: Art Wolfe, Seattle, WA
128: John Shaw, Colorado Springs, CO
133: Zig Leszczynski/Animals Animals, Chatham, NY
135: Arthur Morris/Birds As Art, Deltona, FL
141, 142: Tom and Pat Leeson, Vancouver, WA
150: American Philosophical Society, Philadelphia, PA
154: Francis Lepine/Animals Animals, Chatham, NY
157: Steve Terrill, Portland, OR
161: Library of Congress, Washington, D.C.
164, top: Tom and Pat Leeson, Vancouver, WA
164, bot: John Hendrickson, Clipper Mills, CA
165: Bates Littlehales, Arlington, VA
180, bot: Alan G. Nelson/Animals Animals, Chatham, NY
184: Tom and Pat Leeson, Vancouver, WA
186: Leonard Lee Rue III/Animals Animals, Chatham, NY
196–197: Ray Atkeson/American Landscapes, Portland, OR
216: Steve Terrill, Portland, OR
225, left: Art Wolfe, Seattle, WA
225, top: G.C. Kelley, Tucson, AZ
225, bot: John Shaw, Colorado Springs, CO
238: Ken Cole/Animals Animals, Chatham, NY
239, top: Darrell Gulin, Issaquah, WA
243: Leonard Lee Rue III/Animals Animals, Chatham, NY
244: John Shaw, Colorado Springs, CO
287: Museum of History and Industry, Historical Society of Seattle and King County, Seattle, WA (Neg. #83.10 12252.1)
Back cover: John Shaw (owl); Tim Thompson (beach trail); Tom and Pat Leeson (seal)

ACKNOWLEDGMENTS

The editors gratefully acknowledge the assistance of Kerry Acker, Judith Hancock, Jane Hoffman, Susan Kirby, and Mary Luders. The following consultants also helped in the preparation of this volume: Steve Wang of the Washington State Parks and Recreation Commission, Marjorie Willis of the Oregon Parks and Recreation Department, and Dallas Rhodes, Professor and Chair of Geology, Whittier College.

INTRODUCTION
THE PACIFIC NORTHWEST

Ancient tree trunks rise from shadows to a roof of sunlit branches one hundred feet up. Standing among them, a visitor feels small beside the massive, rough-barked columns, and smaller still in the vast, silent space they define. People do not speak idly of the Northwest's "cathedral forests." Just as in the great Gothic cathedrals of western Europe, one gets a lift here, a feeling of high, vaulted enclosure, as the eye is drawn inexorably up the columns into the dimly seen spaces far above.

Encompassing the states of Washington and Oregon, the Pacific Northwest, where these great trees grow, is a land of spectacular verticals: Washington's Mount Rainier at 14,410 feet, Oregon's Mount Hood at 11,235 feet, and seven other 10,000-foot volcanoes are almost always snowcapped, and the lesser volcanoes and nonvolcanic peaks of the Cascade Mountains extend from Canada to California. "A great many people believed that [the Cascades] were the most beautiful mountains in the United States," writes John McPhee in *Encounters with the Archdruid*. "A smaller and, on the whole, more parochial group felt that . . . [they] were the most beautiful mountains in the world."

Not all the verticals are mountains: Hells Canyon at 7,900 feet is the deepest gorge in North America—the deepest river-cut gorge in the world—and Crater Lake at 1,932 feet is the nation's deepest lake. Other verticals are scattered throughout the two states: the waterfall-rich cliffs of the Columbia River Gorge; Dry Falls, the monumental desert drop over which the Columbia River once plunged; the striking rock spires, rimrocks, and fault scarps of eastern Oregon; the offshore sea stacks, rocky pinnacles that line much of the two states' 500-mile Pacific coastline. Finally, there are the big trees, the forests of Douglas fir, true fir, western hemlock, spruce, redcedar, and pon-

---

PRECEDING PAGES: *In early summer, pink dame's rocket and red Sitka columbine bloom high above the Columbia near Oregon's Crown Point. This stretch of river is part of the Columbia River Gorge National Scenic Area.*

derosa pine that for many people define the region.

European civilization reached the Northwest relatively recently: A Greek navigator sailing for Spain under the name of Juan de Fuca may have visited in the late sixteenth century, but even if he saw the coast, he didn't linger. Spaniards unquestionably came in the late 1700s and briefly maintained a small colony at Neah Bay near the tip of the Olympic Peninsula in the early 1790s. The English captain George Vancouver explored the coast in 1792, and that same year American captain Robert Gray maneuvered his Boston merchant ship the *Columbia Rediviva* into the mouth of the waterway subsequently called the Columbia River. Lewis and Clark followed the river to the Pacific in 1805, and settlers first struggled over the Oregon Trail in the 1840s.

The region had been inhabited millennia earlier. Stone spear points found near Wenatchee, Washington, were made by hunters about 9,000 B.C. at the end of the last Ice Age, and points and fragments found in a cave near Fort Rock, Oregon, date from nearly 13,500 years ago. The early residents built with wood and seldom established year-round settlements, however, leaving no monuments. Recorded history here has been brief, and there are few reminders of even that short span—the Northwest has no equivalent to New England's colonial churches, eighteenth-century houses, or old stone walls. But one can get a sense of continuity, of the passage of time and the brevity of human existence, from the region's old-growth forests and geology.

Some 200 million years ago, the current Selkirk and Blue mountains, which now border Idaho, marked the western coastline of North America. As the Pacific oceanic and the North American continental plates moved toward each other, an inch or two a year, eventually (between 50 and 40 million years ago) North America met and annexed several island microcontinents, which probably originated on the far side of the Pacific. The first "island" became Washington's Okanogan highlands, the second the northern Cascades, a third British Columbia's Vancouver Island. New mountains were thrust upward as the microcontinents slammed into North America and each other.

The Olympic Peninsula is actually a piece of the heavier oceanic crust, which normally is subducted—it slips beneath the lighter continental crust and is drawn back down into the earth's molten inner layer. Instead, this portion of oceanic crust was caught and jammed ever higher between two subcontinents, the northern Cascades and Vancouver Island. Glaciers later gouged out Puget Sound and Hood

ABOVE: *Winter snow covers Mount Shuksan, which rises above Baker Lake. A nonvolcanic peak in Washington's North Cascades, Shuksan is a particularly striking landmark and a particularly difficult climb.*

Canal, isolating the entire Olympic area.

The great Cascades volcanoes were formed as the oceanic and continental plates continued to interact. These volcanic peaks—including ancient mounts Mazama and Mahogany and modern Baker, Rainier, St. Helens, Adams, Hood, and a host of other southern Cascades—form an arc about a hundred miles inland from the California border to Canada. Successive eruptions have built (and in some cases then destroyed) mammoth lava cones and ash layers, which have been eroded and molded by enormous glaciers. Between 17 and 12 million years ago, lava bubbled from large crustal fissures in the eastern sections of both states, leaving thick, relatively flat layers of basalt that form the outcrops and rimrock of the eastern basins and the cliffs of the Columbia River Gorge.

If the rocks evoke the region's ancient history, then old-growth forests are a link to its more tangible past. Trees now living were old when Vancouver first saw the coast, and logs that were already dead when he arrived still exist. In the eastern Okanogan highlands are fossils (needles, seeds, a whole Asian-ink-painting curve of branch) of similar trees that grew here 40 million years ago, the ancestors of modern fir and hemlock, spruce and cedar.

In a sense, the living forest is a relic of a time millions of years ago in the early Eocene epoch. David Rains Wallace writes in his modern classic of natural history, *The Klamath Knot:* "There is still one area west of the Rockies . . . where rainfall and temperatures approximate the benign Eocene environment: the inner coastal ranges of southwest Oregon and northwest California, the Klamath Mountains. In the Klamaths, winters are mild enough and summers moist enough for species to grow together that elsewhere are segregated by altitude or latitude. Several species that once grew throughout the West now survive only in the Klamaths. Perched on my Siskiyou [Mountain] eminence, I again felt suspended over great gulfs of time. The stunted little trees and their giant relatives on the lower slopes were not a mere oddity forest where ill-assorted species came together in a meaningless jumble. They were in a sense the ancestors of all western forests, the rich gene pool from which the less varied, modern conifer forests have marched out to conquer forbidding heights from Montana to New Mexico. Looking out over the pyramidal Siskiyou ridges, I was seeing a community of trees at least forty million years old."

The forests of the Northwest were once even more varied than Wallace described. Fossils show that all kinds of plants grew east of the Cascades, along with the conifers and the exotic modern flora of the Siskiyous: mahogany, ginkgo, and other plants that now appear naturally only in the tropics or in Asia. At the John Day Fossil Beds in eastern Oregon, fossils of palm, banana, and other tropical flora show that this region—now a high desert more reminiscent of the Southwest than of what most people consider the Northwest—used to be a damp tropical jungle.

In temperate rain forests on the Olympic Peninsula, the earth beneath the great trees is never bare, and there are no simple verticals or horizontals. Gray-green epiphytes drip from branches and cling to trunks. Moss envelops everything, softening, thickening, and imparting an otherworldly yellow-green glow. It highlights the edges of logs and rocks, giving the forest a brightness that seems more than physical.

Here nothing is simply dead. A tree trunk takes roughly as long to rot as it does to grow, and from the mossy bulk of a dead log a colonnade of new trees spring up. The trunk grew for centuries, and the younger trees, themselves no saplings, have already been here perhaps a hundred years. Sometimes the nurse log has rotted away, leaving the thick roots of the next generation curved around the space where the log used to lie, like people whose acts are still shaped by some long-forgotten insult or principle.

Although similar in other respects, the ancient fir forests of the western Cascades and the ponderosa pine forests farther east lack the rain forest's nurse logs, its glowing moss and hanging epiphytes, its sense that everything is *alive*. Hiking in the rain forest is a bit like being Jonah inside the whale.

The high country less than a day's hike away is completely different. Even on the coast or in the eastern desert, mountains are never distant in the Northwest—and none are more dramatic than those in the northern Cascades. Climb high in the North Cascades National Park, tie the tent down firmly against the wind, spend the night. In the early morning, sunlight strikes a sea of peaks spreading southward, granite shards rising clear to the horizon like so many waves. At dawn, the white of hanging glaciers is already tinged with blue; yesterday blue ice thundered down mountainsides as the nearest glacier calved. The old-growth fir and hemlock trees, the meadows bright with mountain-heather and lupine, are far below. Up here, all is rock and ice. Almost all, anyway. A group of bucks that arrived soon after sunup, climbing the snowfield from meadows far below, finds small plants to nibble among the rocks. The bucks came, more than likely, to avoid the heat; in summer deer are often seen above 6,000 feet. Nevertheless, their presence up here far above the trees and meadows adds a touch of mystery, which seems appropriate here. The rock slope lies in a different world, beyond timberline, with a glacier crouching on the mountainside above. Another, much larger glacier lies just out of sight to the east, and the valley below is filled with the sound of falling water. Here the water is frozen; only the glacier melt seeps silently among the rocks, without ripples or foam.

OVERLEAF: *Remarkable rock formations catch the afternoon light at the Clarno Unit of Oregon's John Day Fossil Beds. Plant fossils embedded in the volcanic rock here are between 50 and 35 million years old.*

The only waves are the layer on layer of wind-carved rock.

The contrasts between rain forest and high rock, between foggy coast and stark desert, often exist in close juxtaposition. Salt water can be seen from the coastal mountains and vice versa; Hells Canyon lies fewer than 50 miles from the heavily forested, lake-studded 9,000-foot Wallowa Mountains. Salmon that have fed on plankton, herring, and anchovies in the Pacific Ocean swim through the high desert.

There is also much that ties this land together—fauna, flora, climate. Pacific tides touch the western borders of both Washington and Oregon, and whales migrate along the entire coast. Elk and mule deer are found throughout the states; black bears and cougars are scattered in the mountains. Marmots inhabit the rocky alpine meadows, and eagles soar above the landscape both east and west. The Cascades form a north-south axis from Canada to California; volcanoes and the remnants of volcanoes outline their mountainous spine from Mount Baker in the north through the Crater Lake caldera in the south. Great swaths of wildflowers—red and orange paintbrush, blue penstemon and lupine, yellow-centered purple asters and daisies, white tufted bear grass, pink and yellow monkeyflowers—fill the high-country meadows after the snow melts, which, depending on altitude, is anytime from spring to late summer. Creeping phlox grows in rocky areas, and above the tree line, heatherlike cassiope carpets the ground. Near the Columbia River, delicate avalanche lilies enliven wet meadows even before the snow is entirely gone. Rhododendrons thrive near the coast and in the midmontane forests. Fireweed blooms on slopes still bare from clear-cuts or black from forest fires.

Along most of the rainy coast, from the Olympic Peninsula to southern Oregon, Sitka spruce is the dominant tree. In the wettest parts of the coastal and central valleys—even in the Selkirk Mountains near the Idaho border—wherever Pacific moisture is trapped and the ground stays damp, western redcedar grows. At high elevations below timberline, Pacific silver fir, mountain hemlock, subalpine fir, and Engelmann spruce hold sway. In the lower-elevation forests of western Washington and much of western Oregon, western hemlock is the

---

RIGHT: *In Washington's Mount Rainier National Park a gray log, weathered like inland driftwood, rests in a carpet of paintbrush and monkeyflowers, which thrive in the moist soil along a stream near Tipsoo Lake.*

climax species (the plant that would naturally grow and mature here if the forest were left undisturbed for centuries by fire or saw). Douglas fir grows taller in these western forests, and in most of them it is the more impressive and conspicuous tree. Douglas fir succeeds throughout the Northwest wherever rainfall is adequate, but it becomes a dominant tree over large areas only in the western part of the region. Similarly, lodgepole and ponderosa pines thrive on both sides of the mountains, but east of the Cascade crest, they are the dominant trees.

In many ways, the Cascades divide the region as much as they unify it. The mountains are largely responsible for the quick transition from western forests of subalpine fir, hemlock, and Douglas fir to eastern pines and desert. The crucial fact is that rain clouds from the Pacific seldom make it all the way across the Cascades. Forced to higher altitudes, the clouds dump most of their moisture on the western side and have little left by the time they reach the eastern.

The difference in environment becomes obvious in the Cascades themselves. On the eastern slopes, which boast higher summer temperatures and less winter snow than western slopes, timberline—where the stunted, twisted alpine trees give way to white, or mountain, heather, huckleberries, and rock—starts as much as 1,500 feet higher. Down in the woods on a hot summer day, the western side smells like Douglas fir, while the eastern breeze carries the sharper scent of ponderosa pine. Culturally and economically, the Cascades form a boundary between the populous, urban, and generally liberal west and the sparsely populated, conservative east, where dry-land wheat farming, ranching, and irrigated agriculture are still economic staples. When Joel Garreau divided the continent into natural bioregions in his *Nine Nations of North America,* he put western Washington and Oregon in a coastal "Ecotopia" that stretched from northern California to Alaska, while the eastern parts of the states were included in a vast, arid intermountain "Empty Quarter."

In other words, a great deal separates the eastern and western parts of the Northwest, and the only physical feature that binds them together is the Columbia River. Draining more than a quarter-million square miles, the Columbia is the only river that cuts all the way through the Cascades. Older even than the mountains, the river has been flowing to the ocean since before a collision of tectonic plates forced the Cascades up to their current height some two million years ago. The Columbia, its tributaries, and the tributaries of its tributaries reach into the far eastern corners of both Washington and Oregon and drain neighboring states as well.

Physical features aside, various areas of the Northwest share some common history: centuries of Native American inhabitation; early explorations by seafarers such as Vancouver and Gray; and the no-less-epic journeys of nineteenth-century fur traders and settlers. Washington and Oregon were both part of the Oregon Country, which Britain formally ceded to the United States in 1846. Both have depended heavily on timber, fish, and other natural resources throughout much of their history.

The region has also seen some key environmental conflicts, including the fight over the northern spotted owl, one of the hottest environmental issues in the early 1990s. A reclusive bird that lives primarily on wood rats and flying squirrels, the spotted owl was little known until the late 1960s, when an Oregon State University student named Eric Forsman accidentally discovered one in the Willamette National Forest and learned how to call it. Forsman and his colleagues soon determined that the spotted owl lived almost exclusively in old-growth forests. They also noticed that whenever they located an owl, its nest area or a forest close to its nest was about to be clear cut. The scientists alerted the U.S. Forest Service, which devised schemes—all subsequently considered inadequate—for protecting owl habitat. The U.S. Fish and Wildlife Service, however, made no move to list the bird as threatened or endangered, which would have legally prevented the destruction of its habitat on federal lands. Finally, in the late 1980s, an obscure East Coast environmental group petitioned the government to list the owl under the Endangered Species Act. When the government declined to do so, environmental groups sued. In court, not a single scientific witness supported the government's position; the judge sent the government back to the drawing board; in 1990 the owl was finally listed as a threatened species.

Many environmentalists found that the legal requirement to protect owl habitat provided leverage for another concern—preserving old-growth forests. The owl was the legal issue that triggered the enforcement of various laws. Everyone understood from the start, however, that the political fight was not just about birds. The underlying issue was the fate of the owl's habitat, the last unprotected ancient forests in the Northwest.

According to several estimates, 80 to 90 percent of the region's original old-growth forests are already gone. Although there are still

plenty of trees, the new forests are qualitatively different. At its simplest, "old growth" means a bunch of old trees. To scientists and participants in the debate about saving habitat for the northern spotted owl and other wildlife, however, the critical feature of such forests is not age but structure. Characteristic old-growth features include large trees; a multilayered, largely closed canopy of branches; large, dead standing snags; and large rotting logs. The length of time required to develop that structure varies with location and altitude. At low elevations in redwood country, the process can take less than a century. At higher elevations farther north, it may require several centuries. As a rule of thumb, old-growth structure develops in 200 years.

To the forest-products companies and mill towns that depended on old-growth trees from federal forests (big forest-products companies may own their own forests but smaller ones rely on public timber), the protection of old-growth owl habitat seemed like a death warrant. The industry and the mill towns had long been losing jobs through attrition, automation, and recession. And although no one claimed that supplies of old-growth timber were infinite, protecting millions of acres for spotted owls could only hasten the demise of thousands of jobs and the mill-town economies that depended on them. The Bush administration tried to ignore the laws requiring it to protect the owl, but it lost repeatedly in federal court. In 1991, when U.S. District Court Judge William Dwyer enjoined all sales of old-growth timber in western Washington and Oregon, he noted that the government had committed "a remarkable series of violations of the environmental laws."

The spotted owl conflict marked a turning point for the Northwest. Clearly,

ABOVE: *The threatened northern spotted owl has become a symbol of the political battles over the Northwest's remaining old-growth forests.*

LEFT: *The double cascade of Multnomah Falls drops 620 feet beside an old scenic walkway bridge on the Oregon side of the Columbia Gorge.*

OVERLEAF: *Oregon's Drift Creek Wilderness includes this grove of towering Douglas fir trees, ancient survivors that still endure in an old-growth forest.*

the rest of the nation would no longer let the fate of the region's federal forests be dictated by local economic interests. The dispute also helped people understand that an ancient forest is not just trees but an entire ecosystem where numerous creatures besides owls live at least parts of their lives. Residents of old-growth forests may also include the pileated woodpecker, the big red-crested bird that nests in cavities in old trees and sounds like a jackhammer in the woods; the marbled murrelet, a threatened bird that feeds at sea but flies as far as 50 miles inland to nest in old-growth trees; the fisher, a member of the weasel family that makes dens in the cavities of big trees; and many runs of Pacific salmon and steelhead trout, whose spawning streams are sheltered by ancient forests.

Realistically, few people may have worried about marbled murrelets or even spotted owls, but Northwesterners have always cared about salmon. From the beginning, salmon have been the centerpiece of ecosystems, cultures, and self-images in the Pacific Northwest. Even more than the Columbia River, they have bound the region together biologically and culturally.

Five distinct species of Pacific salmon and the seagoing steelhead trout, which has been reclassified as a salmon, begin their lives in fresh water, swim out to sea, and return to fresh water to spawn. They spawn in clear, flowing water with a gravel bottom. After periods of time ranging from a couple of months to several years, the young fish enter the Pacific. There they make ocean journeys that may cover thousands of miles in one to seven years. Finally, as mature fish, they return to the same rivers, the same streams, the same rivulets where they were spawned. Experts believe that they find chemical traces of the vegetation and minerals of their home streams and follow these back to the spawning beds. Arthur D. Hasler, the scientist who largely developed this theory, has described the fish as "following a scent like a foxhound." Once they reach their spawning beds, the salmon lay their eggs and most die. (Steelhead, like Atlantic salmon, can spawn more than once.)

Historically, salmon spawned in virtually every river and stream in the Northwest. All the coastal rivers and those flowing into Puget Sound supported one or more fish runs, as did virtually all the Columbia's far-flung tributaries. Every year before Europeans arrived, 15 or 16 million big fish followed the river into virtually every drainage of central and eastern Washington and Oregon, all the way into Idaho and British Columbia, sometimes gaining thousands of feet

ABOVE: *At the turn of the century, these loggers, photographed near Brinnon, Washington, used double-bitted axes and crosscut saws to fell whole forests of old-growth trees on the Olympic Peninsula.*

in elevation and swimming inland more than a thousand miles.

Growing from little smolts to adults that in some cases weigh more than a hundred pounds, Pacific salmon take protein from the ocean and make it available to inland ecosystems. The hundreds of eagles that appear every winter along Washington's Skagit River—perhaps the second-largest gathering of eagles anywhere in the United States outside Alaska—go there to eat spawned-out chum salmon. Researchers working in Olympic National Park found that salmon were eaten by at least 22 species of birds and mammals, including bears, coyotes, river otters, bobcats, weasels, mink, skunks, raccoons, mountain beavers, Douglas' squirrels, northern flying squirrels, deer mice, shrews, red-tailed hawks, ravens, crows, dippers, jays, and winter wrens. The researchers were

19

surprised to find that black bears had retrieved dead salmon from pools up to five feet deep and that other salmon carcasses had evidently been nibbled by deer.

People have always taken advantage of the salmon runs too. Salmon were an economic staple and a cultural centerpiece for Native American tribes in Washington and Oregon, both west and east of the Cascades. The Makahs, who lived on the tip of the Olympic Peninsula and still hunted whales from dugout cedar canoes in the early twentieth century, caught, dried, and ate salmon. So did the Nez Percé of eastern Washington and Oregon, the horse breeders who are popularly (and probably erroneously) credited with developing the Appaloosa. Salmon vertebrae found at an ancient fishing and trading site in The Dalles, Oregon, go back 8,000 years. Anthropologists calculate that tribes living on the arid Columbia Plateau ate literally hundreds of pounds of salmon per person each year. When Lewis and Clark reached the Columbia River in the fall of 1805, salmon were swimming upstream to spawn, and Native Americans were drying them along the banks. The explorers had never seen anything quite like it. Clark wrote that "the number of dead Salmon on the Shores & floating in the river is incredible [sic] to say." Non-natives were fishing the Columbia River and Puget Sound decades before the end of the nineteenth century. Today people continue to catch fish for both money and sport along the entire northwestern coast.

The regular return of the salmon makes them a uniquely valuable resource to humans and a wide variety of other animals, but it also makes them singularly vulnerable. Since the nineteenth century, salmon fishing has been a kind of economic free-for-all, and even under stringent fishing regulations imposed by the states, people have caught too many fish. More significantly, they have destroyed salmon habitat. Not only has logging raised temperatures in spawning streams by removing trees that shaded the water, but it has also caused erosion that buries spawning gravel under silt. Road construction, the diversion of water for irrigation, and cattle grazing along stream banks have also destroyed spawning beds. Dams are an additional complication. Even where fish ladders have been built to give adult salmon a way upstream, the dams and their turbines have been fatal to large numbers

---

RIGHT: *Wielding long-handled nets, anglers from the Yakama Indian Nation dipnet homeward-bound salmon north of Lyle, Washington. They are fishing the white water of the Klickitat River, a tributary of the Columbia.*

ABOVE: *Nineteenth-century Canadian artist Paul Kane painted Mount St. Helens erupting at night after visiting the area in the late 1840s. He relied on accounts of contemporary eruptions from eyewitnesses.*

of young fish on their way downstream. Among other things, dams slow the natural water current so that young fish—which are basically floating, not swimming—have longer journeys downstream to salt water than evolution has equipped them for; as a result, the fish turn into salt-water creatures while they're still in the fresh-water rivers.

Despite such obstacles, the rivers of the Northwest are still alive with fish, whose migrations follow regular routes and schedules. The native tribes all held first-salmon ceremonies to welcome the fish back each year, figuring that if the salmon felt welcome, they would keep returning. They did, and the tribes knew just when to expect them. For example, people who fished for salmon along the Nisqually River, which meets Puget Sound in the marshes of what is now the Nisqually

National Wildlife Refuge, knew that each spring, when the cottony matter started blowing from the cottonwood trees, the river would soon be filled with fish.

The forests have never been cyclical in the same way, although the lodgepole pine forests of eastern Oregon and Washington burned periodically (their cones release seeds only when they are exposed to heat), and other forests followed centuries-long successions from brush and alder to climax stands of spruce or hemlock. The woods seem to speak of connectedness and continuity rather than cycles.

In these ecosystems, every niche is filled. Under an old-growth forest, below the brown drifts of needles, in the dark, organic soil that contains 200 species of arthropods per cubic foot, fungi called mycorrhizae take nutrients from tree roots as they pass nutrients and water along and protect the trees from microbes that cause fatal root rot. Flying squirrels dig up and eat the fruiting bodies of the fungi and spread the spores. The squirrels, in turn, are eaten by predators, including the northern spotted owl.

The interrelationships are intricate, but close up the images are simple: the thick bark of Douglas firs, ridged like the scales of some prehistoric beast; the straight, vertical rise of the trunks; the emerald glow of a backlit branch. This forest can last a millennium or it can disappear in seconds. Trees like these were incinerated when Mount St. Helens blew in 1980, have been vaporized, burned, or buried by volcanic blasts for millions of years—and have always grown back. The fossils in the sage-covered hills and the eastern highlands dark with lodgepole pine give new meaning to the idea of "ancient forests." They suggest that along with the volcanoes that have risen and fallen and the seacoast that has moved ever west, trees and forests have defined parts of the Northwest for 40 million years.

Volcanoes also define this region, where the earth is, in a sense, alive with volcanic activity. Although most of the underground rumblings are detectable only with scientific instruments, some are harder to miss. In 1980, Mount St. Helens erupted with the force of 27,000 Hiroshima bombs. Roughly 7,700 years earlier, Oregon's vanished Mount Mazama blew itself apart with three times as much force as Mount St. Helens. The eruption that created eastern Oregon's Mahogany Mountain caldera 15 million years ago packed perhaps 200 times as much force. The largest and best-known of the current volcanoes, 14,410-foot Mount Rainier, hasn't really exploded in 2,200 years, but it is still active. A University of Washington seismologist has said, "It's one of the most dangerous volcanoes around—a big, 14,000-foot chunk of mountain surrounded by 2.5 million people." Nobody knows what's next.

The lesson that volcanoes teach is that everything on the surface of the earth can change. Stand at the edge of Crater Lake and remember that once the summit of Mount Mazama rose roughly a mile above this very spot. Or climb to the south rim of the Mount St. Helens crater. Right below, steam rises from vents, and the rock itself—composed of gray cliffs, shards, boulders, all darker than the condensing steam—looks like the set for a science fiction movie or maybe an opera. It could be the surface of some distant, hostile planet. It could be a hidden valley where a fictional knight might seek an evil sorcerer. It could be hell.

Beyond the crater lies Spirit Lake. Not long ago, Spirit Lake was a blue jewel surrounded by trees, the classic white peak of a pristine Mount St. Helens reflected on its surface. It was, in fact, a classic northwestern landscape photo: the white dome of the "American Fujiyama" with a blue lake at its base. Now the lake is filled with great gray floating logs, hundreds and hundreds of them, whole forests mowed down by the blast, forests that disappeared in a matter of minutes on the day the mountain blew. Topsoil in the blast zone also vanished as the whole area was scoured down to bedrock. Life did not disappear. Where soil remained, pocket gophers survived underground, and fireweed and other plants sprang up, just as plants have recolonized the Northwest after eruptions, fires, and glacier flows for millions of years. Today, young trees are growing in parts of the blast zone, and on acres of mud created by melting glaciers, one sees herds of elk. Nevertheless, the stark bedrock, the smoking lava dome, and the ridges and ravines still covered by ghost forests that were killed but not felled by the blast are all reminders that things can change in an instant—and that nature is still bigger than we are.

RIGHT: *Ghost forests cover the slopes and floating logs choke Spirit Lake, striking reminders of the 1980 eruption of Mount St. Helens.*

WASHINGTON

WESTERN WASHINGTON

Western Washington between Puget Sound and the Pacific is the Northwest's Northwest. Geographically the northwesternmost corner of the coterminous United States, it also contains all the elements that people consider quintessentially northwestern: rain forest, glaciated mountains, and wild, rocky coast.

The western third of Washington is bounded on the east by Puget Sound and Interstate 5 and on the west by the Pacific Ocean; it runs south to the Columbia River and north to the Strait of Juan de Fuca, which ties Puget Sound to the Pacific. Some assume that this entire area is the Olympic Peninsula, but it's not. The finger of land that juts north between Puget Sound and Hood Canal is technically the Kitsap Peninsula, and the southern estuaries of Grays Harbor and Willapa Bay and the Columbia River mouth are all carved out of the mainland.

Pushing south 15,000 years ago and covering the Seattle area with 3,000 feet of ice, the last continental glacier gouged a number of deep north-south trenches in western Washington. One became Hood Canal and another Puget Sound, the Northwest's 900-foot-deep inland sea. Its water rising and falling with the Pacific tides, the

---

PRECEDING PAGES: *The icy granite of Mount Challenger and Whatcom Peak looms behind a field of pink heather in North Cascades National Park.*
LEFT: *Silhouetted against the sunset, wave-carved sea stacks rise from the Pacific Ocean at Point of Arches in Olympic National Park.*

---

sound forms a moat separating the Olympic Peninsula from Seattle.

In the nineteenth century and even at the beginning of the twentieth, Puget Sound was a highway, not a moat. Because the terrain was covered with thick old-growth forests, the only convenient way to get around—much less move supplies, logs, or lumber—was by water. Sailing ships took Puget Sound lumber to California, Hawai'i, and the Far East. Steamers carried passengers to the cities and mill towns; tourists rowed out for weekend excursions; families rowed to the store. When people started traveling by car, the sound became a barrier. All of a sudden, travel by boat was neither quicker nor cheaper. The "mosquito fleet" of steamers that crisscrossed the sound did not survive World War II.

The sound today is surrounded by cities, houses, and industry, but despite periodic false alarms and some very real problems, it remains relatively clean and healthy. It is still possible to stand on a beach and see a pod of killer whales swim by or to watch dolphins play in the bow wave of a state ferry. Salmon migrating to and from rivers that drain into Puget Sound—the Skagit, the Stillaguamish, the Snohomish, even the industrialized Duwamish—can still be caught with rods and reels or commercial nets. Divers can explore underwater forests of bull kelp 20 feet long, and find possibly the world's largest octopuses. There are still miles of undeveloped shoreline and uninhabited islands. The pulp mills that began polluting the water in the 1920s and other large industrial plants have largely cleaned up.

The main threat to the sound now is "lifestyle pollution"—the harder-to-control runoff from roads and parking lots, seepage from septic tanks, animal wastes from commercial and hobby farms, and overflow from storm sewers. The challenge is not to bring Puget Sound back from the dead but to keep it relatively healthy.

On a clear day, from a boat on the surface or a street on the shore of Puget Sound, the Olympic Mountains are silhouetted against the western sky. They are the rugged core of the Olympic Peninsula. Although they are not high as northwestern mountains go—the tallest, Mount Olympus, stands a shade under 8,000 feet—they loom more

---

OVERLEAF: *In Olympic National Park, where snow and ice linger on the peaks into summer, a black-tailed mule deer buck pauses in an alpine meadow that is carpeted with western bistort, or smokeweed, flowers.*

than a mile above Seattle's tallest downtown buildings.

No roads cross the Olympic range. The only way to reach the rain forest and wilderness beaches on the far side of the peninsula is to drive around. In writing about the Makah Indians, who were still harpooning whales from dugout canoes on the open ocean in 1864, James Swan noted that "with few intervals, this part of Washington Territory is covered by almost impenetrable forest." When Washington became a state in 1889, no one was known to have ever seen the heart of the Olympics. And the forest was as thick as ever when a party sponsored by the *Seattle Press* set out that same year on a pioneering expedition to cross the mountains. The *Press* expedition took months to struggle up the valley of the Elwha River, crossing the divide into the Quinault Valley at the beginning of 1890. Other explorers followed. Still, close as the Olympics were to the cities and sawmills of Puget Sound, they remained remote for many years.

By the early years of this century, men with guns were slaughtering the great Olympic elk primarily for their teeth—just the incisors, two teeth per elk—which turn-of-the-century male fashion plates wore on their watch chains. A million and a half acres of the Olympic Peninsula had been made a national forest reserve in 1897. Largely to protect the elk, President Theodore Roosevelt in 1909 set aside more than 615,000 acres of that land as a national monument, which formed the core of what became Olympic National Park. The animals—larger and more social than Rocky Mountain elk—became known as Roosevelt elk. Today the park conserves the largest unmanaged herd in the country. Forest-products companies, which resented all that old-growth forest being placed off limits, soon persuaded President Woodrow Wilson to cut the national monument in half. Loggers had not progressed very far into the mountains, though, when Washington environmentalists started pressing for a national park in the 1930s. The lack of logging in the interior made the landscape of the prospective park unique. Most of the Northwest's large protected areas lie at high elevations, where trees are hard to reach or simply do not grow, not in the great lower-elevation old-growth forests that used to cover most of the region. Around the Olympic Mountains, those forests still existed. Local entrepreneurs wanted to be free to cut all the trees between the mountains and the Pacific. Environmentalists sought to save some of them in the new national park. The current conflict between cutting and preserving old-growth trees is nothing new.

The first bill to create an Olympic National Park was introduced in 1935. In 1937, President Franklin Delano Roosevelt visited the Olympic Peninsula, where he was shocked by what he later called the "criminal devastation" of the forests. Finally in 1938, Congress created a 648,000-acre park. At the beginning of 1940, Roosevelt added 187,000 acres, including the rain forests of the Bogachiel and Hoh river valleys. The park started managing most of the wilderness beaches that same year, although it didn't formally take them over until 1953; the northern beaches, which many consider the most spectacular, were added in 1976.

Within the forests that have been saved are specimens of the world's largest Douglas fir, subalpine fir, western hemlock, and Alaska yellow-cedar trees, plus the only temperate rain forest outside New Zealand and Chile. The rainfall patterns of the Northwest are formed by the interplay between Pacific storm clouds and mountains. Farther east, the Cascade Mountains force Pacific rain clouds to higher altitudes, where they unload their moisture, keeping western Washington and Oregon relatively damp and the eastern portions of both states relatively dry. The Olympics get the rain clouds before the Cascades, force them almost as high, and wring out a lot more moisture. The western Olympic Peninsula routinely receives 144 inches—12 feet—of rain per year. Prevailing winds drive the storms right up the west-facing valleys of the Hoh, Queets, Quinault, and Bogachiel rivers, which get lots of rain in the winter and lots of fog in the summer, creating textbook-perfect rain forest conditions.

The park's landscape is extremely compact: The Hoh rain forest lies fewer than 10 miles from the glaciers of Mount Olympus—the third most heavily glaciated peak in the lower 48 states—and only 25 miles from the surf at Ruby Beach. At the northern edge of the park, Mount Angeles rises fewer than 10 miles from the Strait of Juan de Fuca. Although the rain forest is the main feature that qualified Olympic National Park to be declared a world heritage site and a biosphere reserve, the beach alone would make it unique among American national parks.

Short, swift rivers pour down from the Olympics to salt water. Along the sandy southern coast, the rivers end in large estuaries. The Chehalis and the smaller Humptulips rivers flow into Grays Harbor, while the Willapa, Naselle, and North rivers flow into Willapa Bay.

Farther south, the Columbia has made its own estuary. These three estuaries are the largest on the Pacific Coast north of San Francisco, and Willapa Bay is considered the cleanest large estuary in the country.

Although not visually impressive, the coast's three major estuaries are extremely productive. Eelgrass grows in the shallows, creating more dry matter per square meter per year than any other terrestrial food crop except sugarcane. Each year it dies down completely, releasing nutrients for other plants and microorganisms. Algae and small seaweeds live on the eelgrass. Birds feed directly on it, on the seaweeds attached to it, and on the algae, invertebrates, and small fish that depend—often at one or two removes—on nutrients that the dead grass provides. Eelgrass beds are important not only to birds, but also to a variety of mollusks, crustaceans, and fish. Some juvenile salmon use the Columbia River and Grays Harbor estuaries as nurseries before they head out to sea. In the estuaries, the salmon eat bottom-dwelling crustaceans and other invertebrates and swim to the surface to catch insects. Juvenile crabs spend time in the estuaries, too. In the spring, female harbor seals swim into Grays Harbor and Willapa Bay to give birth and nurse their young.

Great flocks of migratory waterfowl and

RIGHT: *At any one time, thousands of migrating western sandpipers may rest and feed on the mud flats of Grays Harbor National Wildlife Refuge; they are among the half million shorebirds that stop here every spring.*

ABOVE: *Because of their fine fur, sea otters were hunted nearly to extinction before World War I; today they again populate Washington's rocky shorelines.*

RIGHT: *A pod of orcas, or killer whales, swims through the San Juan Islands, where the sleek mammals congregate to feed on runs of spawning salmon.*

shorebirds fuel up in Willapa Bay and Grays Harbor every spring. The flocks do not feed north of Point Grenville near Taholah, where the estuaries and broad sand beaches of the southern coast give way to cliffs and rocky headlands, but thousands of seabirds nest on the offshore rocks and islands. Scattered all along the northern coast, those rocks and islands support the largest seabird colonies in the continental United States.

Birds are not the only wildlife along the coast. From beaches or commercial whale-watching boats based in Westport, on the southern edge of Grays Harbor, California gray whales can be seen migrating north in the spring and south in the fall. Orcas and minke whales, Dall and harbor porpoises, Pacific white-sided dolphins, seals, common California sea lions, and endangered northern, or Steller, sea lions all pass along the shore. Sea otters, extirpated by hunters along the Washington coast by 1910, were reintroduced in 1969 and 1970, and a small population now lives north of Destruction Island. The whole area has been designated a marine sanctuary.

This chapter begins in the San Juan Islands, then heads south to Seattle and west across the water to the Kitsap and Olympic peninsulas.

The route continues around the Olympic Peninsula to the wild beaches of Washington's northern coast, and the mountains and forests of Olympic National Park and its five surrounding wilderness areas. It then proceeds south to the estuary refuges of the southern coast and some small sites where coastal old-growth forest has been preserved.

The roads, mostly two-lane, neither invite nor permit freeway speeds. Off the main roads, trailheads can sometimes be reached only by driving up unpaved, often steep and winding, forest service roads, some of which skirt disconcertingly sheer drops down clear-cut mountainsides. Although four-wheel drive is seldom needed, neither is a car with low clearance—or the new Rolls.

EASTERN PUGET SOUND

The deep waters of Puget Sound are full of islands. Some are large and relatively populous. Seven get regular ferry service. Five are connected to the mainland by bridge. The smaller ones are accessible only by private boat. Some small islands have been made into refuges or parks.

The San Juans shelter the largest year-round population of bald eagles

39

in the lower 48 states. Smaller islands support breeding colonies of tufted puffins, American kestrels, and rhinoceros auklets. Whales roam the channels each summer, and porpoises, sea lions, and harbor seals can be seen from the decks of passing ferries. Huge sockeye salmon runs from Canada's Fraser River swim through the northern islands. At the turn of the century, Scandinavian and Slavic fishermen from the Seattle area rowed up to the islands and camped on the beaches to catch Fraser River salmon. Diesel-powered boats are used for fishing now, but Fraser River salmon still support a big commercial fishery—and are still a source of conflict between Canada and the United States. Killer whales, or orcas, swim through the islands too, and on San Juan Island, the town of Friday Harbor contains a whale museum.

About 60 miles north of Seattle, Route 20 heads west from I-5 toward Puget Sound. Before reaching the turnoff for Anacortes and the ferries, detour south on the main branch of Route 20 to **Deception Pass State Park❖,** which straddles a narrow channel between Fidalgo and Whidbey islands. The park is the most visited in the state, and despite impressive views over the turbulent water, its much-used waterfront areas hardly qualify as natural anymore. However, it is an unusually scenic spot, with rocky headlands, sandy beaches, tidal pools, and wooded slopes. Deception also contains a less traveled forest—where black-tailed deer browse among old Douglas fir and bald eagles soar overhead—as well as lakes and coves sustaining a variety of seabirds and waterfowl. To the east, sheltered between Whidbey Island and the mainland in Skagit Bay, **Hope Island State Park❖** is accessible only by boat.

From Anacortes on Fidalgo Island, state ferries leave regularly for the **San Juan Islands.** A rocky archipelago of Puget Sound, the nearly 200 San Juan Islands vary tremendously in size. Some have been inhabited by non-native people since the mid-nineteenth century; others never have been. Some are set aside as refuges or parks; others are feeling the pressures of development. Those not served by ferry are accessible only by plane or private boat. From Anacortes, state ferries go to only four large islands: Lopez, Shaw, Orcas, and San Juan. During

---

LEFT: *On a clear day, the snowcapped volcanic cone of 10,778-foot Mount Baker is a landmark visible from all over northern Puget Sound, including the hundreds of islands in the San Juan chain.*

ABOVE: *Tufted puffins, with their striking orange beaks and feet and pale yellow eye tufts, nest in burrows at the top of cliffs overlooking the sea.*

RIGHT: *A solitary paddler glides across a calm Cascade Lake in Orcas Island's Moran State Park, which was donated to the state in 1920 by a turn-of-the-century shipyard tycoon.*

the summer, especially on weekends, the waiting lines for cars can be excruciatingly long; drivers are advised to arrive early and be prepared to miss a boat. All the ferries carry cars (as well as bicycles, kayaks, and canoes), provide views of the islands, and sometimes allow glimpses of marine wildlife.

In general, the large islands are rural but long-inhabited, so there are no undisturbed woods or wetlands. On Orcas Island, which many consider the most scenic of the larger San Juans, part of **Moran State Park❖** is highly developed and can be crowded, but the park also encompasses a lot of forest and some very big old trees. With luck, a visitor may spot ospreys, common loons, American dippers, bald and golden eagles, belted kingfishers, and old-growth-dwelling Vaux's swifts.

On San Juan Island, **Lime Kiln Point State Park❖** is a good place to spot minke whales, orcas, and Dall porpoises. (It is the nation's first park dedicated to whale watching.) Near the southern tip of the island, American Camp, in the **San Juan Island National Historical Park❖,** where our boys stared down the British during the less-than-epic Pig War of the 1850s, occupies an open plain. Not preserved as a natural area, the plain is nonetheless riddled with rabbit warrens; eagles circle overhead, searching for their rabbit dinners. Hawks cruise the area too, and at night owls appear.

The islands accessible only by private boat start very close to Anacortes. In Padilla Bay, east of Anacortes, one small island (currently closed to the public) contains a bald eagle nest and provides habitat for peregrine falcons. There is a large natural resource conservation

area on nearby **Cypress Island,** north of Anacortes. Although people have summer cabins on Cypress, it qualifies as the last big undeveloped island in the San Juans, and the state has preserved most of it. At many natural resource conservation areas, however, appropriate public uses are yet to be determined.

State parks are the only places on these islands where visitors are permitted, and Washington offers a whole collection of island parks in the San Juans that are accessible only by boat. These **Northern Puget Sound State Parks❖** include **Sucia, Matia, Patos,** and **Clark Island** state parks, north of Orcas; **Jones** and **Doe Island** state parks off the southwestern and southeastern shores of Orcas; **Turn** and **Posey Island** state parks, near the eastern and northern tips of San Juan; **James Island State Park,** just east of Decatur Island; and **Blind Island State Park,** at the mouth of Blind Bay, north of Shaw Island. Sucia, Matia, Patos, and Clark Island state parks all contain wind- and wave-molded sandstone. Most of Matia and Turn islands are managed as parts of a national wildlife refuge.

In addition to the state parks, the **San Juan Islands National Wildlife Refuge❖** includes 83 small islands that are resting and loafing sites for a variety of birds, as well as nesting sites for bald eagles. Double-crested cormorants nest on Colville Island, south of Lopez, and on Bird Rocks. North of the San Juan Islands NWR, Minke whales forage around White Rock and in Speiden Channel, and elephant seals have made appearances near privately owned Speiden Island. Most of the refuge is maintained for wildlife, not people; Matia and Turn islands are the only places where the public is allowed to land. Visitors are asked to stay at least 200 yards away from all the other islands.

The Nature Conservancy manages a **San Juan Preserve System.** All its preserves can be reached only by boat. The sole accessible site is **Yellow Island Preserve❖,** near the southwestern shore of Orcas Island and the northwestern shore of Shaw. The ten-acre island is primarily noted for its spring wildflower displays of Indian paintbrush, blue camas, buttercups, and chocolate lilies, but its shores also offer views of orcas, porpoises, bald eagles, harlequin ducks, and other wildlife. From an ecological point of view, the remarkable thing about the island is a largely undisturbed fescue headland. Native grasses are rare in western Washington because most have long ago been grazed and trampled into oblivion—or so close to oblivion that they have been easily supplanted by nonnative species. Evidently, no one ever bothered taking goats or larger animals to Yellow Island, and even though nonnative plants have made some inroads, the native grasses survive just about intact.

SEATTLE AND ENVIRONS

Although it houses the Northwest's largest concentration of people and cars, Seattle still preserves and protects quite a bit of natural land within its boundaries. Even a modest city park can give kids a sense that the rest of the world has been shut out, that they are free to create a separate world of the imagination. Seattle has more than its share of parks and undeveloped ravines to serve that function. It also has several parks that offer even people older and less imaginative a hint of how the woods looked in the mid-nineteenth century when settlers built their first cabins in the trees of Alki Point.

One is **Schmitz Park❖** off Admiral Way, not far from Alki in residential West Seattle. A real anomaly, the 50-acre park was deeded to the city of Seattle early in this century by a city park commissioner and his wife. It supports the usual alders and salmonberries, sword ferns and second-growth conifers, but it also contains a remnant of old-growth forest with individual trees up to 800 years old. On the other side of the city, **Seward Park❖,** which occupies a small peninsula jutting into Lake Washington off Lake Washington Boulevard, contains some even larger old-growth trees.

East of downtown Seattle, **Lake Washington,** traversed by Interstate 90 on a floating bridge, fills a 240-foot-deep trench carved by the last continental glacier. Surrounded largely by parks and expensive houses, it divided Seattle and the suburbs for decades; now it separates Seattle from other full-fledged cities. Nevertheless, salmon swim through the lake from their spawning beds in the tributary rivers, and in the 1980s there were reports of a sea monster—which turned out to be a huge sturgeon, since deceased, that was presumably released at the end of the Alaska-Yukon-Pacific Exposition in 1909.

In the mid-1950s, Lake Washington was dying. Treated sewage released into it fed huge blooms of algae that died, decayed, stank, and depleted the oxygen in the lake water. To clean up the lake, Seattle-area residents created a regional utility that could take the sewage elsewhere and paid for the necessary pipes and treatment plants. Theirs was the first commitment made in the United States to environmental cleanup on such a large scale and is often cited as an international example of how a dying lake can be saved.

In Puget Sound near Seattle, **Blake Island❖** has been made into a state park. One of the few island parks in the southern sound and the closest one to Seattle, Blake lies between the larger, permanently inhabited islands of Bainbridge and Vashon. Its original forest has long since been logged, but it is covered with a forest of second-growth trees. Privately owned for years. the island now belongs to the state. Indian salmon bakes are held at privately run Tillicum Village on Blake's eastern shore for people who come by tour boat from Seattle (the state also provides a place to moor private boats). Most of the island's woods and four miles of beaches remain undeveloped.

WESTERN PUGET SOUND

A trip to the far side of Puget Sound often starts with a ferry ride. From Coleman Dock at the foot of Marion Street in downtown Seattle, ferries leave for Winslow on Bainbridge Island (a 35-minute trip) and Bremerton on the Kitsap Peninsula. Although the Bremerton run takes an hour, it provides a better sense of Puget Sound's complexity because the route curves around Bainbridge Island and into Sinclair Inlet.

From Winslow or Bremerton, head north for the Hood Canal floating bridge, which connects the Kitsap and Olympic peninsulas. From Bremerton, take Route 304 a short distance south along the water until it intersects with Route 3, which leads to the bridge. From Winslow, a longer drive on Route 305 leads to Route 3. A third alternative, which makes sense as part of a side trip to the Nature Conservancy's preserve at Foulweather Bluff, is to drive north from Seattle on I-5, take the Edmonds–Kingston Ferry exit, ride the ferry from Edmonds to Kingston, follow Route 104 west to the Hansville road, then drive north to Hansville, at the tip of the peninsula, a little east of Foulweather Bluff.

The Nature Conservancy has preserved 93 acres of marsh, forest, and beach at **Foulweather Bluff Preserve❖.** The uplands here were logged in the 1920s and 1930s and then burned. (No one remembers whether the burning was accidental or deliberate.) At present the trees include alders—nitrogen-fixing hardwoods that come up quickly on cleared land—and relatively young conifers. In time, the conifers will take over and grow larger. Even now, the forest, marsh, and beach provide habitat for great blue herons, eagles, buffleheads, and a wide variety of other birds and mammals including river otters and mink. The forest also serves as a watershed for the marshes below. Because a fresh expanse of fill dirt has more economic value than wetlands, marshes tend to fare poorly in developing areas, and many around Puget Sound have disappeared. The freshwater and brackish marshes at Foulweather Bluff rank among the 20 most ecologically significant marshes remaining on Puget Sound.

ABOVE: *The rhinoceros auklet grows a "horn" on its beak in summer, its breeding season, earning this species its name.*
BELOW: *Pelagic cormorants nest on high, inaccessible sea cliffs and dive into the intertidal zone to find their fishy dinners.*

Across the Hood Canal Bridge on Route 104 lies the Olympic Peninsula. Route 104 leads west to Route 101, the main highway that circles the peninsula, traversing nearly 300 miles of strikingly varied landscape from rocky coastal beaches and lush rain forests to clear glacial lakes and snowcapped peaks. At the start of the loop, the road runs through second-growth forest, young tree plantations, and clear-cuts; the towns are unimpressive at best. But the truly grand mountains, trees, and beaches are always close.

At Discovery Bay, a detour north on Route 20 up the **Quimper Peninsula** leads to Port Townsend—a nineteenth-century seaport with historic brick commercial buildings downtown and grand Victorian homes on the bluff—and the **Protection Island National Wildlife**

Western Washington

RIGHT: *At Olympic National Park, snow pockets brighten the steep slopes of Hurricane Ridge. The slender shape of the dark subalpine firs helps them shed heavy winter snows.*

Refuge❖. Port Townsend occupies the northeastern tip of the peninsula; Protection Island lies off the northwestern tip in the Strait of Juan de Fuca. A boat can get within viewing range, although no one is allowed to land on the island or get closer than 200 yards offshore to avoid disturbing the thousands of birds—some 72 percent of all the seabirds in the Puget Sound vicinity—that nest on the island each year. Two kinds of cormorants, tufted puffins, pigeon guillemots, and black oyster-catchers all nest on Protection Island. Some 17,000 pairs of rhinoceros auklets (the forehead of breeding adults sports a pale hornlike knob above the orange bill, hence the name) make up one of the largest colonies in the world.

West of Discovery Bay, beyond the town of Sequim (pronounced "skwim"), a sign on Route 101 announces a right turn for the **Dungeness National Wildlife Refuge❖.** Lying in the rain shadow of the Olympic Mountains, Sequim gets very little precipitation and has become a popular retirement community. Signs lead along back roads to the entrance. The core of the refuge, Dungeness Spit, is one of the longest natural sand spits in the world.

Plodding through the yielding sand of the spit, a visitor leans into the wind that blows steadily from the Strait of Juan de Fuca while a harbor seal, its sleek head dark against the waves, keeps pace along the shore. During spring and fall migration as many as 30,000 waterfowl pass through the refuge and some—such as the black brants—are seen year-round; look to the sheltered east side of the spit where the birds float on placid water. At the end of the spit young eagles may perch startlingly close on wave-smoothed drift logs; harbor seals rest and give birth on the spit. One can sometimes have lunch while seals sun themselves on the beach, cruise in the shallows, make seal noises, and emit seal smells.

OLYMPIC NATIONAL PARK

Farther west on Highway 101 at Port Angeles, where stacks of lumber and big pulp mills line the waterfront, signs indicate the turnoff for the main entrance to **Olympic National Park❖.** Preserved within its boundaries are three totally different ecosystems: mountain (glaciers, high wildflower meadows, and subalpine forest), rain forest (huge old-growth trees hung with mosses and ferns), and seacoast (undeveloped beaches bordered by rocky pinnacles or sea stacks, ancient headlands eroded away from both sides). The Olympic Mountains at the heart of the park were forced up about 50–40 million years ago when the heavy Pacific oceanic plate and American continental plate collided. Edges of the oceanic plate broke off and were thrust upward, eventually forming today's peaks. Marine fossils

ABOVE LEFT: *An Olympic marmot clutches a tasty snack of wild lupine. This marmot species is found solely on the isolated Olympic Peninsula.* **ABOVE RIGHT:** *Bright clusters of the endangered Flett's violet grow in rocky crevices at subalpine levels of Olympic National Park.*

are sometimes found on the old seabed high in the Olympics.

Because the peninsula was isolated—by glaciers first and then by water—flora and fauna species that are found nowhere else prospered here. Sometimes called the endemic 16, they include Flett's violet and fleabane, Olympic magenta painted cup, Piper's bellflower, and the Olympic marmot, Olympic chipmunk, Olympic snow mole, and Mazama pocket gopher. Conversely some species found in the Cascades and Rockies—grizzlies, wolverines, porcupines, mountain sheep, and mountain goats—have not survived in the Olympics; they are referred to as the missing 11).

No road crosses the 1,400 square miles of Olympic National Park, but one can enter the park from virtually any point of the compass by driving up one of the 13 river valleys that fan out around the central peaks. A hiker willing to walk for several days can reach almost any region of the park from any entry point. To find the main entrance, follow the Mount Angeles road to the **Hurricane Ridge Visitor Center❖.** Examples of basaltic pillow lavas, distinctive rock formations

RIGHT: *Softened by the mist, mountain hemlocks—found in the deepest snows and highest forest zones of the Northwest—soar above a carpet of red heather in the mountains of Olympic National Park.*

caused by underwater eruptions, can be seen along the road to Hurricane Ridge. Some 18 miles from Route 101, the ridge provides views of the straits and islands to the north as well as the peaks that surround **Mount Olympus** (7,965 feet). Six of the park's 60 major glaciers are on Olympus, including the well-known **Blue Glacier.** Trails that begin at Hurricane Ridge offer some of the most spectacular mountain scenery, alpine wildflowers (peak bloom is mid-July), and wildlife viewing (black-tailed deer and Olympic marmots are common) in the Olympics, and they connect to a 600-mile trail system that covers the park. In winter, when the trails are buried, Hurricane Ridge is also a good place for cross-country skiing.

Return to Route 101 for a small jog west along the park's circumference. Past Port Angeles and the junction with Route 112, Olympic Hot Springs Road leads up the **Elwha River** and into the park along the route chosen in 1889 by the *Seattle Press* expedition. The Elwha drains the park's largest watershed, and at the turn of the century eight different species of salmon and sea-run trout probably swam up the river to spawn. More than a hundred thousand pink salmon filled the Elwha each fall, and some chinook salmon traveling through it in spring weighed more than a hundred pounds. Two hydroelectric dams, one of which now stands inside the park, barred the salmon from their spawning streams. Although some fish still spawn in the river below the dams, the great fish runs of the past are long gone. There are hot springs at the end of the Olympic Hot Springs Road, as well as trails that lead all the way across the mountains. A very fit hiker with a lot of daylight could cross the Olympics in one extremely long day. Route 101 proceeds along the southern shore of glacially formed **Lake Crescent**; the turnoff at **Storm King** leads to **Marymere Falls,** a 2-mile hike through conifer forests to a 90-foot cascade.

The park's rain-forest valleys and southern beaches lie to the west and south via Route 101. To visit the park's northern beaches turn onto Route 112 just beyond Port Angeles and follow it due west toward

---

LEFT: *The steep, forested shoreline of the Olympic Peninsula rises beyond Tatoosh Island, where seagulls perch on kelp-covered rocks.*
OVERLEAF: *Sunset illuminates the tidal pools, rocks, and ridges of Rialto Beach, where waves and wind constantly pummel the rugged coast.*

ABOVE: *Starfish and sea anemones cling to rocks exposed by the outgoing tide on Washington's northern coast, which is rockier, wilder, and*

Neah Bay. Beyond the community of Sekiu, the Hoko-Ozette road branches southwest off Route 112 to the campground and ranger station at **Lake Ozette.** From the lake, trails head out to the beach. The beaches of Olympic National Park stretch for 57 miles, from the park's southern border near the Queets River north to the edge of the Makah Indian Reservation. They are broken only by three other small Indian reservations, the Hoh, Quileute, and Ozette.

The native peoples have been here for a long time. At Cape Alava, where the northern trail from Lake Ozette reaches the Pacific, a 1970 storm uncovered the remains of a Makah village that had been buried by a mudslide 500 years before and preserved largely intact. Archaeologists found more than 50,000 artifacts, many made of wood or bark that would have turned to dust if exposed to air. The Makahs now display some of the artifacts in a museum at Neah Bay. No artifacts wash upon the beach at Cape Alava, but petroglyphs can be spotted on the rocks.

To continue to the northern beaches, stay on Route 112 straight through the coastal community of Neah Bay. Beyond Neah Bay, head

arguably more important to mammals and seabirds (which nest on off-shore rocks) than the sandier, more accessible shoreline farther south.

cautiously west and then north to the windswept edge of **Cape Flattery,** the northwesternmost point in the contiguous 48 states.

For many years, hikers followed an abandoned dirt road through the woods to Olympic National Park's **Shi Shi Beach.** When the park service acquired Shi Shi, though, it failed to acquire a right-of-way through the Makah reservation, leaving no access to the beach without trespassing—to which landowners strongly object. At this writing, the tribe and the National Park Service are trying to work out a route that will be acceptable to private landowners. Currently, the only legal way to reach Shi Shi is by walking north from Cape Alava. It is a long walk and the Ozette River is often too dangerous to ford. Check with the National Park Service to see if it is possible to reach Shi Shi from Neah Bay. This is arguably the most beautiful beach on the Washington coast, a curve of sand backed by dark, forested bluffs with rocky spires and headlands at either end. A thin line of drift logs lies above the high-water line. Around stream mouths, huge logs are everywhere. Far up the beach, the tall, blocky spires of a headland could almost be the towers

57

of a distant city. Sandpipers rise from the beach and wheel over the surf; as they turn, the undersides of their wings flash white. Bald eagles drift overhead. Black-tailed deer walk across the sand, sun themselves beside drift logs, and browse at the edge of the woods. Hundreds of white gulls rest on the sand while offshore waves break on sea stacks that march into the surf in sawtooth succession. From a distance, small islands are velvety green, crowned with trees. Others are flattened, honed, twisted, hollowed by the sea. In places, seawater has worn archways clear through the rock, like the openings in a cloister. At low tide, when shelves of seaweed-covered rock are exposed at the headlands, a visitor can walk among the towering rocks. Surrounded by the looming stones, one can sit on a drift log and look through a forest of sea- and wind-blasted shapes at the Pacific.

There is one caveat. As visitors stand in the wet sand watching the low water of the rising tide move closer—a sheer cliff of dark rock at their back and the only refuge a shallow cave gouged into the rock—they will understand why the National Park Service and responsible guidebooks tell them to round the points only at low tide and to carry a tide table. This is not just a beach. It's the edge of the ocean. And there's no place to hide from the rising tide or the huge drift logs that waves throw against the shore. Treating this seashore too casually can literally be fatal. That said, the waters are full of life. Sea otters, harbor seals, and sea lions swim along this northern coast. Gray whales migrate between their summer quarters in the Arctic and their breeding grounds off Baja California. Starfish, sea anemones, and other invertebrates live in the tidal pools.

Farther south along the coast on Route 101, a turn north of Forks—the "logging capital of the world"—leads to the ocean at La Push and **Rialto Beach,** which offer more sand, offshore rocks, and opportunity to hike the coast north or south. At Forks, there are also two natural resource conservation areas (NCRAs), containing old-growth forest; some of the trees are 500 years old. Remember, most NRCAs have no signs, clearly defined boundaries, or public-use facilities.

LEFT: *In the temperate valley of the Olympics' Hoh Rainforest, ferns and autumn leaves cover the floor and moss coats trees and logs.*
OVERLEAF: *The diffused sunlight of the rain forest delicately outlines velvety club moss and hanging epiphytes on the branches of a bigleaf maple.*

Outside of the park and the natural resource conservation areas, this landscape is not a comforting one. Along much of the coast, the road winds through vast clear-cuts that evoke photographs of the shattered stumps and flayed earth on a World War I battlefield. The forest-products industry is still big here—although not nearly as big as it once was—and trees are still being cut. Seedlings are soon planted among the stumps, but they must grow for years before they are visible from a passing car. If the site is too high or the soil too eroded, a new forest will not develop for a long, long time. Ancient forests have simply been mined—no one will wait centuries to grow a new one—but the second-growth forests really are a renewable resource. In the long run, those seedlings planted among the stumps will make a difference. In the short run, they don't soften the appearance of total devastation.

South of Forks, at **Bogachiel State Park**❖, an unpaved road and trail head east into the Bogachiel Valley rain forest. On Route 101 past

LEFT: *Olympic National Park began as an elk refuge in 1909 at Teddy Roosevelt's behest. Today the animals' descendants, called Roosevelt elk, wander throughout the misty Hoh Rainforest.*

the Bogachiel River, the North Hoh road leads inland 19 miles to the **Hoh Rainforest Visitor Center❖** in Olympic National Park. The Hoh is the park's best-known rain forest valley, and trails start at the visitor center. The heavily traveled **Hall of Mosses Trail,** a short, self-guided nature loop, winds through old-growth Sitka spruce, western red-cedar, western hemlock, and Douglas fir hung with some 90 species of mosses, ferns, and lichens. The **Spruce Nature Trail** gives a visual primer on how a forest develops. A much longer route, the **Hoh River Trail,** leads all the way through the rain forest, up the Hoh Valley, and then swings south to climb to the **Blue Glacier** on the flank of **Mount Olympus.**

In the rain forest, everything is green. But monochromatic does not mean simple: The greens form a kaleidoscope of different shades, shapes, and textures. Thick moss covers the ground. Grass and shamrock-leaved oxalis rise above it, and above them sprays of fern, mossy logs, saplings, moss-covered alders and maples, and finally huge spruce trunks, like columns in a gargantuan ancient temple. Rows of saplings grow from mossy nurse logs, and rows of trees up to four feet across rise from the spaces where nurse logs used to be. Moss coats some branches so thickly that the leaves are invisible. A clear stream flows over a bed of green plants, their stems combed downstream by the current. Sunlight dapples an open meadow crisscrossed by logs thick with moss. Moss-covered alders form a colonnade, leaning from either side into a corridor of light.

Elsewhere, exposed roots radiate from huge spruce trees; the roots, the ground, and the bases of the trunks are all covered with moss. Where roots lie beneath the surface, waves of moss seem to flow toward the spruce trunks. Not far from the spruce grow cedars so big that their trunks rise like walls, their curvature so gradual that one is not even tempted to try putting one's arms around them. They dwarf even a bull Roosevelt elk grazing among the ferns. Resembling a buckskin horse with antlers, the elk wanders off toward the Hoh River, which is always close. (The river, a milky gray from rock dust ground up by the glaciers from which it flows, supports river otters, harlequin ducks, and spawning salmon.) From off in the trees comes the sound of an elk bugling. Actually, bugling is a rather grandiose term for the surprisingly high, tinny sound these big animals make. A herd of Roosevelt elk in the early morning light is an unforgettable sight, but it sounds like a flock of birds.

Back on Route 101 south of the Hoh River, the highway approaches the ocean and runs close to National Park Service beaches for about 14 miles from **Ruby Beach** past Kalaloch; trails lead from the road down to the sand. Offshore, **Destruction Island** shelters one of the world's seven largest colonies of rhinoceros auklets. Perhaps 85,000 Cassin's auklets nest offshore, along with tens of thousands of storm petrels, 3,000 common murres, and thousands of other birds. Protected since 1907 by the coastal **Flattery Rocks, Quillayute Needles,** and **Copalis Rocks** national wildlife refuges, the hundred miles of rocks, reefs, and islands are all off limits to visitors. The birds can be seen with binoculars from shore. In 1994, the whole area was protected as a national marine sanctuary.

South of the Queets River, Route 101 swings way inland through the Quinault Indian Reservation. Shortly after the highway starts east, unpaved Queets River Road leads into the rain forest along the narrow **Queets River Valley,** which extends like a small tail from the main body of Olympic National Park. Beyond the campground at the end of the road is one of the largest Douglas firs in the world. Farther east on 101, roads skirt both the north and south shores of **Lake Quinault,** ending at the North Fork and Graves Creek ranger stations, where trails lead deep into the southern reaches of the park. Roosevelt elk are common in the area, but because they are shy and attached to their herds casual hikers are unlikely to see them. Some 13 miles from Graves Creek, a trail enters **Enchanted Valley,** passes the world's largest-known western hemlock, and finally reaches **Anderson Glacier.**

Lake Quinault's South Shore Road also leads to a trailhead for the **Colonel Bob Wilderness❖,** which adjoins the southern side of the park. The Colonel Bob Wilderness and the Olympic National Forest's four other wilderness areas all function as extensions of the park. This one includes both rain forest and alpine slopes and provides a sweeping view from the top of 4,492-foot **Colonel Bob Mountain.** Beyond Lake Quinault, southeast of Humptulips, a detour off Route 101 on the narrow East Hoquiam road leads to the state's **Olympic Wildlife Area❖,** where thick forest cut by streams provides habitat for Roosevelt elk, black-tailed deer, and black bears.

Continuing the loop around the Olympic Peninsula, follow Route 101 to Aberdeen, head east toward Olympia via Routes 12 and 8, and turn north again on Route 101, which follows the western edge of Hood Canal. To the west lie more of the wilderness areas that surround Olympic National Park. At Hoodsport, Route 119 (Lake Cushman Road) winds around **Lake Cushman** to forest roads and trails that enter the park and **Mount Skokomish Wilderness❖,** where the **Hamma Hamma River,** habitat for elk, deer, bears, and eagles, and nine major peaks are all jammed into fewer than 17,000 acres. The closely monitored, rare Olympic mountain rockmat, a strange low-growing plant that resembles the stone it grows on, has also been found in the Mount Skokomish Wilderness.

Farther north on Route 101 at Duckabush, the Duckabush and Mount Jupiter roads lead to the **Brothers Wilderness❖.** Several different forest roads reach trailheads. The wilderness contains much steep terrain, including the 6,866-foot twin peaks of the **Brothers,** which form perhaps the most striking single feature of the Olympic Mountains' eastern profile. Mountain lions and Olympic marmots live within the wilderness. A trail up **Mount Jupiter** follows the narrow spine of Jupiter Ridge; the lower portions of the path are edged by blooming rhododendrons in late spring. Higher up, the trail provides views of Puget Sound and eventually of the densely wooded valleys and wild peaks of the interior.

Just south of Quilcene, Big Quilcene River Road and connecting forest roads lead up to the **Buckhorn Wilderness❖,** which at nearly 45,000 acres is by far the largest of the wilderness areas around Olympic National Park. Several forest roads lead to the start of trails that run along the Big Quilcene, Dungeness, and Gray Wolf rivers. **Mount Townsend** reaches 6,280 feet in the northeast, and **Mount Fricaba,** the highest peak in this section of the peninsula, rises 7,134 feet in the southwest. Black bears, cougars, and bobcats are all found here.

Beyond Quilcene, Route 101 completes its peninsular loop at the junction with Route 104, where travelers can turn east toward the Hood Canal Bridge and the Seattle-bound ferry. From the ferry dock, the Olympics look very close. In the early morning, sunlight glints off snowfields on their crests, and in the evening they are silhouettes against the setting sun.

THE SOUTHERN COAST

On the Pacific coast north of Grays Harbor on dead-end Route 109, **Griffiths-Priday State Park❖** lies at the mouth of the Copalis River. Not really a natural preserve, the park includes a sand spit that may provide habitat for the endangered snowy plover. (At the northern edge of Grays Harbor, a sand spit in **Damon Point State Park❖** is home to these shorebirds.) Snowy plovers, pale, sand-colored birds, are at the extreme northern end of their breeding range here, and the state of Washington has considered them endangered for some time.

Along the north shore of Grays Harbor, at the western edge of the town of Hoquiam, Route 109 passes the **Grays Harbor National Wildlife Refuge❖.** A key feeding area for shorebirds heading north along the Pacific Flyway—their last major stop until they reach Alaska's Copper River delta—the Grays Harbor refuge supports up to half a million birds at a time during the peak spring migration. It is one of the nation's four most important staging areas for migratory birds.

Nevertheless, the refuge isn't scenic. Tucked into **Bowerman Basin,** which lies behind the airport on the industrialized northern side of Grays Harbor, it consists largely of mud, grass, and shallow water. Before landfill for a World War II airport created Bowerman Basin, shorebirds had numerous places to feed around Grays Harbor. Now, of the estimated million birds that use the estuary at peak times, fully half concentrate in Bowerman Basin.

RIGHT: *The Northwest's temperate climate and acid mountain soils are particularly congenial to the native Pacific rhododendron, whose dense clusters of pink flowers brighten the coastal woods each spring.*

ABOVE: *Huge flocks of migrating shorebirds—thousands of dowitchers, dunlins, and sandpipers—stop each spring at Bowerman Basin in Grays*

Incredibly, the refuge was almost buried under industrial fill in the name of environmental protection. In the late 1970s, after prolonged negotiation with federal agencies, the Port of Grays Harbor agreed to preserve most of the estuary's remaining undeveloped shoreline and dump new fill in only one isolated spot—Bowerman Basin. The negotiators had somehow failed to consider all those shorebirds. To make a long story short, the basin became a refuge, and now crowds of people come every April to see huge flocks of western sandpipers, dunlins, and other shorebirds.

Follow Route 101 south to Willapa Bay. On the east side of the bay beyond the town of South Bend, a little coastal old-growth forest survives. Farther south, near the mouth of the Naselle River, eight acres of ancient forest are preserved. Neither of these old-growth areas are open to or can accommodate public use, but the old-growth redcedar forest of South Nemah is a rarity: an unlogged drainage in the Willapa Hills. The

Harbor. After rest and feverish feeding, the birds continue en masse up to their arctic breeding grounds on Alaska's Copper River delta.

rest of the area has been largely denuded, its old forests long since sliced up by huge saws in the mills that have fallen on hard times for lack of raw material. Remnants of the old forest are few and far between.

A little farther beyond the Naselle River stands the headquarters of the **Willapa National Wildlife Refuge❖**. Divided into several sites, the Willapa refuge was created in 1937 primarily to protect the black brant, a stocky goose marked by a thin white collar around its neck. The site still provides prime winter habitat for the brant, as well as trumpeter and tundra (formerly known as whistling) swans; Aleutian, cackling, lesser, and dusky Canada geese; and a wide variety of other birds. Up to 150,000 shorebirds use the bay at the peak of spring migration, and up to 100,000 waterfowl visit at the peak of fall. Over the course of a season, perhaps a million birds drop in.

Willapa Bay has been a center of the oyster industry since the 1840s, long before Washington became a state. At first, people harvested the small native Olympia oysters that grew here naturally. The Olympias are long gone, but the industry remains; for generations, it has relied on Pacific oysters, which are native to Japan. In the town of South Bend, which styles itself "the oyster capital of the world," huge piles of shells still stand beside the packing houses. The oyster industry provides an economic incentive to keep Willapa Bay clean.

In the southern part of the bay near refuge headquarters, **Long Island** features a dense stand of old-growth redcedar and hemlock trees. Accessible only by small boat, the island has been logged since the turn of the century, but somehow a 274-acre cedar grove was spared. The 4,000-year-old grove was not formally protected until the 1980s, when the federal government swapped second-growth timber to the Weyerhaeuser Company for part of it and then bought the last 155 acres. The cedars are the island's prime attraction but not its only one. It is the largest estuarine island on the entire Pacific coast; surrounded by tidal marshes and tidal flats, it provides significant habitat for deer, bears, elk, and other mammals.

Farther south on Route 101 is Ilwaco, a sport-fishing center near the mouth of the Columbia. Route 103 proceeds from here up the Long Beach Peninsula (promoters claim that this truly is the longest beach in the country). Driving on the beach is a very popular local custom, so on a summer afternoon, keep a sharp eye out for jeeps, campers, and kids on mopeds. Nevertheless, the beach is huge, remarkably clean, and sometimes totally deserted first thing in the morning.

The tip of the peninsula contains another part of the Willapa National Wildlife Refuge and **Leadbetter Point State Park❖,** a tract of sand dunes and woods that adjoins the refuge and provides some of the same opportunities to see wildlife—black brants, sandpipers, swans, brown pelicans. Even relatively large and noisy groups of people have been known to spot bears here.

Head back east on Route 4 along the Columbia River toward Interstate 5. A turn just before Cathlamet leads to the **Julia Butler Hansen National Wildlife Refuge for the Columbian White-Tailed Deer❖.** Named for a long-time state legislator and congresswoman who lived in Cathlamet, this wildlife refuge is the only one in Washington established primarily to protect mammals. The diked riverfront land and Columbia River islands (accessible only by boat) that compose the

ABOVE: *Categorized as omnivores, black bears enjoy roots, berries, insects, and dandelion heads. They are also the largest predators on the Olympic Peninsula, which also harbors bobcats and cougars.*

refuge provide habitat for Columbian white-tailed deer, which, according to Lewis and Clark, were once plentiful from The Dalles to the mouth of the Columbia. They are now an endangered species. Winter brings tundra swans, Canada geese, and other birds. Deer—and elk too—are easiest to spot in the evening or early morning.

In 1792, when the sailing ship *Columbia Rediviva* first entered the river that bears its name, fifth mate John Boit wrote that near the river's mouth, the water "abounds with excellent Salmon, and most other River fish, and the Woods with plenty of Moose and Deer." Most of the riverbanks have long since been hunted out, trapped out, cleared, plowed, and built upon. The great salmon runs have dwindled. But the millions of fish that still pass this point each year, the white-tailed deer that survive in the refuge, and the sheer numbers of birds that feed in the great estuaries of the coast hint at the abundance that the crew of the *Columbia Rediviva* first found.

CHAPTER TWO

CENTRAL WASHINGTON

From Puget Sound to the foothills farther east, central Washington is dominated visually by the Cascade Mountains, a line of volcanoes and jagged peaks that runs from Canada to the Columbia River. To the north two 10,000-foot volcanoes, Baker and Glacier, form the centerpieces of vast wilderness areas. The heavily glaciated peaks of the North Cascades are protected by one national park, and 14,410-foot Mount Rainier, farther south, is the focus of its own magnificent national park. Mount St. Helens, in the early stages of renewal after its 1980 eruption, is now a national monument.

The mountains are not the whole show, however. Wolves and grizzlies roam the northern Cascades. Eagles and trumpeter swans congregate along the Skagit River. Wildflowers bloom as soon as the snow melts off alpine meadows, and pockets of old-growth forest still grow in isolated valleys. On the region's southern edge, the scenic Columbia River Gorge marks the great river's passage from the arid eastern plateau.

Formed over many eons, the Cascades are a combination of volcanic and nonvolcanic peaks. The northern Cascades are the oldest. Part of an ancient microcontinent that smashed into the North American mainland between 50 and 40 million years ago, these peaks were forced up by the collision of the two continental land masses.

LEFT: *In early summer, native wildflowers (purple lupine, red paintbrush, white western bistort, and creamy western pasque flowers) light up a meadow below the rock and glacial ice of 14,410-foot Mount Rainier.*

Many mountain-building and erosional periods have followed and have gouged out valleys and lakes, leaving a forest of granite and gneiss, festooned with hanging glaciers.

The Cascades' volcanoes are generally younger than the nonvolcanic peaks. They have formed along inland arcs that parallel the intersections of the oceanic and continental plates. Successive bands of volcanoes have risen slowly, leaving some in splendid isolation like Mount Rainier, leaving others close to nonvolcanic peaks.

Because of the formidable mountain topography of this region, few roads travel east-west. Therefore, as a starting point for forays into the rugged interior, the route for this chapter uses the main north-south highway, I-5, which parallels the eastern edge of Puget Sound. Working gradually south, the chapter begins in the northwestern corner of the state at the Mount Baker Wilderness and then proceeds along what has been called the most scenic mountain highway in America, Route 20, to explore the Skagit Valley, North Cascades National Park, and the vast Pasayten Wilderness. Glacier Peak, the largest wilderness area in the Northwest, comes next, followed by the Alpine Lakes Wilderness area, less than an hour from Seattle. The itinerary then moves south, visiting various preserves around Tacoma, Mount Rainier National Park and the six wilderness areas surrounding it, and winding up in the blast zone at Mount St. Helens in the southwestern section of the state.

The roads through the mountains are often narrow, steep, and winding, containing sheer cliffs, sharp drop-offs, and frequent switchbacks. Travelers who want to take long looks at the mountains should use the frequent scenic turnouts. The summer months bring thousands of visitors; planning trips during off-season—late spring or early fall—helps avoid the crowds.

Mount Baker

Driving north on I-5 from Seattle, travelers do not leave the metropolitan area until they are past Everett, where Boeing builds its huge 747s. On a clear day, views of Mount Baker—which from Seattle is never more than a white jag on the northern horizon—grow steadily larger and more distinct, making the peak the principal visual presence of northern Puget Sound.

Central Washington

ABOVE: *Every winter up to 500 bald eagles congregate along the Skagit River to feed on spawned-out chum and other salmon.*
RIGHT: *In the shadow of Mount Baker, the coastal Skagit Wildlife Area shelters thousands of waterfowl each winter.*

South of Bellingham, there is a small protected area where bogs and wetlands provide an outdoor laboratory for Western Washington University. (The area is currently not available for public use, although its status may change in the future.) Closer to Bellingham, Route 11 west and south leads to **Larrabee State Park❖,** where trails meander through the woods to mountain lakes and views, and wildflowers such as bleeding heart, trillium, Indian paintbrush, and columbine brighten the coastal terrain.

At the northern end of Bellingham, turn east from I-5 onto Route 542 toward **Mount Baker,** a classically shaped snowcapped volcano in the northernmost section of the **Mount Baker–Snoqualmie National Forest❖.** Called "Koma Kulshan," or steep white mountain by the Nooksack tribe, Mount Baker is second only to Rainier as a Washington scenic icon. Its upper slopes are almost totally covered by

glaciers. Only about 300,000 years old, Baker is still considered an active volcano (indeed, many expected it to blow before Mount St. Helens), and steam clouds sometimes waft from a summit crater.

The surrounding **Mount Baker Wilderness❖** includes a great deal of mountain rock and ice plus dense fir, hemlock, and cedar forests and the drainages of the Nooksack and Baker rivers. From the town of Glacier, Route 542 ascends 24 miles—first gradually through dense forest and then more steeply to the timberline—providing views of river gorges, glacial lakes, alpine waterfalls, and Mount Shuksan to the east. Before the route dead-ends at Artist Point, Forest Road 32 branches east to the Hannegan Campground, where a 47-mile hiking trail leads farther east into the wildest parts of the North Cascades. Hikers can start out in the Mount Baker Wilderness, enter North Cascades National Park, cross the mountains at Whatcom Pass, and wind up on the shore of Ross Lake.

Route 542 ends in the northern part of the **Mount Baker National Recreation Area❖.** From here trails lead off into the wilderness and up toward the mountain's 10,778-foot summit to the south. The ascent is a climb rather than a hike and reaching the summit safely requires ice axes, ropes, and crampons. Ice and crevasses must be crossed, but college women wearing wool and carrying alpenstocks made it in the 1920s, and today a fit climber can go from the parking lot to the summit and back in one day.

The southern section of the Mount Baker National Recreation Area, accessible from Route 20 to the south, contains **Baker Lake,** an alpine reservoir where camping, boating, and fishing are permitted, and **Shannon Lake,** home to the largest colony of nesting ospreys in the state.

THE SKAGIT VALLEY

The Skagit Valley is a swath of flat, fertile, often flooded agricultural land that follows the Skagit River west from the foothills of the North Cascades to Puget Sound. "Great islands of craggy rock arch abruptly up out of the flats," the novelist Tom Robbins writes in *Another Roadside Attraction,* "and at sunrise and moonrise these outcroppings are frequently tangled in mist. . . . It is a poetic setting, one which suggests inner meanings and invisible connections. The effect is distinctly Chinese. . . .

"The Skagit Valley, in fact, inspired a school of neo-Chinese painters. In the forties, Mark Tobey, Morris Graves, and their gray-on-gray disciples turned their backs on cubist composition and European color and using the shapes and shades of this misty terrain as a springboard, began to paint the visions of the inner eye."

The main stem of the **Skagit River** arises in Canada and flows to salt water from North Cascades National Park. Two major tributaries, the Sauk and Suiattle, start deep in the Glacier Peak Wilderness to the south. The Skagit is one of only three Washington rivers—and the only one in this part of the state—that have been designated national wild and scenic rivers. (To be eligible for wild and scenic designation, a river must flow freely and contain at least one outstanding scenic, recreational, geologic, wildlife, historic, or archaeological feature.)

South of Mount Vernon, a turn west from I-5 onto Route 534 leads to the **Skagit Wildlife Area❖** at the river's mouth. The tidal flats, salt marsh, and farmland of the wildlife preserve are managed to provide habitat for wintering waterfowl. Some 27,000 lesser snow geese migrate here each fall from the Arctic; there are also hundreds of tundra, formerly whistling, swans, 24 duck species including mallards, teal, wigeon, and pintail, and various raptors.

North of Mount Vernon at Burlington, turn east on Route 20 and follow it up the river. Baker Lake Road east of Sedro Woolley and Baker River Road at Concrete lead to trails that enter both the national park and the **Noisy-Diobsud Wilderness❖** on the western edge of the park, where some very steep, forested terrain is split by Noisy and Diobsud creeks. Just west of Rockport, **Rockport State Park❖** contains some old-growth Douglas fir forest as well as several campsites and hiking trails.

On both sides of Rockport, between Concrete and Marblemount, lies the **Skagit River Bald Eagle Natural Area❖.** Every winter as many as 500 bald eagles feed on spawned-out chum and other salmon in this corridor along the Skagit River. (Perhaps another hundred eagles feed along the Sauk, the Suiattle, and other tributaries.) This is one of the biggest gathering spots for eagles in the lower 48 states. The Skagit produces the largest run of chum salmon on Puget Sound; the fish return each winter to spawn and die, and eagles return every year to eat the fish. Prime time for eagle-watching is January, but from late November until mid-March they can be viewed from a car, raft, or boat. No foot traffic is allowed in the area in these winter months. The best vantage points from Route 20 are the Miller Steelhead Park, Washington Eddy Lookout, and Sutter Creek Rest Area.

OVERLEAF: *Early morning sun lights Mount Challenger and Whatcom Peak. The exposed rock typifies the austere landscape of the North Cascades, which display more naked granite than the mountains farther south.*

THE NORTH CASCADES

Marblemount is the western gateway to **North Cascades National Park❖,** a spectacular area of jagged peaks and coniferous forests, wildflower meadows and mountain lakes, waterfalls and glaciers. Route 20, which becomes the North Cascades Highway, is the only driving route through the mountains. Completed in 1972, the road clings to rock faces above steep river gorges. Because of deep snow and avalanches, it is closed every winter.

The national park is not an isolated preserve. Divided by Route 20 into northern and southern units, it forms the core of a complex that includes the Ross Lake and Lake Chelan national recreation areas and is largely surrounded by national forests and wilderness areas, including the two largest in the Northwest, Pasayten and Glacier Peak. Encompassing several million acres, the area contains big trees and deep lakes, mountain streams and green valleys, but it is primarily distinguished by its rock and ice.

Not volcanic in origin, the North Cascades were once at the bottom of an ancient sea and were thrust higher than the rest of the Cascade range by crustal upheavals millions of years ago. In the southerly parts of the Cascades, volcanic rock still covers the relatively isolated peaks that soar above the surrounding plateau. The taller peaks rise in jumbled proximity to one another.

In summer all through the park, more than 300 melting glaciers keep water running down rivers, cascading over precipices, and seeping down rocks. The glaciers also create their own miniature weather systems, probably augmenting the variety of habitats and therefore the number of plant and animal species that live in the park. More plant species have been identified here than in any other national park: as many as 1,700. Even without the glaciers, there would be a wide range of environments: from the dry eastern side of the mountains to the wet western side, from the river valleys to the snowcapped peaks.

More than 100,000 acres of the park are considered possible habitat for the spotted owl, although only a few owl pairs have been found so

---

RIGHT: *Created when Seattle City Light dammed the Skagit River more than a half century ago, Ross Lake cuts through the center of the mountainous park, enabling visitors to travel deep into the North Cascades.*

ABOVE: *Found throughout Washington's mountains, the cougar is a superb jumper, reluctant swimmer, and solitary hunter.*

RIGHT: *The gray wolf, the ecosystem's top predator, reappeared in the North Cascades in the late 1980s.*

far. Other residents include black bears and a number of mountain lions, as well as wolves, coyotes, bobcats, and mountain goats.

The presence of grizzly bears in these mountains was big news at the end of the 1980s. Grizzlies had clearly lived in the Cascades years before and were still occasionally reported, but the reports were all unconfirmed. No one had positively identified a grizzly since the 1960s. Although a five-year state study beginning in 1986 failed to photograph or capture any of these huge brown creatures, it did positively identify grizzly footprints. The big bears were back—or more likely, they had never left. There weren't many, and they had just stayed out of sight. (The bears need a lot of room. Although North Cascades National Park and its surrounding wilderness areas cover roughly 3.5 million acres, there is no way to ensure the bears' survival unless their habitat is protected not only in and around the national park but also north of the border in Canada.)

North Cascades National Park and its surrounding wilderness and recreation areas may not be large by grizzly bear standards, but on a human scale, they add up to a lot of space. The 360 miles of maintained trails, ranging from gentle to expert, are long and varied enough for hikers to spend days in the woods; and the glaciers and peaks are steep enough for serious climbers. Plenty of alpine scenery is visible along Route 20 (often touted as the most beautiful mountain highway in the country) or from overlooks such as those at **Goodell Creek, Gorge Creek Falls, Diablo Lake,** or **Washington Pass.** But no roadside view can capture the scale or essence of these mountains. North Cascades National Park is primarily a place to explore on foot.

At Marblemount, partially paved Cascade River Road branches off Route 20, heading southeast for 25 miles to trails leading into the peaks at the southern end of the park. The **Cascade Pass Trail** climbs four miles to wildflower meadows (carefully rehabilitated in recent years) and views of the Cascade and Stehekin valleys. The trail follows an ancient transmountain path first used by Native Americans and early explorers such as Alexander Ross; additional trails continue south to Lake Chelan.

At Diablo, farther east along Route 20, more trails lead north into the park and the **Ross Lake National Recreation Area❖.** Bordered by Canada to the north and the Pasayten wilderness to the east, the recreation area runs through the center of the park and then angles up to occupy its northeastern corner. **Ross Lake,** which stretches from Route 20 to the U.S. border, is both extremely scenic and wholly unnatural. It was created when Seattle City Light dammed the Skagit River to produce hydroelectric power. The dam and a resort lie at the southern end of the lake, but the water provides a travel corridor deep into the northern section of the national park; water taxis deliver hikers to trailheads far from any highway. Canoes and small motorboats can also be rented.

The nation's largest stand of old-growth western redcedar grows near the western shore of Ross Lake in **Big Beaver Valley.** (This is one case where an old geographical name really stands for something: An active beaver pond is still located here.) City Light planned for years to raise the dam and therefore the water level, which would have flooded the cedar grove (plus a good deal of lower British Columbia). United States and Canadian environmentalists successfully fought the plan, which has now been abandoned. Although the southern end of Ross Lake is developed, the northern portions are very wild. The first evidence that gray wolves had returned to the North Cascades was wolf paw prints found on the lakeshore in the late 1980s.

Beyond Diablo, more trails branch off Route 20. The **Happy Creek Forest Walk,** south of the road, is a short boardwalk path with interpretative signs that winds through old-growth forest; the trail to **Rainy Lake** is short and paved; the one to **Lake Ann** winds two miles through big Douglas firs. Longer trails start from the Colonial Creek Campground and from various points indicated by signs along the roadside, leading into the park and the **Okanogan National Forest❖,** some 1.7 million acres containing the Pasayten and Lake Chelan–Sawtooth wildernesses.

A turnoff at Mazama leads to trailheads for hiking, mountain biking, and cross-country skiing in the huge **Pasayten Wilderness❖.** This vast, empty land of high country and pine forest connects the North Cascades to the drier Okanogan highlands to the east. Although the western edge of the Pasayten is indistinguishable from the mountains and forests of the North Cascades, the eastern edge is much drier and more open. Stretching north to the Canadian border—people sometimes hike into the Pasayten's Cathedral Rocks area from British Columbia's Cathedral Park—the Pasayten lies far from any major population center. It is the second-largest wilderness area in the Northwest.

Past Mazama and Winthrop—mountain-biking centers in the summer and cross-country skiing territory during the winter, when the North Cascades Highway (Route 20) is closed—turn south on Route 97 and follow the signs to Chelan at the southern end of Lake Chelan. Unlike Ross Lake, **Lake Chelan** (the Wapato Indian word for deep water) is a natural body of water. Nearly 50 miles long and extremely deep (1,500 feet), the steep-sided lake is a kind of inland fjord. Regular boat service takes visitors from the town of Chelan, north of Wenatchee, to the small resort town of Stehekin, which lies within the **Lake Chelan National Recreation Area❖,** an appendage of the national park.

No through roads lead to Stehekin. The town is accessible only by boat, floatplane, or foot. Hikers can make their way from the western side of the mountains to the lake, or come down from the north through Cascade Pass to Cottonwood Camp and catch a government shuttle bus to Stehekin along the dead-end road. The status of Stehekin as a recreational area has long been the subject of bitter controversy: environmentalists are trying to restrict human activity so that it will be

---

RIGHT: *Enveloped by light mist and surrounded by graceful conifers, tall stalks of creamy white bear grass rise above an alpine meadow in the Cascades. Red paintbrush and lavender iris carpet the ground.*

compatible with the surrounding wilderness; residents are trying to preserve their community.

To the east and north of the lake, touching the southeastern corner of the national park, the **Lake Chelan–Sawtooth Wilderness**❖ rises from the lakeshore to almost 9,000 feet on North Gardner Mountain. The terrain encompasses peaks and valleys, meadows and lakes, and supports Douglas fir, Engelmann spruce, and sagebrush, as well as elk, deer, cougars, mountain goats, and bears.

BOULDER RIVER AND GLACIER PEAK

Not far as the crow flies from the heavily populated, heavily developed north-south freeway corridor but well off the beaten track, the route to Glacier Peak includes some of the most impressive and least crowded places in western Washington. To reach the Boulder River and Glacier Peak area, turn east from I-5 toward Arlington on Route 530 along the North Fork of the Stillaguamish River. Six miles west of Darrington, Forest Road 2010 heads south to trails into the ancient forest of the

Boulder River Wilderness❖.

This close to Puget Sound, virtually no large areas of old-growth forest survive at low elevations. First, loggers took everything they could move to salt water with ox teams and muscle. Next, they took everything they could winch to a logging railroad—using prodigious engineering ingenuity to run rail lines almost everywhere. Finally, they ran roads to places even the logging railroads had not reached and used trucks to haul out everything that was left. Over the years they logged farther and farther from salt water, farther and farther up the slopes. After more than a century of logging, there is only an occasional clump of huge old trees in a ravine or on a slope that the men with axes, crosscut saws, and chain saws overlooked. The clumps are

ABOVE: *A colorful bird with a distinctive song first described by Lewis and Clark in 1806, the western tanager lives in mountainous areas throughout Washington.*

LEFT: *Every fall, vine maples—small, scrubby trees whose leaves turn a brilliant red at the end of summer—brighten the understory of the evergreen forests of the North Cascades range.*

small, though, and the trees, although huge by any conventional standards, are not the real crème de la crème. In this context, the survival of a whole valley full of low-elevation old growth verges on the miraculous. But that has happened in the lower Boulder River drainage.

Along the Boulder River grows the last sizable low-elevation old-growth forest in the Cascades. The landscape is punctuated by streams and snowcapped peaks. The trail along the river can also be enjoyed in winter, when mountain trails lie under many feet of drifted snow.

To reach Glacier Peak, follow Route 530 to the town of Darrington and turn south along the Sauk River on Forest Road 22 or the Mountain Loop Highway—which isn't much of a highway but does get close to the mountains. Five miles later, after crossing the White Chuck River, Forest Road 23 heads east to the trailheads for the huge **Glacier Peak Wilderness❖,** where more than half a million acres of roadless, undeveloped wilderness surround 10,541-foot **Glacier Peak.** Full of lakes, streams, waterfalls, and lesser peaks, the Northwest's largest wilderness also contains a great many active glaciers. The **Pacific Crest National Scenic Trail❖**—the long-distance mountain trail that winds over the Sierra Nevada and Cascade ranges for more than 2,600 miles from Mexico to Canada—curves more than halfway around Glacier Peak, which is perhaps the most remote of the region's 10,000-foot volcanoes. Large enough in its own right, the Glacier Peak Wilderness is bordered on the south by the Henry M. Jackson Wilderness and on the north by North Cascades National Park.

THE ALPINE LAKES

The country's northernmost interstate and the main route east from Seattle, I-90 is one of the few highways that crosses the Cascades. Before reaching the Cascades proper, I-90 passes close to hiking trails that lead through the grandiosely named Issaquah Alps. In fact, the Tradition Lake trailhead on **Tiger Mountain** off Exit 18 is the most popular hiking spot in Washington. Easy trails, with fine views in clear weather, lead through second-growth forest to the talus caves and wetlands of **West Tiger Mountain Natural Resource Conservation Area,** and through miles of a state forest that—in a radical departure from past practices—is being managed for wildlife and recreation as well as timber production. This NRCA differs from many others in Washington in that there are facilities for public use, although as at all NRCAs, the area was designated primarily to protect habitat. Tiger Mountain is a critical link in a proposed Mountains-to-Sound Greenway that will preserve and connect wildlife habitat, trails, views, and historic sites in the freeway corridor extending from salt water to the eastern slopes of the Cascades.

As one approaches the town of North Bend on I-90, the isolated crags of **Mount Si❖** seem to rise straight from the valley floor. Far and away the most distinctive landmark along the corridor between Seattle and Snoqualmie Pass, Si was a trademark image of the short-lived but much-discussed 1980s television show *Twin Peaks*. Leaving the freeway at North Bend, head east of town to Mount Si Road, which leads to a very large parking lot and a very steep trail up the mountain. The heavily used trail, which gains 3,200 feet in 4 miles, provides views west, south, and north. On a clear day, a hiker can see Mount Rainier and the Olympics and get a bird's-eye view of the Snoqualmie Valley and the towns below. Just to the east lie miles of clear-cuts, but the trail up Si has been protected since 1976 by a conservation area, which was expanded in 1990; it is now large enough to preserve the new forest that will eventually grow among the stumps.

Seattle's **Cedar River Watershed❖** lies east of North Bend, a short drive from the freeway on Cedar Falls Road but accessible only by special arrangement with the city of Seattle's water department. Although much of the watershed has been logged, use of the area has been restricted since the turn of the century, when Seattle residents started drinking Cedar River water. The watershed now acts as a de facto refuge, providing core habitat for perhaps 40 cougars and 600 elk, as well as very rare nesting sites for common loons. Some of the elk are flattened trying to cross I-90, but quicker or luckier animals have migrated as far as Mount Adams, 70 miles southwest. Cougars have followed the forested ridgelines all the way to the Seattle suburbs. Trees on much of the land are second-growth, but some Douglas firs are 700 years old.

A more accessible patch of ancient forest grows a little farther east, near the Denny Creek freeway exit, along the **Asahel Curtis Nature Trail❖.** Named for an early-twentieth-century Seattle photographer, the nature trail offers an easy look at a particularly fine stand of huge (some 250 feet), old (some 600 years) trees.

The same exit also leads to trailheads for **Pratt Lake, Melakwa Lake, Granite Mountain,** and other destinations in the **Alpine Lakes Wilderness❖.** Less than an hour's drive from the Northwest's largest city, the wilderness contains 393,000 acres of mountains and forests and more than 700 lakes. Seeing much of the Alpine Lakes area—or any

OVERLEAF: *Surrounded by alpine firs, rocks, and pink heather, mile-high Lila Lake on Rampart Ridge in the southern portion of the Alpine Lakes Wilderness reflects the peak of Mount Hibox (right) on nearby Box Ridge.*

other major wilderness—obviously requires more than a day, but this is nevertheless a great place for day hikes. Some visitors complain about the lack of solitude on the more accessible trails, and any place this close to the city will inevitably attract plenty of people. But hikers who go at an off-time—say, first thing on a Tuesday morning right after school has started in September—may have even a popular trail all to themselves.

Early in the season—which at higher elevations may be well into the summer—many trails climb through the vivid reds of paintbrush, the delicate orange recurved petals of tiger lilies, the thick white flower spikes and shiny green tufts of bear grass. Late summer brings the powder blues and wine purples of ripe berries. Go to one of the hot, huckleberry-covered slopes in later summer. Take along a child old enough to like berries but not yet walking, let her crawl through the trailside dust grabbing handfuls of blue fruit, and feel like a mother bear.

A hiker who tries swimming in one of the lakes—even on a hot summer day—is more likely to feel like a polar bear. Not much used as swimming holes, the cold alpine lakes provide the foregrounds for some of the wilderness's classic landscape views: a crystal-clear lake lies in a rocky cirque, while the peaks behind it—dark with trees or bright with the glare of sunlight on naked rock—appear twice, once silhouetted against the sky and once reflected on the mirrored surface of the water.

Climbers can see many more peaks, layer upon layer of them. On a clear day, the higher the vantage point, the more tiers of mountains are visible. For those who get high enough, the isolated white cone of Rainier or Glacier usually anchors the scene as successive ridges and lesser peaks roll on to the horizon. Sometimes fog fills the valleys, foreshortening the vista so that each ridgeline seems to crowd the one behind it. Sometimes clouds descend, dissolving the distant peaks and allowing nearby crags to advance and float alone in the mist. Then, surrounded by the chiaroscuro of dark trees on gray rock, hikers may feel as though they have stepped into a Chinese landscape painting.

Several easily accessible trails into the Alpine Lakes start at **Snoqualmie Pass,** where I-90 crosses the Cascade crest and meets the

---

RIGHT: *Actually clones growing from the same large root system, stands of aspens turn an identical golden yellow in the fall. Here they brighten a stream bed near the Cascade crest in the Alpine Lakes Wilderness.*

RIGHT: *Nesting pairs of common loons are not generally found in Washington, but several couples have been spotted in the de facto wildlife refuge of Seattle's Cedar River Watershed.*

LEFT: *An angler tries his luck in the morning stillness of Rachel Lake, which lies in the Alpine Lakes Wilderness east of Snoqualmie Pass.*

Pacific Crest Trail, which follows the mountains from Canada to Mexico. Although only 3,020 feet high, the pass gets 35 feet of snow each year and is western Washington's largest ski center. The interstate's Snoqualmie Summit exits lie close to parking lots and trailheads for both northern and southern segments of the Pacific Crest Trail.

Hikers can also enter the Alpine Lakes Wilderness from Route 2, which parallels I-90 to the north. West of Leavenworth, in the **Wenatchee National Forest❖,** Icicle Road (Forest Road 7600) leads south and west to some of the region's most spectacular hiking trails and to sheer granite cliffs that are heavily used by rock climbers. In fall, larch trees turn golden among the lakes and granite. Where Route 2 crosses the Cascades at 4,000-foot **Stevens Pass,** the Pacific Crest Trail meets pavement again. (Hikers can cover the 67 miles between the passes at Stevens and Snoqualmie without crossing any roads.) North of Route 2 lies the **Henry M. Jackson Wilderness❖,** named for the late U.S. senator from Everett, Washington, who sponsored the National Environmental Policy Act in 1969. This wilderness, which bridges the gap between the Alpine Lakes and the huge Glacier Peak Wilderness farther north, contains peaks, lakes, glaciers, and forests of fir, spruce, and hemlock. Descending westward from Stevens Pass on Route 2, turn north on a county road near the town of Gold Bar for **Wallace Falls State Park❖,** where a 2.5-mile trail through a mixed second-growth forest follows the Wallace River to the 250-foot waterfall.

MOUNT RAINIER

Southwest of the Seattle–Tacoma urban corridor lie six wilderness areas that surround one of the most beautiful natural preserves in the

97

LEFT: *Actually a species of antelope, the long-haired mountain goat is native to the Cascades and was introduced in the 1920s to higher elevations of Mount Rainier National Park.*

RIGHT: *At more than 14,000 feet, Mount Rainier—which Native Americans called Tahoma—is the Northwest's highest peak. On clear days its glaciated summit is visible from Puget Sound as well as the cities of Seattle and Tacoma.*

country, **Mount Rainier National Park❖.** The tallest peak in the Cascades, visible a hundred miles away on a clear day, **Mount Rainier** is probably the greatest single scenic icon of the Northwest. No wonder—in how many places can one stand at sea level and see, sometimes literally on a boat deck, a massive snowcapped volcano rising three miles into the sky.

To reach Mount Rainier, drive south from I-5 in the Tacoma area on Route 7. North of the town of Eatonville on Route 161, which parallels Route 7, the **Northwest Trek❖,** a wildlife park, gives visitors a chance to see Roosevelt elk, woodland caribou, mountain goats, and bighorn sheep, which roam freely here; lynx, bobcats, cougars, badgers, and other animals are in more traditional zoo exhibits. Return to Route 7, heading south and then east on Route 706. Just before the national park entrance, Forest Road 59 leads north to the **Glacier View Wilderness❖.** Only 3,050 acres, Glacier View includes 5,500-foot Mount Beljica, several lakes, and a variety of conifers.

Mount Rainier, soaring to 14,410 feet in splendid isolation, is the highest of a chain of volcanoes that dominates the Cascade Range. Probably about a million years old, Rainier rose gradually from the base of older volcanoes as continuous eruptions formed its graceful cone. For eons, glaciers have gouged deep chasms and erosion has carved the distinctive rocky ridges that radiate from the mountain's flanks.

The high slopes of Mount Rainier are all rock and ice, but the base is not. Despite the harsh environment, there are stands of huge old-growth trees and vast flower meadows. At higher elevations, where

snow lingers into the summer, fragile alpine flowers bloom in July or August. This part of the mountain, between the dark forests and the perpetual ice, was the most attractive to naturalist John Muir. Everywhere there are views of the huge white peak. Seen close-up from a bare ridge or at a distance from a meadow rich with flowers, it fills the field of vision. And that's appropriate—in Mount Rainier National Park, the mountain itself is always the main attraction.

From the Nisqually entrance (the only gate open year-round), the road climbs 19 miles to Paradise, on the southern slope of the mountain, passing close to some enormous trees. At **Kautz Creek** dead trees and debris still remain from a flash mud flow in 1947. **Longmire** offers a visitor center, lodge, trailheads, and small museum devoted to the natural and geologic history of the area. The park contains more than 300 miles of trails. They branch off Route 706 to the south into the Tatoosh Range, jagged pinnacles that originated some 30 million years ago, and to the north toward Rainier. The 93-mile **Wonderland Trail,** which crosses the road near Longmire, takes hikers all the way around the mountain's base (it can be hiked in shorter segments).

Paradise, with its lodge, visitor center, and classic views of the mountain, is the most heavily used part of the park. In late summer, short walks on paved trails lead to meadows blooming with more than 40 species of wildflowers—yellow glacier lilies, blue lupines, red Indian paintbrush, indigo gentians. From Paradise, one can take longer, more difficult hikes into the rough country on the mountain's southern flank. A steep hike leads straight up to **Camp Muir** at 10,000 feet, the most popular route to the summit. Most climbers spend a short night at Muir, then head for the summit before dawn.

Native Americans called the huge volcano Tahoma or Tacoma, meaning great mountain. In May 1792, from a ship on Puget Sound, Admiral George Vancouver noted in his log the sighting of a "high, round mountain covered with snow." He named it for a friend, Admiral Peter Rainier. In 1833, William Tolmie, a young Scottish doctor in charge of the Hudson's Bay Company post at Nisqually House, and several Native

---

Left: *Late summer brings wildflowers to the high meadows of Mount Rainier National Park. Along Paradise Trail are delicate western pasqueflowers, which send up long-stemmed, fuzzy white seedpods.*

101

ABOVE: *With neither Gore-Tex clothing nor polypropylene ropes, these climbers navigated the crevices of Mount Rainier on August 20, 1913.*

RIGHT: *Waves and pinnacles of ice jut from the jagged surface of Mount Rainier's Tahoma Glacier, seen here from 5,600-foot Emerald Ridge.*

Americans hiked into what is now the park, saw water cascading off the glaciers, and climbed into the snow. "From a natural amphitheater," writes historian Murray Morgan, "they could see a torrent of rain and snow melt pouring off North Mowich glacier in a 300-foot waterfall. Several peaks were within striking distance. Tolmie chose the one that seemed to have the most snow and, after a nice cup of tea, started up."

Twenty-four years later, an American army officer made it to 14,000 feet. In 1870, General Hazard Stevens and Philemon Van Trump reached the top. They spent the night on the summit, where a volcanic steam cave saved them from freezing to death. In the 1890s, Van Trump's advice to would-be climbers of Rainier included wearing a good set of woolen underwear. Twenty years after Stevens and Van Trump reached the summit, a young teacher named Fay Fuller became the first woman to climb the mountain. She wore a straw hat and used an alpenstock made from an old shovel handle.

Nearly 8,000 people attempt the summit each year, and some 2,500 succeed. Novice climbers can sign up with the Mount Rainier Guide

Central Washington

Service for a day of instruction and, weather permitting, a guided climb to the top. Nevertheless, scaling Rainier isn't the proverbial walk in the park. Every year people die on the mountain, in falls or avalanches. Many forget just how dangerous Rainier can be: It may not have erupted in a big way for 2,200 years, but it's still an active volcano. The clearest threat to nearby population centers is probably not an eruption spewing lava and poisonous gas but one that simply melts the glaciers, creating huge mud flows like the one that swept all the way to Puget Sound 5,000 years ago.

Mount Rainier's 27 major glaciers trap some 156 billion cubic feet of water. Covering about 40 square miles, these hanging rivers of year-round ice constitute by far the largest single-peak glacier system in the lower 48 states. Glaciers give Rainier its look. Climbers cross them on the way to the summit, and even casual hikers can get as close to glaciers as they wish—although because boulders often tumble off the ice, smart hikers do not want to get too close. And everyone sees glacial water churning through canyons and plunging over cliffs.

Near the Stevens Canyon Entrance to the park (east from Paradise along Route 706) is the **Grove of Patriarchs,** where an easy nature trail winds through gigantic western redcedars, western hemlocks, and Douglas fir that are between 500 and 1,000 years old. From Route 410 in the northeastern section of the park, a road travels west to the White River Entrance and the **Sunrise Visitor Center,** which at 6,400 feet is

the highest point in the park accessible by car. From here trails lead in all directions through tundralike terrain populated with dwarfed trees and fragile alpine vegetation; gray pumice pellets from an 1800s eruption dust the ground. Visible from trails at Sunrise, **Emmons Glacier**, measuring four miles long and one mile wide, is Rainier's largest.

In the northwestern section of the park, accessible only from the north via Route 165, the Ipsut Creek Campground lies just three miles from the **Carbon Glacier,** the shiny charcoal-gray ice pack that has proceeded farthest down the mountain's flanks. The surrounding

Carbon River area receives the park's heaviest rainfall and is home to a rare inland temperate rain forest.

Wilderness areas surround the park on all sides. To the south beyond the Ohanapecosh Visitor Center on Route 123 and Route 12, forest roads lead west into the **Tatoosh Wilderness❖.** The Tatoosh ranges from forested river bottomlands to high meadows. In clear weather, hikers in the Tatoosh Wilderness enjoy views of the region's three highest peaks, Mount Rainier, Mount Adams, and Mount Hood.

Along Route 12 farther east the **Goat Rocks Wilderness❖,** includes the Northwest's highest section of the **Pacific Crest National Scenic Trail❖.** On its way from Mexico to Canada, the trail reaches 7,600 feet here—hikers should take the risk of sudden weather changes and hypothermia seriously, even in summer—passing close to the Packwood Glacier and the 7,930-foot summit of Old Snowy. The Cowlitz, Klickitat, and Tieton rivers all rise in the Goat Rocks Wilderness, and below timberline stand forests of hemlock, true fir, western white pine, and Alaska yellow-cedar.

Proceeding from the eastern part of Mount Rainier National Park, Route 410 climbs through Chinook Pass, where the Pacific Crest Trail heads north into the Norse Peak Wilderness and south into the William O. Douglas Wilderness. Near the northeastern corner of the national park, the **Norse Peak Wilderness❖** is forested with Douglas fir, true fir, hemlock, pine, and Engelmann spruce. The valleys, peaks, and lakes provide habitat for lynx, cougars, fishers, and wolverines, as well as elk, deer, and bears.

The **William O. Douglas Wilderness❖** is named for the late U.S. Supreme Court justice who grew up in nearby Yakima, Washington, loved the northwestern landscape, and returned each summer to hike the Cascades. As a private citizen, Douglas successfully fought to keep the federal government from building a road along the Olympic Peninsula's wilderness beach and from expanding Bumping Lake to store more irrigation water for the Yakima Valley by flooding forest near Goose Prairie. As a judge, he framed the question in a dispute between

---

LEFT: *Masses of pink monkeyflowers—***Mimulus lewisii,** *named for the explorer Meriwether Lewis—bloom among blue lupine and yellow composite flowers near a mountain stream in the Goat Rocks Wilderness.*

public and private power companies in a way that made possible the preservation of Hells Canyon, shared by Oregon and Idaho. The wilderness named for Douglas offers a wide range of terrain, including pine and fir forests, hundreds of small lakes, 7,766-foot Mount Aix, and habitat for cougars, lynx, fishers, wolverines, elk, deer, and bears.

The **Clearwater Wilderness Area❖** lies to the north of Mount Rainier and is accessible via forest roads that wind south off Route 410 east of the town of Enumclaw. The wilderness contains old-growth forest, lakes, alpine meadows, and the Clearwater River. North of 410 and farther west from Enumclaw on the White River, some old-growth forest survives in the **Federation Forest State Park❖,** where the Fred Cleator Interpretive Trail is a designated national recreation trail.

TACOMA AND SOUTH TO MOUNT ST. HELENS

South of Seattle lies the city of Tacoma. Founded in the nineteenth century as an unvarnished mill town, it boomed briefly as the terminus of the first transcontinental railroad to the Northwest; after the depression of 1893, it fell hopelessly behind Seattle in the race to become the commercial and population center of the state. Now Tacoma boasts spectacular views of Mount Rainier (the mountain is closer to this city than to Seattle and consequently looks a lot bigger), a splendid bay with so much chemical pollution in its sediments that it has been designated a Superfund hazardous waste cleanup site, great turn-of-the-century buildings downtown, and some terrific parks.

From I-5 turn west on Route 16 and follow the signs to **Point Defiance Park❖.** Occupying a peninsula jutting into Puget Sound, Point Defiance is one of America's great urban parks. Certainly not wilderness, it nonetheless contains miles of undeveloped saltwater beach and many acres of trees, some of them very large. Not far from Point Defiance, right off Route 16 and surrounded by the city, lies the **Snake Lake Nature Center❖,** a 54-acre preserve with resident foxes, wood ducks, and great blue herons.

Between Tacoma and the state capital of Olympia, I-5 descends into a wide, flat expanse of field and marsh spreading north to Puget Sound. This is the delta of the Nisqually River, which starts at a glacier on the southern slopes of Mount Rainier. The **Nisqually National Wildlife Refuge❖** lies near the river's mouth, just off the freeway. It includes an estuary, tidal flats, freshwater marshes, patches of woods, and open fields. This diverse habitat attracts a wide variety of birds, particularly migratory ducks and geese in the fall, goldfinches, warblers, and swallows in the spring, and year-round residents such as great blue herons and red-tailed hawks.

In the 1960s, when the ports of Olympia and Tacoma wanted to dredge and fill the Nisqually delta to create a massive new port, environmentalists stopped them. Subsequently, the Weyerhaeuser Company decided to build a log export facility near the refuge on land that had remained undeveloped because the DuPont Company had manufactured dynamite there and kept most of the area as a buffer. Environmentalists lost the fight against that project, but then Weyerhaeuser canceled its log-exporting plan. Now houses and commercial buildings are planned for the site and for another on the opposite side of the refuge. Already in easy earshot of the freeway, the railroad tracks, and the nearby military base at Fort Lewis, the Nisqually delta may eventually be hemmed in by thousands of homes.

Closer to Olympia, a very determined traveler can detour to **Hope Island State Park❖,** which is accessible only by boat. Largely undeveloped, this small island in southern Puget Sound was owned by a single family and has recently been acquired by the state. A swing through Olympia leads to the state's **Woodard Bay Natural Resource Conservation Area.** From downtown head north on East Bay Drive until it becomes Boston Harbor Road and finally turn northeast on Woodard Bay Road. From the shore of Woodard Bay, an arm of Henderson Inlet (which is in turn an arm of Puget Sound), the conservation area extends inland to encompass wetlands and old-growth cedar. South of Olympia, beyond Chehalis, a side trip from I-5 east on Route 12 and south on the Jackson Highway leads to **Lewis and Clark State Park❖,** which contains some old-growth forest, too.

None of these sites prepare visitors for the **Mount St. Helens National Volcanic Monument❖.** Volcanoes may be as much a part of the natural history of the Northwest as trees, but going from second-growth forest to the blast zone north of the mountain is like making a science-fiction trip between worlds.

On the morning of May 18, 1980, Mount St. Helens erupted with the force of 27,000 Hiroshima bombs. It felled trees up to 17 miles away,

109

ABOVE: *Mount St. Helens erupted on Sunday morning, May 18, 1980, blasting an enormous ash cloud over 22,000 square miles of the Northwest. In eastern Washington ash had to be shoveled away like drifted snow.*

killed 57 people, and deposited ash over 22,000 square miles. (The mountain erupted on a Sunday morning. On a weekday, loggers would have been working in the woods north of the volcano, and hundreds more people would probably have been killed.) In some places downwind the air was so thick with falling ash that people had to turn on their headlights at midday. Entire forests of huge old-growth trees were vaporized. Farther from the blast, trees were blown down as if sliced by a scythe. Close in, whole ridges were scoured down to bedrock. David Johnson, a geologist working for the U.S. Geological Survey, was observing the mountain from a ridge that he believed was a safe distance away. He simply vanished in the blast. So did his truck.

The eruption came as no big surprise. People had assumed for years that sooner or later Mount St. Helens would go off. In the early 1870s, Charles Nordohoff, predicting that the explosion would be sooner, wrote of two men trapped on the summit overnight who survived beside a volcanic vent so hot that they had to run into the snow periodically to cool off. In the spring of 1980, geologists expected the mountain to erupt any day. They didn't know how powerful the blast would be, but they figured St. Helens was a dangerous place. People were warned to leave the area. Most did. A crusty octogenarian named Harry Truman, who ran a resort beside Spirit Lake, became a media star and folk hero by refusing to leave. He had lived beside the lake with a houseful of cats for many years, and he thought he knew the mountain.

He was wrong. Truman and his cats were buried under 300 feet of rock, ash, and mud. The perfect white cone of the mountain lost 1,300 vertical feet. Incredibly, despite the devastation, some creatures survived in the blast zone—pocket gophers were, by and large, safe underground; they appeared later like survivors of a bombing emerging from their shelters—and others returned within a year. Some places in the blast zone still look lunar, but others are being covered by flowers, shrubs, even trees.

Herds of elk now live in the desolate mud flow area along the Toutle River. Here hot mud formed by melting glaciers raised the river level by as much as 66 feet, burying houses, knocking out bridges, and ultimately depositing millions of tons of sediment downstream in the Cowlitz and Columbia rivers. The big elk climb the forested hills to forage, but much of the time they stay along the river, standing, walking, and lying down right on the mud.

To reach Mount St. Helens, take Exit 49 from I-5 and follow Route 504 east about five miles to the **Mount St. Helens Visitor Center,** which provides panoramic views as well as exhibits devoted to the eruption. Continue along Route 504 into the devastated area north of the mountain. At the end of the road, just eight miles from the crater stands the new **Coldwater Ridge Visitor Center;** from its observation deck one can look across Coldwater Lake, created when volcanic debris clogged a creek, and at the mountain's desolate north slope. Because it is a national monument, the area, with its charred stumps and snags, has deliberately not been replanted.

To climb the mountain or reach hiking trails on the southern side, take 504 west, then head south on I-5 to Woodland and turn east on Route 503. There is a climbers' register at Yale Reservoir. Past Cougar, Forest Road 83 leads to a network of roads and trails on the mountain's southern side, which has heavy layers of ash from earlier eruptions but wasn't touched in 1980. From this side one can climb to the

ABOVE: *Elk now frequent the banks of the Toutle River, still gray from the torrent of mud unleashed by Mount St. Helens' melting glaciers.*

top of Mount St. Helens, overlooking the crater. (All climbers need permits, and early in the season before the snow has melted, they need climbing gear and some climbing knowledge—enough to avoid the cornice, the seductive ridge of unsupported snow built up at the edge of the sheer rock cliff that drops straight down to the crater floor.) Route 503 leads back west to the freeway. It is also possible to take forest roads around the eastern side of the mountain, a route that passes additional trailheads and connects with Route 12 and then I-5.

From the summit of Mount St. Helens, the crater and the logs floating on Spirit Lake are visible in a single glance. Behind them looms Mount Rainier—unspoiled but still active. Perhaps—not tomorrow or next year but maybe centuries or millennia in the future—it will be the next Mount St. Helens. The U.S. Geological Survey has established the Cascades Volcano Observatory to monitor activity in the area and provide warning of possible eruptions. However, someday inevitably Rainier or some other Cascade volcano will destroy the forests, melt the glaciers, and cover the landscape with ash. Geologists don't know now when or where the next eruption will come, but they are certain that Mount St. Helens wasn't the largest. And it won't be the last.

RIGHT: *Amid the jumble of logs felled by the eruption, plants have begun colonizing the rich soil around Spirit Lake and Mount St. Helens.*

EASTERN WASHINGTON

People tend to lump everything east of the Cascades under the heading "eastern Washington" and to assume that this area in the rain shadow of the higher peaks to the west is all bone-dry. Much of it is semiarid, especially in the central basin: the fossilized tree trunks embedded in sage-covered hills at Ginkgo Petrified Forest State Park, the shrub-steppe environment of the arid lands ecology research area on the Hanford Nuclear Reservation, the sand and sparse vegetation of the Juniper Dunes Wilderness. But the landscape east of the Cascades also includes the pine-darkened ridges of the Pasayten Wilderness near the Canadian border and the old-growth western redcedars of the Salmo-Priest Wilderness, the great wheatfields of the Palouse Hills, the forested Blue Mountains of the southeast, and the 190-foot cascade at Palouse Falls. Eventually nearly everything—rivers, lakes, glaciers, and creeks—drains into the vast Columbia River Basin. Flowing south from Canada through pine forests, the Columbia turns west in the arid tri-cities region of Pasco, Richland, and Kennewick and makes its final run to the sea through a deep gorge shared by Washington and Oregon. Big hydropower dams across the river and its major tributaries have eliminated the free-flowing waterways that once allowed

LEFT: *In the arid country of southeastern Washington, the Palouse River, swollen with spring runoff, charges south to meet the Snake, creating its own rainbow as it plunges 190 feet over Palouse Falls.*

salmon to penetrate the entire Columbia basin, reducing wild salmon populations dramatically and destroying whole salmon runs that once spawned in hundreds of miles of inland streams. As some—perhaps slight—compensation, the dams have also formed extensive marshes and wetlands that support a wide variety of birds. Thousands of ducks, geese, and wading birds nest and winter in this area.

In northern sections of the region, a lack of development and proximity to the forests and mountains of British Columbia have preserved remnant populations of large mammals. Pine forests of the Okanogan highlands—actually a subcontinent from the Pacific that docked here 100 million years ago—shelter what may be the largest lynx population south of the Canadian border. Resembling the Rockies more than they do the Cascades, the Selkirk Mountains in the far northeastern corner of the state were once the edge of the North American continent. Grizzly bears and woodland caribou, both endangered in the lower 48 states, inhabit the Salmo-Priest Wilderness in the Selkirks. These mammal populations cross the border freely and probably could not survive without habitat on the Canadian side— habitat now threatened by logging and development. Smaller, less imperiled mammals and birds in this region include coyotes, mule deer, badgers, ground squirrels, rattlesnakes, golden eagles, and magpies.

The natural pine forests of eastern Washington (and eastern Oregon) have been drastically altered by generations of logging and fire suppression. In the late 1980s, when the forests were stressed by a region-wide drought, insects and disease started killing the trees. Pine and spruce forests east of the Cascades are mottled with the reddish brown of dead needles, dead branches, and dead trees. There are plenty of suspects for the forest's plight: Spruce budworms and mountain pine beetles damage and often kill the trees. Dwarf mistletoe diverts a tree's nutrients and forms big "brooms," which can overwhelm foliage and stunt the tree's growth. Tussock moths, western pine beetles, Douglas fir beetles, half a dozen root diseases, and an assortment of other ailments kill or weaken trees or interfere with normal growth.

OVERLEAF: *The topography of the Columbia River Gorge is a testament to the forces that created it, from the ancient basalt cliffs eroded by the river to Mount Adams, formed by volcanoes and carved by glaciers.*

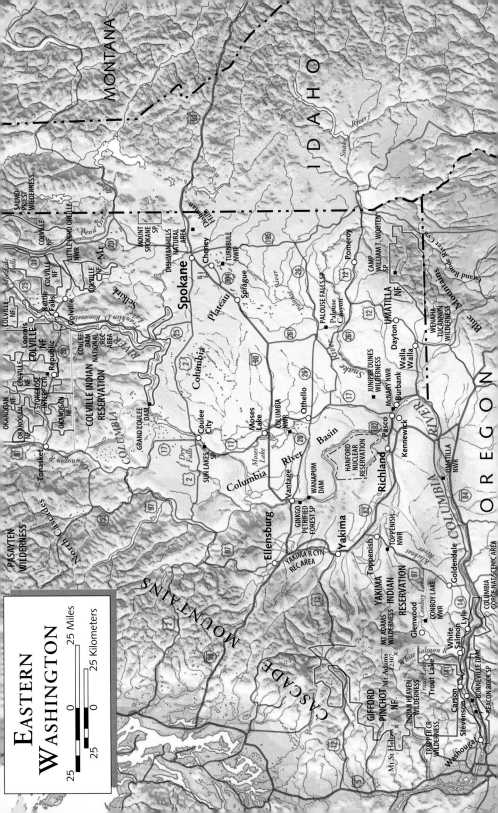

LEFT: *During spring migration to their arctic breeding grounds, Canada geese rest and graze at Washington's wildlife refuges.*
RIGHT: *On alert in a field of purple penstemon, a great horned owl awaits prey; this predator hunts animals as large as house cats, opossums, and great blue herons.*

Bugs and disease are not the only culprits. Early loggers liked to think that if they cut the big trees, little ponderosa pines would have a chance to grow and the forest would perpetuate itself. Unfortunately, when the big trees were gone, so was the source of seeds. The young trees that grew up were not pines but a tangle of alpine fir and other species, which often became infested with parasites. When the wildfires that had regularly cleared the slopes of fir seedlings were suppressed, the resulting thick stands of Douglas fir and alpine fir grew to maturity where they did not belong. These species created a multilayered forest canopy where bugs spread easily. Spruce budworms, for instance, hatch high in the canopy and spin threads on which they descend to the branches below them. The crowding of firs in the unburned forest placed extra stress on the trees, making them exceptionally vulnerable to bugs and disease.

This chapter starts in the arid central portion of the state and proceeds to Washington's remote and heavily forested northeastern sections. Next it enters the dry hills of southeastern Washington, where the scarcity of water has left large areas almost untouched by humans. Finally the route leads through Washington's side of the Columbia River Gorge to the wilderness areas of the state's southern Cascades. The main landmark here is Mount Adams, a relatively little known but impressive 12,307-foot volcano that is the second-highest mountain in the Northwest.

COLUMBIA PLATEAU

Interstate 90 goes east over Snoqualmie Pass, through and beyond the Cascades and the town of Ellensburg, into the dry, rolling country

above the Columbia River. From the exit at Vantage, just before the freeway crosses the river, signs point to **Ginkgo Petrified Forest State Park❖.** The landscape is all rock and dry soil, slicked in places by flash floods and dotted with the gray-green of scattered sage. In this bleak setting, the plant fossils of the park provide evidence that the climate used to be very different here. Petrified tree trunks, ridged and solid as old Greek columns, lie half buried in the stark hills. Even without explanatory signs, the grain of the wood and the texture of the bark indicate that these cylinders are no ordinary stone. Some of the trees growing here millions of years ago were Douglas fir and spruce, species that are now familiar on the wet western side of the mountains. Others, elms and chestnuts, are associated with different parts of the country. The namesake ginkgos are now native to northern China and Japan. On trails through the park, visitors may spot bald eagles, prairie falcons, ravens, white-throated swifts, sage thrashers, sage sparrows, and meadowlarks. Deer, elk, and coyotes have been seen here, as have Pacific rattlesnakes.

Interstate 90 continues east across the Columbia toward Spokane. At Moses Lake, take Route 17 south to Route 26 west; beyond the town of Othello lies the **Columbia National Wildlife Refuge❖.** With 23,500 acres, the refuge is the largest in the state, encompassing rugged canyons, eroded cliffs, and rough, sage-covered terrain. Seepage from

121

the Columbia Basin Irrigation Project has created a vast network of lakes and wetlands that provide nesting sites for a variety of migrating birds and a wintering area for more than a hundred thousand ducks and geese, including Canada geese, mallards, and tundra, formerly whistling, swans. American avocets, long-billed curlews, and other wading birds nest here. The refuge also shelters cliff dwellers: red-tailed hawks, American kestrels, great horned owls, and cliff swallows. American coots and great blue herons visit the refuge, as do an increasing number of migrating sandhill cranes.

Now a National Natural Landmark, the water-gouged **Drumheller Channels** area of the refuge contains prime examples of the Channeled Scablands created by Ice Age floods, which eroded deep canyons, coulees, and potholes in the underlying volcanic basalt. These unusual geologic formations occur only in eastern Washington. A self-guided auto route circles the refuge. People who want to get out of their car can canoe, hike, or follow any of three interpretative habitat trails (marsh, riparian, and shrub-steppe upland).

Continuing east on I-90, turn off beyond Sprague on Route 904 to Cheney. Cheney Plaza Road leads south to the **Turnbull National Wildlife Refuge❖,** a collage of more than a hundred lakes and marshes broken by patches of ponderosa pine. Turnbull is a fall stopping place on the Pacific Flyway for thousands of ducks, geese, and other migratory birds and is particularly important to diving ducks such as redheads, canvasbacks, and scaup. White-tailed deer, elk, badgers, beavers, and other mammals also inhabit the refuge, which visitors can see from trails and a five-mile self-guided auto route. Here, too, the landscape is marked by the Channeled Scablands.

At Spokane take the Sprague Avenue exit off I-90 for the **Dishman Hills Natural Resource Conservation Area❖,** which lies on the eastern outskirts of Spokane, above a garish commercial strip of car dealerships and fast-food restaurants. Following dirt paths through pine trees and rock outcroppings, however, one quickly forgets the surroundings. The terrain is open and parklike, and indeed, the hills are well used as a park. There are big ponderosa pines, and a visitor who looks closely in spring may spot a mariposa lily with its three large lavender petals. Despite the runners, cyclers, and equestrians, the groups of school kids, and the proximity of private homes and car lots, the Dishman Hills can provide a real sense of solitude.

North of Spokane, Route 2 soon intersects Route 206, which dead-ends at **Mount Spokane State Park❖,** the largest state-owned park in Washington. A paved road climbs to the summit, which provides views of three states. Part of the mountain has been developed for downhill skiing, but miles of trails wind through the second-growth conifer forest and mountain meadows that cover most of the slopes. The southeastern section of the park has been set aside as a natural area.

THE SELKIRK MOUNTAINS AND OKANOGAN HIGHLANDS

Continuing north, Route 20 and then Route 31 follow the Pend Oreille River to the mountainous northeastern corner of the state, where the Selkirk Mountains are home to wildlife found nowhere else in Washington. At Metaline Falls, narrow, winding Boundary Road (Forest Road 2975) leads northwest into the **Colville National Forest❖.** In the spring, the one-acre **Flume Creek Mountain Goat Viewing Area❖** affords a rare opportunity to see these long-haired, sure-footed creatures as well as moose and deer. Farther north is **Crawford State Park❖,** where the main attraction is the underground trail at **Gardner Cave,** the second-largest limestone cave in Washington.

East of Metaline Falls, **Hall Mountain** rises over Sullivan Lake. From December through February, this is a good place to spot bighorn sheep. Native to the state, bighorn sheep were decimated by domestic cattle diseases earlier in the century and are now being successfully reintroduced to their former habitats. Sullivan Lake Road runs past the Sullivan Lake Campground to Forest Road 22 and then Forest Road 2220, which climbs, in time, to trailheads for the **Salmo-Priest Wilderness❖,** bordered by Canada to the north and Idaho to the east.

Relatively small and ringed by clear-cuts, the Salmo-Priest Wilderness is beleaguered but very wild. Lower, less rugged, and drier than the Cascades to the west, the Selkirk Range provides hikers with a longer season and a chance to walk all day without meeting anyone else. Pacific moisture that has survived the trip across the higher mountains to the west descends on the Selkirks, supporting plant species seldom seen on this side of the Cascades. The 500-acre **Salmo Research Natural Area** near the trailhead contains a wide variety of plant populations, including a western white pine forest, a western larch forest

ABOVE: *Found throughout the mountains of Washington, Roosevelt elk migrate to lower elevations each autumn to avoid the deep winter snows.*

RIGHT: *Autumn comes to the remote Selkirk Mountains, which provide habitat for grizzly bears, lynx, wolverines, moose, and smaller mammals.*

(which turns a brilliant golden yellow each fall), a subalpine fir/Cascade azalea/fool's huckleberry community, a western hemlock/queen's cup (bead lily) community, and a western redcedar/devil's club community.

Beside a wide stream, where the ground is wet underfoot and brush loaded with rainwater or morning dew soaks a hiker's pants, a trail runs through a stand of cedars. A single 20-mile loop with several icy stream crossings leads past old-growth cedars, through meadows of wildflowers—steep slopes covered with intense reds, blues, whites, and yellows—and along a knife-edge ridge offering mountain views in all di-

rections. Because the Salmo-Priest wilderness is so remote and so accessible from the wild country of eastern British Columbia, lynx, cougars, pine martens, wolverines, moose, and grizzlies are seen here (although very rarely by casual hikers). Some hold that rare, endangered woodland caribou, of which only two small U.S. populations are known, stray here from Canada. All the large mammals depend on the connection

125

between the Salmo-Priest and the mountains that extend into British Columbia. Logging north of the border could sever the north-south link and leave U.S. populations totally isolated.

From the wilderness, head south and then west on Route 20 into the densely forested Okanogan highlands. About 13 miles southeast of Colville, side roads (which are hard to find and follow; it is advisable to call and get directions) lead to the state's **Little Pend Oreille National Wildlife Refuge❖**. Surrounded by logging and farming country, this is a rugged, largely forested area laced with roads and trails. At lower elevations pine forests provide habitat for white-tailed deer; elk; mule deer; black bears; different species of wildcats; smaller mammals such as red, northern flying, and Columbian ground squirrels; and a variety of birds.

Route 20 crosses the Columbia River at Kettle Falls, which was a great American Indian salmon-fishing site until it was flooded by the Grand Coulee Dam. West of the Columbia River, in the pine forests of the Okanogan highlands, lies the old gold-mining town of Republic. Here extraordinary beds of Eocene fossils are owned by the town and the nonprofit Stonerose Foundation. The sites are unprepossessing, but the plant fossils dug by both experts and amateurs—the **Stonerose Interpretive Center❖** in town rents rock hammers by the day—are both beautiful and scientifically significant.

No other site in the country—and perhaps in the world—has yielded so many different Eocene fossils of temperate plant species, including the earliest known precursors of the apple, blackberry, wild currant, clematis, rhododendron, madrona, hemlock, true fir, and many others. It also claims the second-oldest horse chestnut and cherry, oldest salmon, and oldest moth with a proboscis. Nearly 50 million years ago, these leaves, branches, and bugs were washed into a lake, where they were buried by volcanic ash. Over millions of years, both the plant fragments and insects were compressed into sedimentary rock. The town of Republic now lies in the old lake bed.

More than 200 different plant species have been identified so far, and new species keep appearing. Because plants once occupied

ABOVE: *Found in the Selkirks and North Cascades, the once populous grizzly bear is now endangered in the lower 48 states. The huge omnivore, which can weigh 1,500 pounds, is the Northwest's largest predator.*

LEFT: *The isolated Selkirk Mountains, adjacent to the wild regions of eastern British Columbia, are the only area in the Northwest where moose commonly can be seen.*

much wider ranges, the Republic fossils include species now found only on other continents. Some leaves are so well preserved that under a microscope even their smallest veins are visible. The quality of the fossils contributes to their aesthetic appeal. These are not blotchy fragments that only a paleobotanist could love. Leaves and branches curve gracefully, and the image of a single leaf in a slab of rock shows great delicacy.

Back on Route 20 near Republic, go due west to the town of Tonasket, crossing the Okanogan River and following signs for the town of Loomis. There, turn north on Sinlahekin Road and west on Toats Coulee Road, which eventually runs out of pavement but leads to side

Above: *The lynx is a formidable winter predator: Broad furry paws enable it to move easily across deep drifts, and long antennalike ear tufts amplify even snow-deadened noises.*

Right: *Morning light strikes glacier-carved rock spires in the Pasayten Wilderness, a rugged area of some half million acres in north-central Washington.*

roads and trails into the eastern portion of the **Pasayten Wilderness❖** in the **Okanogan National Forest❖.** The eastern Pasayten lacks the concentration of peaks found in the North Cascades, but beyond the huge open meadows and bare slopes rise massive stone buttresses and glacier-carved pinnacles that look as if they had been lifted from the Alps.

East of Tonasket, dense forests provide habitat for what may be the largest surviving lynx population in the lower 48 states. Resembling a small bobcat with big feet, the lynx eats a wide variety of small woodland animals but depends heavily on a single species, the snowshoe hare. The hares, in turn, subsist primarily on lodgepole pines between 15 and 40 years old, eating the tender tips of small branches. They must find branches that grow far enough above ground to stay clear of the winter snow but not so far up that a hare cannot reach them. Indirectly, therefore, lynx depend on lodgepole pines.

Both species can find the lodgepole habitat they need in the federal and state forests of the western Okanogan, but the land here is not protected from logging. In addition, after decades of fire suppression, the lodgepole stands are aging, and insects are invading, laying the groundwork for cataclysmic fires that could leave the lynx with nowhere to go. The only major fire that struck near the heart of lynx country, when 400,000 acres burned in 1994, probably did more good than harm. Future fires may be less benign. For now, the animals can roam freely to and from Canada. Preserving land where lynx can cross the border without traversing developments or clear-cuts is a prerequisite for saving the graceful wildcats.

SOUTHEASTERN WASHINGTON AND THE COLUMBIA RIVER BASIN

South of the Okanogan highlands lies the great Columbia Basin. From above the town of Kettle Falls south to the Grand Coulee Dam, the once free-flowing Columbia and Spokane rivers have been impounded into the enormous Franklin D. Roosevelt Lake. More than 130 miles long and bounded by 660 miles of shoreline, the lake is the centerpiece of the **Coulee Dam National Recreation Area❖** and also falls within the Colville and Spokane Indian reservations. Migratory waterfowl gather here, and bald eagles soar overhead in fall and winter. Route 25, which follows the lake's upper eastern shoreline, has many scenic sections.

South of Coulee City is **Sun Lakes State Park❖.** Between 11,000 and 13,000 years ago, ice blocked the Clark Fork River near present-day Missoula, Montana. When the ice gave way, floods washed over eastern Washington, cutting deep canyons known as coulees into the underlying volcanic basalt and creating strange and distinctive land-scapes called the Channeled Scablands. Here a 3.5-mile-wide, 400-foot-high natural drop in the terrain afforded a spectacular site for a waterfall,

RIGHT: *Aggressive and poisonous, the subtly colored northern Pacific rattlesnake preys on small mammals in the deserts and dry coulees of eastern Washington.*

LEFT: *Pink long-leaved phlox blooms among the big sagebrush—which grows in places too dry even for ponderosa pines—in the Juniper Dunes Wilderness.*

Richland, is the only place in the river's main stem where salmon still spawn. Big chinook lay their eggs in the gravel of Vernita Bar, near the place where the abundance of salmon first impressed Lewis and Clark. In October 1805, Clark and two other men took a small canoe 10 miles above the mouth of the Snake River to an island where Indians were drying fish. "The number of dead Salmon on the Shores & floating in the river is incrediable to say," Clark wrote on October 17. "The waters of this river is clear, and a Salmon may be seen at the deabth of 15 or 20 feet." One can still be impressed by the quantity of wildlife along the river (if not by William Clark's creative spelling). Vernita Bridge, north of Richland where Route 240 crosses the Columbia, is a good launch site for canoes and rafts. Gliding down the Hanford Reach, one can see salmon, bald eagles (in winter months), deer, coyotes, and many shorebirds and waterfowl.

Off Route 12 in Burbank, near the confluence of the Columbia and Snake rivers, up to 150,000 migratory waterfowl rest and feed each fall and winter in the marshes, cropland, and islands of the **McNary National Wildlife Refuge❖**. In late spring and summer, when waterfowl are scarce, avocets, long-billed curlews, and American white pelicans use the refuge. Year-round residents include northern harriers, red-tailed hawks, pheasant, great blue herons, and in the wetlands yellow-headed blackbirds.

BLUE MOUNTAINS

Follow Route 12 east through Walla Walla into southeastern Washington, to the rugged **Wenaha-Tucannon Wilderness❖** in the **Umatilla Na-**

tional Forest❖. Beyond Dayton, turn southeast onto Tucannon Road, following it past **Camp William T. Wooten State Park❖** to Forest Road 4712, which leads to trailheads for the wilderness. Farther northeast on Route 12 near the town of Pomeroy, other roads run south to wilderness trailheads. A wintering area for Rocky Mountain elk, the Tucannon valley is home to white-tailed deer, mule deer, and bighorn sheep, as well as many game birds (Merriam turkeys, valley and mountain quail, chukar and Hungarian partridge, pheasant, and doves), and is noted for its large and varied woodpecker population, including pileated, hairy, downy, white-headed, and northern three-toed.

The steep canyons and pine-covered slopes that fracture the Blue Mountain landscape near Hells Canyon in northeastern Oregon continue on this side of the border. A little of the canyon does, too. There are no big mountains, but plenty of sharp ascents. Off Route 129 the

ABOVE: *North America's largest shorebird, the long-billed curlew spends most of the year in warmer climes but nests at the McNary National Wildlife Refuge every spring.*

LEFT: *Silhouetted at sunset against sky and lake, mallards are among the thousands of waterfowl that congregrate every fall on the marshes at the McNary refuge.*

Grande Ronde River Canyon❖ winds through the extreme southeastern corner of the state. Hawks, owls, and eagles glide above the steep river gorges, and mountain and western bluebirds visit in the spring. Between Dayton and Pomeroy on Route 12, Route 261 leads northwest to **Palouse Falls State Park**❖. The Palouse River plunges 190 feet, creating one of the best-known spectacles in southeastern Washington, and flows between the sheer rock walls of Palouse Canyon.

THE COLUMBIA RIVER GORGE AND SOUTHERN CASCADES

Carrying the water that has fallen on a quarter million square miles of the Northwest, the Columbia River flows through the Cascade Mountains below thousand-foot volcanic cliffs. The Oregon side, with its chain of parks and waterfalls, is better known, and a freeway there

135

carries most of the interstate traffic. For travelers more interested in scenery than speed, Washington's Route 14 (the Lewis and Clark Highway), winds around and through the rocks of the northern side, in sight of the Oregon cliffs.

East of the gorge, pick up westbound Route 14 where it intersects I-82, just before the freeway crosses the Columbia into Oregon. The **Umatilla National Wildlife Refuge❖** complex stretches for 20 miles along both sides of the river (refuge headquarters are in Oregon). From Route 14, Christie Road provides the best access into the refuge for anyone who wants to get out of the car. The sheer number of wintering and migratory waterfowl raises its marshes, sloughs, farm-land, and sage-covered hills a cut above most other refuges. Up to 50,000 Canada geese and 500 pairs of long-billed curlews, as well as other birds, nest here; deer and other mammals frequent the uplands; salmon, sturgeon, and other fish use the water. The appearance of the migratory birds, however, is the main event. Nearly half a million ducks have been seen here on a single day.

Continue west on Route 14, with its views of the river and the Oregon shore. West of Lyle, the Klickitat and White Salmon rivers meet the Columbia in the **Columbia River Gorge National Scenic Area❖**, a section of the river from The Dalles to Washougal that became the first national scenic area in the United States.

To reach Mount Adams and other parts of the southern Cascades, take Route 141 north from the town of White Salmon. The road follows the **White Salmon River,** one of only three Washington streams that are part of the national wild and scenic rivers system. The lower portion of the White Salmon, where it flows through a rocky gorge to the Columbia, has been classified a wild river, as have the lower reaches of the **Klickitat River,** which rises on the Yakima Reservation north of Mount Adams and flows into the Columbia east of White Salmon. Route 142 follows the Klickitat up a narrow canyon from Lyle most of the way to Goldendale.

At B Z Corners, Glenwood Road heads east from Route 141 to

LEFT: *Flanked by steep coulees, the Palouse River winds toward its conflu-ence with the Snake through an area first inhabited 10,000 years ago.*

OVERLEAF: *From a hilltop near Goldendale, rolling grasslands stretch toward Oregon, visible beyond the dark basalt cliffs that outline the Columbia.*

Conboy Lake. Here, in the marshes, meadows, and forest of **Conboy Lake National Wildlife Refuge❖,** are nesting sites for common snipes, the only nesting sites in the state for sandhill cranes, winter habitat for tundra swans and bald eagles, and a spring migration stop for Canada geese, mallard, and pintail. Both mountain and western bluebirds can sometimes be spotted. (Many local residents have built special blue-and-white nesting houses to attract the mountain bluebird, which is now endangered.)

Continue north on Route 141 to Trout Lake and various sites within the **Gifford Pinchot National Forest❖** in the southern Cascade range. To reach the **Mount Adams Wilderness❖,**

ABOVE: *The delicate six-petaled magenta flowers of the grass widow appear soon after snowmelt on grassy slopes and open pine forests in the Columbia River Gorge area.*

LEFT: *The snowy volcanic cone of Mount Adams, the second-highest peak in the Pacific Northwest, is reflected in Takhlakh Lake in the Gifford Pinchot National Forest.*

take Forest Road 23 from Trout Lake. The centerpiece of this wilderness is 12,307-foot Mount Adams, the Northwest's second-highest peak. Like the region's other major mountains, Adams is a volcano. It is eminently climbable, and routes of widely varying difficulty lead to the summit. Around the mountain lie rolling forests, alpine meadows bright with summer wildflowers, marshes, and streams. To the east, the wilderness borders the Yakima Indian Reservation.

Along forest roads west of the town of Trout Lake lie large ice caves created by molten lava and a 12,000-acre lava bed, which is embellished with curiously shaped formations and unusual cracks and crevasses. Forest Road 24 leads to the **Indian Heaven Wilderness❖** along the Cascade crest, where subalpine meadows and more than 150 small lakes and ponds are sprinkled among true fir forests. Farther west is **Trapper Creek Wilderness❖,** best reached from Carson by driving north along Wind River Road to the trailhead at Government Mineral

141

LEFT: *Unlike other bluebird species, the endangered mountain bluebird prefers open habitats—on sagebrush plains, in mountain meadows, at timberline—and hovers as it forages for grubs and other food.*

RIGHT: *Just below the Bonneville Dam, a volcanic monolith towers 848 feet above the Columbia; in 1805 Lewis and Clark named it Beacon Rock.*

Springs. A very small wilderness area—only 6,250 acres—Trapper Creek contains both old-growth Douglas fir and rocky peaks.

Back on the Columbia, between Carson and Stevenson, is the **Table Mountain Natural Resource Conservation Area.** Not just a river vantage point, the conservation area includes forest, wetland, and vertical rock. Farther along on Route 14 just east of Washougal, the **Pierce National Wildlife Refuge** is open to the public only by special permission. The river bottomland of the refuge provides habitat for a wide variety of wildlife, including one of the last chum salmon runs on the Columbia.

Nearby **Beacon Rock State Park❖** rises above the river. Some claim that next to the Rock of Gibraltar, Beacon Rock is the largest known monolith in the world. It's not (there's plenty of lith but it's not really mono), but stretching out from the top are great views of the Columbia River Gorge, the dramatic Oregon cliffs, and snowcapped Mount Hood (a constant visual presence along this section of the river). Although its tributaries may still be untamed, the Columbia—the Indians called it simply the Big River—is not. Massive hydroelectric dams such as nearby Bonneville have turned the once wild and even frightening river into a series of lakes. But its gorge still provides a striking transition between the dry and wet sides of the mountains. In a sense, the transition is older than the mountains: The river flowed here long before the Cascades arose.

142

WESTERN OREGON

The 350-mile-long Oregon coast lacks the wilderness beaches of Washington's Olympic Peninsula, but its high, windswept headlands, massive offshore rocks, long views along sandy beaches, and miles of dunes make it arguably more spectacular. The Coast Range is the western edge of a large slab of ocean crust that broke off approximately 40 million years ago. The lip of ocean crust gives geologists a glimpse of the rock that usually exists only on the deep ocean floor.

The road along the coast, Route 101, is long, popular, and mostly two lanes wide, which can make the drive extremely slow, but an impatient driver has many opportunities to cut east through the coastal mountains and speed up on Interstate 5. Although no single site qualifies as a main attraction, Oregon's coast is one of its most dramatic regions. Managed by the Oregon State Parks Commission, the entire beach, from vegetation line to high-water mark, is public domain. (The state legislature declared the beaches public in 1967. The following year, ruling against a motel owner who challenged the new law, a judge held that even before the law was passed "the public had acquired recreational easement rights in the beach.") Many individual parks, some little more than turnouts with restrooms and picnic tables, offer access to the beach.

PRECEDING PAGES: *At Ecola State Park, waves slide ashore on the sand; distant rocks and mountains mark the western edge of the continent.*
LEFT: *Highlighting tufts of dune grass and solitary sea stacks, dawn breaks at the mouth of the Pistol River on the southern Oregon coast.*

Near Florence, about 145 miles south of the Washington-Oregon border, are the Oregon dunes, the largest coastal dune area in the United States. Unlike the shorelines to the north and south, this 40-mile stretch of coast has no high headlands or sea stacks (offshore rocks) to keep the sand from moving on, off, and along the shore. (High points along the rest of the coast are either volcanic basalt hard enough to withstand the ceaseless pounding of the waves or soft sedimentary rocks that are slowly eroding away.) Because no basalt flowed into the dunes area and no other volcanic action left rocks here, the shoreline is low, and sand has piled up behind the beach.

The character of the coast changes around Port Orford, about 85 miles south of Florence and 50 miles north of the California border. Farther north the Coast Range and northern Klamath Mountains form a barrier between the coast and inland valley. To the south, the Klamaths rise directly from the shore. The Klamath Mountains of southwestern Oregon and northwestern California belonged to the ancient coastal mountain range that also included the Blue and Wallowa mountains and followed the edge of the old North American continent. One hundred fifty million to 100 million years ago, the Klamaths were somehow cut off from the continent and became an island. (They are now about 60 miles west and 50 miles north of their starting point.) Gradually, the sea separating the Klamaths from the continent filled with sediment, forming a plain that connected them to the mainland once again.

The land along the ocean is actually an extension of California's northern coastal mountains. Sandstone and other sedimentary rocks now found here were originally scraped off the ocean floor and subjected to harsh pressures and high heat as they were crushed against the hard rocks of the coastal mountains. In the process the soft sediments crystallized into jade and other stones. The Klamaths also contain the oldest rocks in Oregon, large masses of granitic rock dating back more than 150 million years. Some vegetation here is found nowhere else in the Northwest, some nowhere else in the world.

This chapter begins in the city of Portland and then heads west toward the Pacific. Sections then describe the coast from the Washington border to Florence, the Oregon dunes between Florence and Bandon, and finally the southwesternmost portion of the state, the Siskiyou and Klamath mountains.

Astoria

WASHINGTON

LEWIS & CLARK
NAT WILDLIFE REFUGE

30

Seaside

SADDLE MTN
STATE PARK

26

COLUMBIA

RIVER

Cannon Beach

OSWALD WEST SP   Neahkahnie Mt

Manzanita

NEHALEM BAY SP

SAUVIE ISLAND
WILDLIFE AREA

84

30

FOREST
PARK

Portland

Mt Hood
X 11235

CAPE MEARES SP & NWR
THREE ARCH ROCKS NWR
OCEANSIDE STATE WAYSIDE
Netarts Spit

Tillamook

Lake
Oswego

TRYON CREEK
SP

Oregon City

CAPE LOOKOUT SP

CAPE KIWANDA SP

MOLALLA RIVER
SP

Pacific
City

SALEM

Lincoln
City

C
O
A
S
T

R
A
N
G
E

W
I
L
L
A
M
E
T
T
E

R
I
V
E
R

W
I
L
L
A
M
E
T
T
E

V
A
L
L
E
Y

M
O
U
N
T
A
I
N
S

26

Depoe
Bay

101

YAQUINA HEAD
OUTSTANDING NAT AREA
Yaquina Head

Newport

DRIFT CREEK
WILDERNESS

Waldport

Yachats

CUMMINS CREEK
WILDERNESS

ROCK CREEK
WILDERNESS

CARL G. WASHBURN
MEMORIAL SP

DEVIL'S ELBOW SP

DARLINGTONIA STATE
WAYSIDE

Florence

Dunes

OREGON
DUNES
NAT
REC AREA

5

Reedsport

38

Oregon

DEAN CREEK
ELK VIEWING AREA

GOLDEN & SILVER
FALLS SP

C
A
S
C
A
D
E

Coos Bay

SHORE ACRES

Bunker Hill

Charleston

SUNSET BAY

SOUTH SLOUGH NAT EST
RESEARCH RESERVE

CAPE ARAGO SP

BULLARDS BEACH SP

BANDON MARSH NWR

BANDON SP   Bandon

Coquille River

Klamath

5

CAPE BLANCO SP

GRASSY KNOB
WILDERNESS

WILD ROGUE
WILDERNESS

Port Orford

SISKIYOU

HUMBUG MTN SP

NAT

Rogue River

FOREST

Illinois River

KALMIOPSIS

Grants
Pass

199

WILDERNESS

Chetco River

Cave
Junction

46

Mountains

OREGON CAVES
NAT MON

Mts

Brookings

LOEB SP

O'Brien

Crescent
City

101

RED
BUTTES
WILDERNESS

Siskiyou

CALIFORNIA

WESTERN OREGON

25   0   25 Miles

25   0   25 Kilometers

hen in great quantities in the Columbia R.
bout 40 miles above us by means of skiming
scooping nets. on this page I have drawn
likeness of them as large as life; it
perfect as I can make it with my
en and will serve to give a
neral idea of the fish. the
ays of the fins are barey but
t sharp tho somewhat pointed.
e small fin on the back
xt to the tail has no
ys of bone being a
aranaus pellicle.
the gills have
ch. those of the
ight each, those
e 20 and 2
t of the back
e fins are of
of a bleuish
e the lower
of a silve=
art. the
chid the
cond of
e puple
silver

thin n
the fins
eleven ray
abdomen ha
of the pinnae
haff formed in f
has eleven rays. all
a white colour. the b
dusky colour and that o
part of the sides and bell
ng white. no spots on a
first bone of the gills n
eye is of a bleuis cart, and th
a light gaald colour nearly wh
of the eye is black and the iris o
white. the under jaw exceeds the up
the mouth opens to great extent, fold
that of the herring. it has no teeth.
the abdomen is obtuse and smooth; in thi
differing from the herring, shad, anchovy
&c of the Malacapterygious Order & Class
Clupea

PORTLAND AND ENVIRONS

Situated at the confluence of the Willamette and Columbia rivers, Portland and its suburbs are never far from flowing water. To the east, Mount Hood, the highest peak in the state, can be seen from any part of the city. And in this urban setting **Forest Park❖** has been called the nation's largest inner-city wilderness. Although "wilderness" may be stretching things a bit, this park in the heart of the state's largest metropolitan area contains mature second-growth Douglas firs and a 5,000-acre forest traversed by deer, coyotes, and the occasional cougar, as well as 50 miles of trails. This is, in fact, the world's largest forested park existing inside a city. More than 110 species of birds and 60 species of mammals use the park, as well as great numbers of Portlanders. Spring brings wildflowers: white trilliums, then the tiny whitish spikes of vanilla leaf, the aptly named inside-out flower, and later, dozens of other species.

Nearby, **Tryon Creek State Park❖** in the suburb of Lake Oswego offers a nature center and 14 miles of hiking trails amid Douglas firs, western redcedars, and black cottonwoods. Visitors can hear woodpeckers and squirrels and sometimes see beavers, great blue herons, or black-tailed deer. Thirteen miles south of Oregon City, **Molalla River State Park❖** contains one of the largest great blue heron rookeries in the Willamette Valley. From February to July herons nest on an island in the upper branches of cottonwood trees; waterfowl, songbirds, and ospreys use the park, too.

Just north of Portland on Route 30 (turn right across the Multnomah Channel), a combination of river shoreline, wetlands, grassland, and deliberately planted grain crops in the **Sauvie Island Wildlife Area❖** attracts more than 200 different bird species. The population of wintering waterfowl on Sauvie Island can hit 200,000, and bald eagles spend the winter here, too. The area also contains a hundred-acre community of wapato, a plant which forms starchy roots that were an important food for Native Americans in much of the Northwest. Sauvie

---

LEFT: *In an 1805 journal entry, Meriwether Lewis described and drew an eulachon, a small, oily smelt much valued by Native Americans.*

OVERLEAF: *As the sun sets over the Pacific, two shorebirds forage in the rich tidal pools that pattern the beach at Cape Lookout State Park.*

Island's wetland areas are best seen by canoe.

Beyond Sauvie Island, Route 30 follows the Columbia River to the coast. Toward the river's mouth, east of Astoria and accessible only by boat, the islands and sandbars of the **Lewis and Clark National Wildlife Refuge❖** are a major stopover for waterfowl on the Pacific Flyway, pro-

viding wintering and resting habitat for tundra (formerly called whistling) swans, Canada and snow geese, and mallard, canvasbacks, goldeneyes, and buffleheads. These are only the first of Oregon's many refuge islands that have been preserved exclusively for wildlife.

ABOVE: *Common murres, which lay their pear-shaped eggs on narrow ledges, nest on the sheer sea cliffs along the northern Oregon coast.*

RIGHT: *Weathered drift logs and polished sea rocks mark the high-tide line at a beach near Cape Meares, a dramatic headland near Tillamook.*

THE NORTHERN OREGON COAST

The **Oregon Islands National Wildlife Refuge** stretches the length of the coast, providing habitat for a wide variety of seabirds and marine mammals. Landing on any of the coastal rocks or islands or approaching within 500 feet of them is forbidden, but if one has binoculars some of this wildlife can be seen from the coastal parks. In the spring and autumn, **Cape Meares State Park❖** near Tillamook affords a fine vantage point. Other good viewing spots include Coquille Point in **Bandon State Park❖** (south of the town) and the lighthouses at Yaquina Head, north of Newport, and Heceta Head, north of Florence.

Although the islands are off limits, the coastal mainland offers a long string of accessible parks. At Astoria, Route 30 meets Route 101, which follows the coast all the way to the California border. Just off Route 101 below the town of Seaside, a 14.5-mile trip inland along Route 26 (also called the Sunset Highway) leads to the trails and rare plants of **Saddle Mountain State Park❖,** at the end of Saddle Mountain Road, just past Necanicum Junction. Remnant populations

of plant species that moved south ahead of the glaciers during the last Ice Age—such as Saddle Mountain bittercress, Saddle Mountain saxifrage, alpine lily, pink fawn lily, hairy-stemmed checkermallow, sedge, and trillium—still grow on the upper slopes of the mountain. A trail leads to the 3,283-foot summit.

Back on Route 101 at the coast, ten miles south of Cannon Beach, **Oswald West State Park❖** offers hikers a trail through an old-growth coastal rain forest of Sitka spruce, hemlock, and cedar. Ancient Sitka spruce trees up to 12 feet in diameter slowly increase their girth on Cape Falcon; rare purple-flowering checkermallow grows on the headlands. Another hiking trail leads through salal and salmonberry shrub lands to the top of Neahkahnie Mountain. At **Nehalem Bay State Park❖,** just south of Manzanita, a herd of elk wander a two-mile sand spit. The park also contains estuarine wetlands and a rare native sand dune community.

Farther south, near the town of Tillamook, a turn west onto the **Three Capes Scenic Loop** and then Cape Meares Loop Road leads to **Cape Meares State Park❖,** where visitors can walk through more old-growth spruce. The light is always soft under the big trees, in sharp contrast to the base of the seaside cliffs, where waves break on the rocks in full sunlight. The "Octopus Tree," a huge multibranched old spruce ten feet in diameter, grows near the picnic areas. Occupying one of the coast's many dramatic capes, the park is right next to the **Cape Meares National Wildlife Refuge❖,** where cliffs on the rocky headland provide nesting sites for tufted puffins, common murres, and pelagic cormorants. Although access to the refuge is limited to two trails, the birds can also be seen from the park, as can harbor seals and California sea lions.

Cape Meares is the northernmost park on the Three Capes Scenic Loop. About two miles south of the Cape Meares Lighthouse, **Three Arch Rocks National Wildlife Refuge❖** can be seen (but not visited) from the beach in **Oceanside State Wayside❖.** Binoculars are essential for viewing the quarter-million seabirds that nest at the refuge—including tufted puffins, Brandt's and pelagic cormorants, and common murres—or the northern, or Steller, sea lions and harbor seals that patrol the coastline.

Farther south are **Cape Lookout State Park❖** and **Cape Kiwanda State Park❖.** There is more old-growth forest at Cape Lookout, where registered state natural areas occupy the cape and five-mile-long Netarts Spit, one of Oregon's most primitive ocean shores. At low tide,

ABOVE: *Inundated by drifts of fine white sand, a rhododendron gamely produces flowers at the Oregon dunes. Remnants of an old forest, now overrun by the shifting hills of sand, appear at the top of the slope.*

seals haul out at the end of the spit, and gray whales migrate south past the point in November. Whale-watching cruises from Depoe Bay, north of Newport, can provide closer views.

The Three Capes Scenic Loop rejoins Route 101 just past Pacific City. A highly developed beachfront stretches south for the next 40 miles to Newport, a fishing center. Just above Newport, the **Yaquina Head Outstanding Natural Area❖** juts out into the Pacific, creating opportunities to view harbor seals, California sea lions, and in every month but October and November, gray whales migrating to and from Alaskan waters. Pigeon guillemots—distinguished by their jet black bodies, white wing patches, and bright-red webbed feet—along with other seabirds, nest there.

Below Newport, several small wilderness areas protect slices of the uplands that rise abruptly from the sea. Northeast of Waldport, the **Drift Creek Wilderness❖** includes old-growth Douglas fir and part of the Drift Creek drainage, providing habitat for northern spotted owls and for runs of chinook salmon, coho salmon, and steelhead trout,

also classified as salmon. Below Yachats, right off the coastal highway, is the **Cummins Creek Wilderness❖.** From a steep ridge here, hikers can look between nine-foot-diameter spruce trees to the Pacific. Western redcedars and Douglas firs grow here too, along with a thick understory of ferns and salal, which bears drooping arcs of pinkish flowers from May through July. Cummins Creek is the only Oregon wilderness area with an old-growth Sitka spruce forest, and its major streams support important runs of Pacific salmon. Its forests provide essential nesting habitat for the marbled murrelet, a threatened species of seabird that feeds at sea but nests in old-growth forests, putting it at the center of legal battles over land use. The **Rock Creek Wilderness❖,** a bit farther south, includes similar habitat.

The adjoining **Carl G. Washburne Memorial State Park❖** and **Devil's Elbow State Park❖** south of Cummins Creek contain old-growth forest sheltering tall native rhododendrons. Trails lead to the beach and to undisturbed blowout ponds (formed in sand or light soil by wind activity) in an old-growth forest. Five miles north of Florence, in the **Darlingtonia State Wayside❖,** a boardwalk winds through a wetland of Port Orford cedar and darlingtonia (*Darlingtonia californica*), a large insectivorous plant. The darlingtonia is also known as the pitcher plant or cobra lily, because its hooded leaf and upright growth make it resemble a cobra about to strike. The hood surrounds a mouthlike well of leaves that lures insects, which are digested in a pool of liquid at the base of the plant.

THE OREGON DUNES TO BANDON

South of Florence, the hills recede inland, and the next 40 miles of coast are the **Oregon Dunes National Recreation Area❖.** The dunes often seem like a different world. In the early morning when no one else is around, a walker in the dunes finds four different reminders of the infinite: the ocean, the empty beach, the sea of beach grass, and the dunes themselves. Some of these shifting sand hills, up to 500 feet high, are covered with dark spruce thickets; some are as bare as the Sahara.

LEFT: *A world unto themselves, the Oregon dunes are the creation of sand washed onto a low beach—one of the few spots on the Oregon coast unprotected by rocky headlands—and blown inland by the wind.*

Inland, where the surf can be heard but not seen, nothing indicates direction but the sun. The dunes roll away to all points of the compass. And they move: Memorize a landscape now, come back in a few years, and it may be different. A trip to the dunes is like a voyage on the ocean: an ocean of sand, an ocean of rippling beach grass, an ocean filled with the sound of invisible waves.

The wind naturally shifts the sand around. Early in this century, people planted European beach grass near the mouths of rivers—which were important transportation corridors—to help hold the sand in place. These grasses have now spread throughout the area, stabilizing the foredunes, just beyond the beach, so that not much sand drifts inland from the shore. As the wind blows sand eastward behind the foredune, it scoops out a crater. In wet weather, water accumulates there, creating new wetlands called deflation plains. When sand blows eastward, no new sand blows in from the beach to replace it. As a result, the whole dune area is moving to the east, and eventually, if nothing changes, the heart of the current dune area may run out of sand.

But the dunes have been shifting for millennia. The trees crowning some of the dunes are remnants of a woodland that once covered much of this area, until dunes expanded into forest. The late science-fiction

RIGHT: *The Douglas iris, named for the early 19th-century Scottish naturalist who is also commemorated by the Douglas fir, grows all along coastal areas of southern Oregon.*

LEFT: *European beach grass, not native to the Oregon coast, was planted there early in the 20th century to stabilize the shore and river mouths.*

writer Frank Herbert, whose classic *Dune* series of novels is set on a desert planet, once said that these dunes were where he learned about ecology. (Some people have always assumed that Herbert's fictional planet was modeled on the Oregon dunes. Herbert said it was not.)

To a person on foot in the sand, the dunes stretch on and on. There's plenty of solitude, but in some places there are also plenty of people roaring around on off-road vehicles (ORVs), which are permitted in national recreation areas. (The places without vegetation in nearly half of the dunes' 32,150 acres are open to motorized vehicles. The dunes are considered a great place to ride, and although most ORV riders stay where they belong, some do not.)

To walk into the dunes, start from the Waxmyrtle Campground off the Siltcoos Beach turnoff south of Florence or the Dunes Overlook a little farther south, roughly ten miles above Reedsport. More than 400 species of wildlife inhabit the area, including shorebirds, gulls, eagles, and black-tailed deer. Among the birds are ruddy ducks, cinnamon teal, great blue herons, northern harrier hawks, great flocks of western sandpipers, and a few western snowy plovers, federally designated a threatened species. Three miles east of Reedsport off Route 101 on Route 38, the **Dean Creek Elk Viewing Area❖** offers almost certain views of the big Roosevelt elk, which can be easily seen from a car.

The Dunes National Recreation Area ends north of Coos Bay. From town, a 23-mile detour northeast off Route 101 on the Coos River Highway leads to **Golden and Silver Falls State Park❖,** where the

161

LEFT: *Related to jellyfish and to coral, tentacled sea anemones cling to coastal rocks and open like flowers in the salt water of the Pacific Ocean.* RIGHT: *Along the often foggy coast near Coos Bay, a light-house stands sentry on the cliffs at Cape Arago, a spot where Sir Francis Drake may have anchored his ship the* Golden Hind *in 1579.*

main attractions are two waterfalls, each more than a hundred feet high. There is also a small old-growth forest and groves of pungent myrtlewood. The park is off Route 101 at Bunker Hill, across Isthmus Slough, off the Coos River Highway.

Southwest of Coos Bay, take the Cape Arago Highway from Charleston to **Cape Arago State Park❖,** a dramatic cape where explorer Sir Francis Drake may have anchored his ship the *Golden Hind* in 1579. Although much of Cape Arago has been developed with lawns and pic-nic tables, one can scramble down to the water's edge. The park pre-serves a stark headland where a visitor can be absolutely alone with the Pacific. Standing at the ocean's rocky rim at sunset, with seabirds wheel-ing in the dim light, one feels truly on the edge of the continent.

Cape Arago, Sunset Bay, and Shore Acres state parks form one con-tinuous strip. **Sunset Bay❖**—a fine place to watch the sun go down—contains a bit of old-growth forest and perhaps the most protected swimming cove on the whole coast. **Shore Acres❖,** which includes both a formal garden and a trail through native plant communities above the sea, is a prime spot for winter storm watching. Harbor seals, California sea lions, and northern elephant seals gather on the offshore rocks; they can be seen—and heard—from the Simpson Reef Viewpoint.

For a change from rocks and headlands, return toward Charleston along the Cape Arago Highway, turn south on Seven Devils Road, and stop off at the 4,500-acre **South Slough National Estuarine Research Reserve❖,** the first estuarine sanctuary in the nation. Right after Seven

ABOVE: *Harbor seals haul out on rocks and congregate at river mouths; in spring, they swim into estuaries to give birth.*

LEFT: *The snowy plover's subtle coloring makes it easy to miss— and to protect. The species is now threatened on the Pacific Coast.*

RIGHT: *With its distinctive thick red bill, the black oystercatcher actually pries mussels, barnacles, and limpets off the rocks.*

Devils Road joins Route 101 north of Bandon, flanking the ocean, are the remote sand beach and wildflower-sprinkled dunes of **Bullards Beach State Park❖,** where black turnstones and surfbirds occupy the jetty along with black oystercatchers, marked by flat, bright-red bills and flesh-colored legs. Bullards Beach provides public viewing access for **Bandon Marsh National Wildlife Refuge❖,** a salt marsh and estuary that lies between the highway and the Coquille River. Here a tremendous diversity of shorebirds, wading birds, raptors, and waterfowl rest and feed in the salt marsh and mudflats. Near the shore, little brownish birds—least and western sandpipers—bob in the waves, and dunlins and black-bellied plovers scurry along. About a mile south, near the jetties and rocky areas, black oystercatchers fill their beaks with food, alongside turnstones and harlequin ducks. Bandon Marsh is famous for hosting the occasional Asiatic species that accidentally flies in for a visit—in 1994, such sightings of Asian species lured birders from as far as the East Coast.

THE SOUTH COAST AND KLAMATHS

Between the towns of Bandon and Port Orford, the Cape Blanco Highway leads to **Cape Blanco State Park❖**. Except for the large Beaver Marsh, which is a registered state natural area, the park is hardly pristine, but the beach below the lighthouse provides unobstructed views of ocean, driftwood, the northward curve of beach, and a thicket of slender sea stacks just offshore. Both here and at Cape Arago, gray whales can be seen swimming south in November and December and north in March, April, and May. At peak times, 30 to 40 whales an hour pass any given point on the coast. Red-tailed hawks, deer, and porcupines can also be spotted occasionally. A thick growth of salal, salmonberry, thimbleberry, and huckleberry bushes feed wildlife as well as knowledgeable hungry hikers.

South of Cape Blanco, Route 101 curves east to **Humbug Mountain State Park❖**. For a sweeping view of the coast, climb a three-mile trail to the top of 1,748-foot **Humbug Mountain,** which on its west side drops dramatically to the surf below. Unusual for Oregon, the park's vegetation includes tan oaks and Coast, or California, live oaks, which are more common farther south.

Route 101 continues to hug the narrow shoreline south to California; but north and south of Port Orford, roads climb inland to the wilderness areas and rivers of the Siskiyou National Forest and the Klamath Mountains. Just north of Port Orford, Grassy Knob Road leads southeast to the all-but-trailless **Grassy Knob Wilderness❖,** part of the **Siskiyou National Forest❖**. Old-growth Douglas fir and Port Orford cedar forests on the steep slopes here provide habitat for northern spotted owls and other old-growth-dependent terrestrial species; the trees' boughs shade streams that are home to salmon and steelhead. The Port Orford cedar is just one of the plant species that grow only along the coast of southern Oregon and northern California; it is closely related to the Alaska yellow cedar, which also grows at higher elevations in western Oregon and Washington and along the coasts of British Columbia and southeastern Alaska.

South of Grassy Knob Road, Elk River Road follows the **Elk River❖** along the southern boundary of the wilderness. Although small, the Elk is the most productive salmon river in Oregon per mile; it flows into the Pacific south of Cape Blanco. Upstream, 19 miles of the Elk are protected as a national wild and scenic river. The upper two miles of the north fork are federally designated as wild, which means that there are no roads and no logging near the water; the less primitive lower 17 miles are classified as recreational, which means that development exists along its banks but has not substantially altered them. Some of the high country that drains into the Elk River is protected by the Grassy Knob Wilderness.

Through this corner of Oregon, a series of wild rivers plunge west from the Siskiyou Mountains toward the sea. The best known is the **Rogue River❖,** which meets the ocean at Gold Beach. Flowing through the heart of the **Wild Rogue Wilderness❖,** the river is federally designated as wild for 33 miles; an additional 51 miles are classified as scenic or recreational. The **Illinois River❖,** which empties into the Rogue just downstream from the wilderness, is also part of the national wild and scenic river system, classified as wild for nearly 30 miles and scenic for almost 18 more. Salmon swim up the Illinois and Rogue into the mountains to spawn. Rafters and kayakers can descend both the rivers, and the trail along the Rogue can be hiked in its 40-mile entirety or portions sampled on day hikes.

Reaching the Rogue wilderness requires a winding drive of a little more than 30 miles up the Rogue's south bank on Jerry's Flat Road, off Route 101 right after the bridge across the river's mouth. Follow this road, which becomes unpaved Forest Road 33, past the point

---

RIGHT: *Gold miners once lived and worked along the Rogue, which is now protected as a national wild and scenic river for 84 miles and is paralleled by a 40-mile trail through the Wild Rogue Wilderness.*

where the Illinois enters the Rogue River to the start of the trail up the Rogue, just beyond Foster's Bar.

Sometimes the river flows placidly between stone-lined banks, and sometimes it churns audibly over boulders. Small waterfalls plunge over rock rims into stone pools. The trail climbs well above the Rogue along the edge of precipitous slopes covered with unusual wildflowers, then descends almost to the riverbank. Periodically, it passes cabins, resorts, or remnants of old mining equipment. Always following the river, it leads under big Douglas firs and hemlocks resembling forests much farther north, crosses tan oak hillsides reminiscent of northern California, and enters groves of myrtlewood. The oaks jutting from arid hillsides shade the trail, and the myrtlewoods—actually California laurels—cover it with a litter of slender leaves. The Douglas firs' massive trunks rise from a brushless, parklike forest floor.

The mixture of vegetation found along the Rogue characterizes southwestern Oregon, and there may be no easier place to appreciate the combination than **Loeb State Park❖,** up North Bank Chetco River Road from the town of Brookings. A nature trail follows the Chetco River through the grove of virgin myrtlewood that the park was established to protect; the dense growth of myrtlewood and the leaves covering the ground make the park feel like a jungle. The long, shiny myrtlewood leaves, when crushed, yield a smell every bit as pungent as eucalyptus (a native of Australia that grows widely in California). The Loeb nature trail connects with a Forest Service path that leads uphill through big Douglas firs and a grove of redwoods. Although the redwoods are at the northern edge of their natural range, the trees are no scrawny outliers—they are enormous.

Farther up the Chetco River in the Siskiyou Mountains, more rare plants grow in the **Kalmiopsis Wilderness❖,** part of the **Siskiyou National Forest❖.** North Bank Chetco River Road leads to Forest Service roads that reach the edge of the wilderness; other roads give access from the west off Route 199. The **Chetco River,** which brings salmon into the wilderness, is part of the national wild and scenic river system, and is federally designated as wild for the first 25 miles below its headwaters.

The dry ridges of this rough country enclose valleys of old-growth forest and the namesake kalmiopsis shrub, a relative of the rhododendron, which grows nowhere else. David Rains Wallace suggests in *The*

Klamath Knot that it is easy to envision the legendary northwestern hominid known as Bigfoot or Sasquatch living in this remote region. "There are places in the Klamaths where . . . a harmony between forest and hominid is imaginable," he writes, "where the sense of aloneness and strangeness turns into something else. I found one such place a day's walk up the Chetko from strange, lonely Taggart's Bar. . . .

"I dropped into a little bench of Douglas firs and sugar pines so big that it took me a moment to adjust my perceptions to them. Some of the firs were more than eight feet in diameter, and it was disorienting to see them looming behind full-grown oaks and madrones that would have been large trees in another setting. An eight-foot-tall, hairy person would have seemed on the right scale for them."

There is no quick and easy way from the southwesternmost portion of the Oregon coast to I-5, the inland freeway leading back north or to the eastern approaches to the Siskiyous. Forest Road 23, which connects the lower Rogue River with Grants Pass, gives travelers a real feel for the mountains. Although the Siskiyous do not have the high, jagged peaks characteristic of the Cascades, this is very rugged country: The complexity of its convolutions compensates for what the range lacks in stature. In a storm, when clouds sweep up like breaking waves and lightning flashes illuminate the dark ridges, the landscape is full of drama. Forest Road 23 is winding, hilly, and narrow, and few people take it. The alternative is to follow the coastline into California almost to Crescent City, then head northeast to Grants Pass along Route 199, also called the Redwood Highway. (It passes through miles of redwoods.) Even though individual trees may lack the grandeur of the better-known redwoods farther south along old Route 101, a real forest remains here, not just a remnant strip along the road.

Back in Oregon, rugged tracks and unpaved Forest Service roads lead to the **Kalmiopsis Wilderness❖** and the **Red Buttes Wilderness❖,** also part of of the **Siskiyou National Forest❖.** To drive into the Kalmiopsis Wilderness, turn off Route 199 beyond Cave Junction on Eight Dollar Mountain Road, which becomes Forest Road 4201. Illinois River Road and Eight Dollar Mountain Road also lead to the upper portions of the Illinois River from Route 199 between Cave Junction and Grants Pass. Take Route 199 north and I-5 east to Medford, then turn south to Jacksonville to enter the main part of the Red Buttes Wilder-

Western Oregon

RIGHT: *Along the Chetco River near Brookings, a clump of massive redwood trees has sprouted from an old stump; ferns and tan oak, a broadleaf evergreen, populate the understory.*

ness, which encompasses old-growth forest at lower elevations and, higher up, flower meadows and sweeping views.

Apart from the redwoods, the main attraction between the ocean and Grants Pass is **Oregon Caves National Monument❖,** a half hour's slow drive east on Route 46 from Route 199. The centerpiece of the national monument is a network of caves that the California poet Joaquin Miller christened "the Marble Halls of Oregon" in 1907. A deer hunter found the caves in 1874, when he followed a dog that had tracked a bear underground. The caverns include a subterranean chamber 250 feet long and harbor eight species of bats, including the endangered Townsend's big-eared bat. These days, the caves can be visited on an approximately half-mile-long, 75-minute tour run by a private concessionaire. Decades ago, concessionaires who managed the caves blasted new tunnels, rerouted underground streams, installed bright lights and asphalt paving, and made other improvements that the National Park Service is now trying to remove. The Park Service is spending more than half a million dollars to haul out rubble, close artificial openings, rip out asphalt paving (replacing some of it with concrete and other surfaces), install more subdued lighting, and return streams to their natural courses. Lights, pavement, and railings will remain, but the lights will shine on scenes that more closely resemble nature's creation.

170

Even without paying the entrance fee, one can follow trails into the surrounding forest. The Big Tree Trail winds past a number of massive Douglas firs, finally reaching a fir that measures 12 feet across and dwarfs them all. Its top has broken off—really huge firs are usually truncated in this way—but the remaining trunk is still very much alive. Probably 1,200 to 1,500 years old, the tree was alive and growing when Sir Francis Drake and the Spanish explorers cruised the Oregon coast.

CENTRAL OREGON

Central Oregon, as the term is used in this chapter, describes a great north-south swath of the state comprising several very different topographic and physiographic areas: the forests and volcanoes of the western and high Cascades, the southern wetlands of the Klamath Basin and Warner Valley in the heart of basin-and-range country, the surreal blue of Crater Lake, the lava flows near Bend, the wildfowl refuges among the farms of the lush Willamette Valley, the waterfalls of the Columbia River Gorge, and 11,235-foot Mount Hood.

Oregon's only national park lies in this region, amid the unbroken string of five national forests that stretch the length of the state along the Cascades. Part of the continent-spanning 2,638-mile Pacific Crest National Scenic Trail runs from Washington to California through the forests and the park.

The western Cascades started erupting about 40 to 35 million years ago, the high Cascades about 8 million years ago. The high volcanoes are mostly composed of andesite or rhyolite rather than the dark basalt exposed along the Columbia River Gorge. Basalt is a volcanic rock that flows rather liquidly as magma (rock in its molten state) and tends to spread out. Andesite, usually lighter in color, is less fluid when molten

LEFT: *A whitebark pine tree shaped by the ferocious winds grows in the snow above Crater Lake. The deepest lake in North America occupies a vast caldera formed 7,700 years ago by the eruption of Mount Mazama.*

and piles up into tall cones. Rhyolite, a light-colored volcanic rock, usually can produce violent eruptions, appearing as clouds of ash charged with steam. Geologists assume that the eruption of Mount Mazama, which produced Crater Lake, was one of rhyolite magma.

Geologically, the volcanic mountains and the Willamette Valley to their west have little in common. Some geologists think the valley is a collection of basins created by a complicated accumulation of faults. Heavily populated today, the Willamette Valley has always been Oregon's center of human settlement, and its fertile land was the main magnet that drew pioneers west along the Oregon Trail. Although its cities now contain most of the state's people, much of the valley remains rural and unpaved, thanks largely to Oregon's early, stringent, statewide land-use planning. The area is mainly agricultural, and its soil still produces virtually all the nation's hazelnuts, some of its best wine grapes, rich harvests of tree fruit and berries, and a variety of other crops.

The valley follows the course of the Willamette River from Portland to Eugene. In the mid-1960s, the Willamette was perhaps the most polluted waterway in the Northwest. Twenty-one municipalities and more than 600 industries dumped wastes into it. Then, in 1966, Tom McCall was elected governor on a frankly environmentalist platform. As a Portland television newscaster, McCall had made a documentary on the Willamette entitled "Pollution in Paradise." His election was a signal that the people of Oregon were ready to protect the state's remaining natural environment, including the river. The 1967 legislature—which also made Oregon's beaches public—started passing environmental laws. Soon industries needed permits to discharge wastes into the Willamette, and municipalities along the river had to provide secondary sewage treatment. Within five years, pollution in the Willamette had been reduced by more than 90 percent. People were swimming in it. Salmon were spawning in it. The cleanup became one of the Northwest's great environmental success stories.

The Willamette Valley runs roughly parallel to Oregon's northern Cascade Mountains, which differ in important respects from the state's

---

OVERLEAF: *Each spring hundreds of wildflower species, including yellow balsamroot and purple lupine, bloom in a fragile Nature Conservancy preserve near the southern edge of the Columbia River Gorge.*

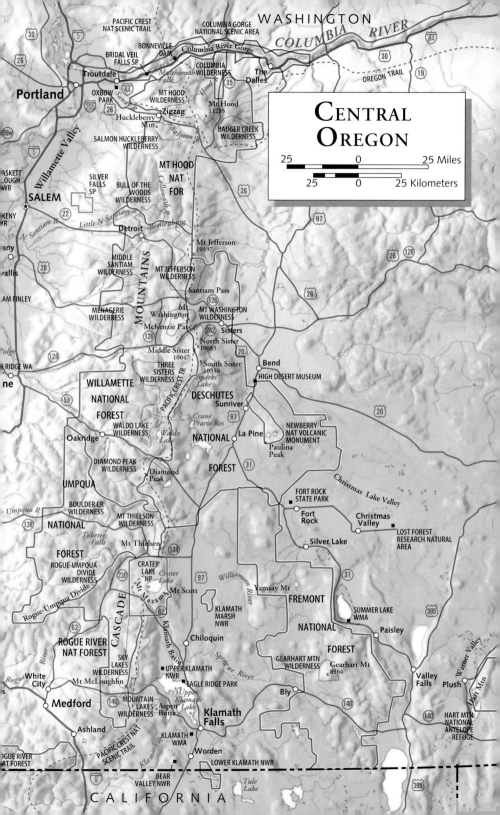

southern Cascades. South of McKenzie Pass, which can be considered the boundary between the two, volcanoes have spewed out rhyolites, suggesting that they may be ready, sooner or later, for tremendously powerful eruptions like the one that produced Crater Lake.

Just south of McKenzie Pass, the Three Sisters peaks mark the southern boundary of glacier country; from the Three Sisters north, all of the big mountains have glaciers on their slopes. The trees change around McKenzie Pass too. South of the pass, on western slopes at elevations of 5,200 to 6,600 feet, stands of red fir dominate the forest; on the eastern slopes, forests of red fir push north to the vicinity of Crater Lake. Below the pass, from the Rogue-Umpqua Divide 80 miles south to the California border, a mixed-conifer type of vegetation including Douglas fir, white fir, ponderosa pine, sugar pine, bigleaf maple, and orange-barked madrona flourishes at elevations of 2,450 to 4,600 feet. White firs continue nearly 80 miles farther north from the Umpqua Divide to McKenzie Pass. The big Cascade flower meadows are found from Mount Jefferson, just above McKenzie Pass, north to Canada. Farther south, the evidence of volcanic eruptions lies closer to the surface, and open areas on the volcanoes' flanks tend to be arid pumice plains.

Because the Cascades run like a backbone nearly straight down the area covered in this chapter, exploring the region thoroughly requires time-consuming mountain road journeys through the range—not exactly a quick zip on the interstate. Some roads are closed in winter, and unpaved forest roads can be rough going for passenger cars.

The Columbia River Gorge, which stretches east from Portland, was formed when the river cut its way through the flows of basalt that covered the area 17 to 12 million years ago. The prehistoric Bretz-Missoula floods, which periodically raised the river's level to a thousand feet, later scoured away loose rock. During these tremendous deluges, the Columbia carried more water than all the rivers currently on earth. The floods occurred periodically near the end of the last Ice Age. They came from Glacial Lake Missoula, formed in Montana when a retreating glacier left an ice dam across the Clark Fork River. When the ice

RIGHT: *Upper Klamath Lake, Oregon's largest, forms part of a network of lakes and marshes that attracts numerous migrating waterfowl and the largest population of wintering eagles in the lower 48 states.*

ABOVE: *Nearly extinct by 1930 due to habitat loss, the trumpeter swan (top) has made a successful comeback; the garrulous eared grebe (bottom) frequents marshes and ponds and breeds in large colonies.*

melted and became thin enough to float, the lake rushed out beneath it as a tremendous wall of water, scouring the land across three states in its race to the Pacific. When the ice dam froze again, the water in the lake began to build and prepare for yet another flood.

This chapter begins east of the Klamath Mountains in the wetland refuges of the Klamath Basin. The route then loops to the east, visiting the wet oases of the Warner Valley, the high, arid areas around Hart Mountain in the national antelope refuge, and the desert of Christmas Lake Valley. We then proceed to Crater Lake National Park—where the nation's deepest lake occupies the caldera left by an enormous volcano—and the forests and wilderness areas around it. The route winds through volcanic landscapes to Bend, then plunges into the wilderness areas of Oregon's central Cascades with their old-growth forests, glaciers, lava flows, and high volcanic peaks. Finally, the itinerary heads north for a tour of the wetland refuges in the

180

ABOVE: *Millions of ducks and geese visit the Klamath Basin each year. Some of those taking off from Upper Klamath Lake, however, may become dinner for the growing number of bald eagles that now winter here.*

Willamette Valley, a trip to the cliffs and waterfalls of the Columbia River Gorge, and a look at the wilderness areas around Mount Hood.

THE KLAMATH BASIN

East of Grants Pass lie the wilderness areas in the southern end of the **Winema❖** and **Rogue River❖** national forests, the wetland refuges of the Klamath Basin, and Warner Valley. To reach the area, leave I-5 at Medford on Route 62 north, turning east at White City onto Route 140, which provides access to the Sky Lakes Wilderness, a watershed for Upper Klamath Lake. The smaller **Mountain Lakes Wilderness❖,** also accessible from forest roads that branch off Route 140, was preserved as a primitive area for decades before the Wilderness Act was passed in 1964. It lies a bit farther south, just west of the lake. Its high point, on the edge of the basin, is 8,208-foot Aspen Butte. Even before the Mountain Lakes and Sky Lakes wildernesses were protected, loggers left parts of them

181

alone simply because the areas were so remote and the timber growing at high elevations tended to be small. As a result, both contain extensive old-growth forests of pine, fir, mountain hemlock, and other species.

The wildlife areas of the Klamath Basin focus not on trees but on wetlands. When viewed from Mount Scott in Crater Lake National Park and other high points in the southern Cascades, the Klamath Basin spreads southward, flat and green. It looks as if it used to be underwater, and in fact, most of it was covered by one of the lakes that formed at the end of the last Ice Age. Early non-native settlers created the green fields by draining and filling the lakes and marshes that they found here. Wetlands still punctuate the basin (Upper Klamath Lake is Oregon's largest, and other lakes and marshes dot the landscape), but they cover only a small fraction—according to one estimate, 25 percent—of the area that they once did.

Water flows into the Klamath Basin from three sides. Rain and snow that fall on the southern Cascades wind up in the basin, as does much of the precipitation that strikes Yamsay Mountain to the east. The Williamson River rises well east of Crater Lake National Park and flows south into Upper Klamath Lake. The lake, in turn, drains into the Klamath River, which flows into northern California, then west to the Pacific. (According to some geologists, sand ground up by Cascade glaciers and carried by the Klamath to the coast formed much of the extensive Oregon dunes.) Chinook salmon and steelhead used to follow the Klamath River upstream all the way to Upper Klamath Lake, but California's Iron Gate Dam now blocks their way. The basin's main surviving fish populations are bottom-dwelling suckers, including two endangered species.

Dams enable California to use Klamath River water for agriculture, and Upper Klamath Lake is managed as an irrigation reservoir. If the demand for water is high, the lake is drawn down, and the marshes around it dry up. Although the fluctuations in water level make life difficult for the wildlife in the marshes, the habitat north of the lake is not affected, and up along the Williamson River, the marshes are largely pristine.

So far, the demands of agriculture have had little impact on the upper basin's birds. In both spring and fall, migratory waterfowl use the basin as a staging area where they rest and eat during migration. They treat the lakes and marshes as a single integrated system, moving from one body

of water to another. The waterfowl, in turn, provide food for the wintering eagles, which fly in from other parts of Oregon, Washington, British Columbia, Idaho, and Montana to dine on ducks, scoters, teal, and other delicacies. The eagles take birds that are naturally sick or weakened or birds that have been wounded or killed by hunters.

The eagles seem to be prospering. In the mid-1980s, hundreds of them congregated in the Klamath Basin every year, and in the early 1990s, the population rose to a thousand. As the basin's winter population rose, the winter population in Montana declined; evidently kokanees, landlocked salmon on which the birds feed in Montana, have become scarcer, so eagles that used to winter there now fly to the Klamath Basin. By 1994, the basin's gathering of bald eagles was the largest in any state except Alaska. The birds are so numerous, says one refuge official, that "they lose that magic"; as in parts of Alaska, seeing an eagle becomes routine.

The lakes and marshes of the Klamath Basin are protected by a network of national wildlife refuges. At the northern end of Upper Klamath Lake, accessible from Route 140, cattail and bulrush marshes in the **Upper Klamath National Wildlife Refuge❖** provide nesting and breeding habitat for American white pelicans, two species of egrets, three species of herons, double-crested cormorants, white-faced ibis, and black-necked stilts, among numerous other species. Because the refuge is a watery marsh, one needs a small boat to see much of the birdlife; a six-mile stretch of water off Rocky Point Road is a designated canoe trail. Not far from the Upper Klamath refuge is Klamath County's 640-acre **Eagle Ridge Park❖,** on a peninsula jutting into the lake. The forests and wetlands of the park, reached by a four-mile drive on a gravel road (which can be difficult in bad weather) off Route 140, offer places to see bald eagles, American white pelicans, and a wide variety of waterfowl, including Forster's terns and western grebes.

North of the lake and the town of Chiloquin, off Route 97 from the town of Klamath Falls, the marshes, meadows, and woods of the **Klamath Marsh National Wildlife Refuge❖** provide nesting sites for sandhill cranes, cinnamon teal, American coots, and a variety of other waterfowl. South of Klamath Falls on Route 97, the state's **Klamath Wildlife Management Area❖** attracts more than 200 bird species and provides winter habitat for up to 1.5 million waterfowl each year. It is

183

also one of only two places in the world where an extremely rare Oregon plant, the Applegate milkvetch, is known to grow.

A bit farther southwest, off the Keno–Worden road, the thick pine and fir forest of the **Bear Valley National Wildlife Refuge❖** provides night roosting sites for wintering bald eagles. The refuge is closed to the public, but there are viewing areas outside its boundaries. Eagles prefer tall trees with open branch structures, and along the western side of the Klamath Basin, the trees fitting that description are ponderosa pines. The eagles wait on ponderosa pine snags for their duck dinners to appear, and they roost in the trees every night.

Just east, across Route 97, lies the northern portion of the internationally known **Lower Klamath National Wildlife Refuge❖** (most of the refuge is actually in California). Nearly a million waterfowl use the Lower Klamath and Tule Lake refuges during the peak of fall migration on the Pacific Flyway. The wealth of bird species—more than 275—is impressive, but less visually striking than the sheer number of individual birds funneling through the area on their way south from their breeding grounds in the late fall. Flocks of more than 100,000 snow geese may fill the air. Wintering eagles feed there daily. West of Worden, visitors can see dozens of bald eagles fly in every morning for a day's foraging. Good roads and self-guided tours crisscross the refuge, making it an excellent choice for a driving trip.

WARNER VALLEY AND THE HIGH LAVA PLAINS

From Klamath Falls, Route 97 heads north to Crater Lake, and Route 140 swings east across a southern section of the state to the high, arid plains east of the Cascades, traversing several areas of interest to birders, wildlife viewers, geology enthusiasts, and lovers of relatively unpopulated backcountry. East of the Klamath Basin wetlands on Route 140, northeast of Bly, the **Gearhart Mountain Wilderness❖** in **Fremont National Forest** includes not only its namesake mountain but also Haystack Rock, Palisade Rocks, and creeks flowing out of the high country in all directions. Some of the water from Gearhart Mountain winds up

---

LEFT: Freshly arrived at the rookery, an American white pelican gives his lower jaw a stretch. One of the continent's largest birds, the white pelican is noted for its stocky body, long neck, flat bill, and nearly 10-foot wingspan.

185

ABOVE: *Millions of pronghorn, among the world's fleetest animals, once roamed the western plains. Today they number only 30,000 and need the protection of preserves.*
RIGHT: *In the late autumn, the landscape of the Hart Mountain National Antelope Refuge evokes images of Africa's Serengeti.*

in the Sprague River, which joins the Williamson above Upper Klamath Lake. Once a shield volcano, this high area—all of it above 5,800 feet—contains striking lava rock formations and habitat for mule deer, Rocky Mountain elk, black bears, cougars, and bobcats. (It is also surrounded by natural features with such classic western names as Dead Horse Creek, Dead Cow Creek, Whiskey Spring, Swede Flat, and Dutchman Flat.)

In the high desert beyond Lakeview, drive north and east on Route 140 for the Plush Cutoff road to the natural wetlands of the **Warner Valley,** another oasis in the vast basin-and-range region of the intermountain West. Way off the beaten track for most people, the Warner

Valley has always been on a main thoroughfare for birds. Great flocks of waterfowl migrating along the Pacific Flyway stop at the valley's lakes, potholes, marshes, meadows, grazing land, and dunes. White-faced ibis, long-billed curlews, sandhill cranes, American avocets, and other species nest here.

The writer William Kittredge, who grew up on a Warner Valley ranch in the 1930s and 1940s, has written in *Owning It All* that "we understood our property as others know their cities, a landscape of neighborhoods, some sacred, some demonic; some habitable, some not, which is as the sea, they tell me, is understood by fishermen. It was only later, in college,

187

that I learned it was possible to understand Warner as a fertile oasis in a vast featureless sagebrush desert." Kittredge and his family drained swamps, diked fields, and irrigated dry soil, turning a natural landscape into productive farmland. In their own minds, he writes, "we were doing God's labor and creating a good place on earth, living the pastoral yeoman dream. . . . And then it all went dead, over years, but swiftly. You can imagine our surprise and despair, our sense of having been profoundly cheated. . . . We felt enormously betrayed. For so many years, through endless efforts, we had proceeded in good faith, and it turned out we had wrecked all we had not left untouched. The beloved migratory rafts of waterbirds, the green-headed mallards and the redheads and canvasbacks, the cinnamon teal and the great Canadian honkers, were mostly gone along with their swampland habitat."

Recognizing, if not resolving, the conflict between wildlife and livestock grazing, the federal Bureau of Land Management created a Warner Wetlands Area of Critical Environmental Concern. Some of the remaining wetlands have been preserved—although there is still controversy over how much grazing should be allowed in the area—and if the Warner Valley is not as it was in Kittredge's boyhood, it should continue to be a stopping place for migratory birds.

The **Hart Mountain National Antelope Refuge❖** occupies the high ground east of the Warner Valley. Rising 3,600 feet from the valley floor, it can be reached by driving east and north on the Hart Mountain Road from Plush, or from the east by following Rock Creek Road off Route 205 south of the Malheur National Wildlife Refuge (see Chapter 6). The Hart Mountain refuge was established in 1936 to provide sanctuary for the area's remaining herds of pronghorn (often wrongly called antelope), but for decades it was a cattle range. After conservationists sued federal wildlife officials, cattle were banned from the range in 1990.

The refuge's nearly quarter-million acres of high desert, sparsely forested ridges, and wooded canyons provide habitat not only for the pronghorn but also for California bighorn sheep. The original sheep population died out in the early 1900s, a victim of excessive hunting and diseases introduced by domestic sheep, which grazed on the range. The several hundred bighorns that flourish there now are descendants of animals reintroduced in 1954 from British Columbia.

Many species of wildlife use the range too, changing with the season and the type of habitat. Bighorn sheep, mule deer, golden eagles, and prairie falcons inhabit the high western portions of the 8,000-foot plateau. In spring, summer, and fall, the nearly 2,500 pronghorn stay closer to the lakes and ponds of the lower eastern portion, in the sagebrush country and meadows. In the winter, they desert the plateau entirely for the Sheldon antelope refuge in Nevada, 30 miles away. Throughout the year, the mule deer prefer the shelter of brittlebrush and aspen groves. In the spring, groups of sage grouse perform intricate courtship and mating rituals. Mountain bluebirds, black-capped chickadees, rosy finches, lazuli buntings, black-headed grosbeaks, rufous-sided towhees, and hummingbirds all appear seasonally.

People visit Hart Mountain to hike and camp—and fish and hunt—as well as to view wildlife, but this country is not easy to reach. In some seasons the unpaved roads are impassable; even when the snows have melted and spring mud has dried, visitors may not want to attempt a trip to the area unless their cars have plenty of clearance.

Another haven for birds is the **Summer Lake Wildlife Area❖,** reached by taking Route 140 west to Route 395, then taking 195 north to Route 31 at Valley Falls. Approximately 40 miles north on Route 31, beyond Paisley, the wildlife management area provides lake and marsh habitat for more than 200 bird species. Summer Lake is visited by up to 200,000 migrating waterfowl every fall. Species to be seen along the shores include plover, snipes, curlews, stilts, and phalaropes, sharing the area in season with great blue and black-crowned night herons, mallard, pintail, redheads, and canvasbacks, among many others. Tundra (formerly whistling) and trumpeter swans, nesting snowy plover, and snow geese all inhabit the refuge; visitors are most likely to see the geese and tundra swans.

Continuing north, Route 31 leads to the **Christmas Valley Scenic Byway,** less than 20 miles north of the town of Silver Lake. The byway extends 102 miles east on paved and gravel roads through the desert and volcanic landscape of south-central Oregon, passing the 2-mile long, 60-foot deep Crack-in-the-Ground, the Devil's Garden, and an enormous lava flow. Six miles into the byway, just beyond the town of Fort Rock (named for an old volcano that formed an island in an Ice Age lake), is **Fort Rock State Park❖,** where golden eagles, prairie falcons, white-throated swifts, and violet-green and cliff swal-

lows fly above the rock formations. In winter, pronghorn use the park.

North of the byway, about 22 miles east of the community of Christmas Valley, the **Lost Forest Research Natural Area**❖ preserves a relict ponderosa pine forest in an arid area of sagebrush, a green island in the dry land. The Lost Forest recalls a time before the desert lapped at the eastern foothills of the Cascades. Pine woodlands once covered the area, but now the closest other forest is 40 miles away. South and west of the forest lie 16,000 acres of shifting sand dunes. Nearby Fossil Lake, the remnant of a lake that once filled the whole Fort Rock basin, preserved the bones of flamingos and mammoths. Visitors should make sure to check conditions before setting out because the unpaved roads in the area can be impassable in wet weather. Route 31 continues north to Route 97, which leads south to Crater Lake and the Cascades area, and north to central Oregon and the Bend area.

CRATER LAKE

All the Cascade wilderness areas contain lakes, but by far the most spectacular is **Crater Lake,** the centerpiece of Oregon's only national park. To visit the lake and **Crater Lake National Park**❖, take Route 97 south to Diamond Lake Junction, turn west on Route 138, and follow it about 15 miles to the northern entrance to the park. (This entrance is open from June to early October. Reaching the park in winter is more difficult because it receives about 50 feet of snow between October and May, when most of the roads are closed. The entrance from Route 62, south of the park, which leads to the Rim Visitor Center, stays open all year.)

Crater Lake lies in a caldera formed some 7,700 years ago when the vanished Mount Mazama exploded with three times the force of Mount St. Helens's 1980 blast. Mazama was probably 12,000 feet high before a massive eruption blew an estimated 25 cubic miles of tephra (volcanic solids) out of its core. The explosion deposited at least six inches of pumice over an area of 5,000 square miles, and a thinner layer over some 350,000 square miles—as far north as Alberta and Saskatchewan,

LEFT: *The deep, unearthly blue water of Crater Lake is remarkably pure because, in the closed ecosystem, all of it originates as snow or rain. The water fills about half of the 4,000-foot-deep caldera.*

ABOVE: *The weathered remnant of an ancient volcanic dike, the island formation fancifully known as the Phantom Ship "embarks," with its rocky "sails" unfurled, from the lake's southern shore.*

as far east as Yellowstone National Park. A river of burning ash flowed 40 miles down the Rogue River Valley. Native American artifacts found under layers of volcanic ash in many sites indicate that people must have seen Mazama erupt and collapse.

With its insides spattered over a good deal of western North America, the mountain's cone could no longer support itself and collapsed into the volcano. The resulting caldera was 4,000 feet deep; over the centuries, water has filled it roughly halfway to the top. Ringed by sheer rock cliffs up to 2,000 feet high, Crater Lake is the deepest lake in the United States. A sounding done with piano wire in 1896 put the lake's depth at 1,996 feet. A more recent attempt with sonar recorded 1,932 feet. Even when seen from a jet at 30,000 feet, the water is an unearthly blue color, perhaps the deepest blue water anywhere. (Legend has it that a small gray thrush taking a dip in the lake was transformed into the intensely colored mountain bluebird.) During the summer the 33-mile Rim Road is open all the way around the lake, and visitors are advised to use the many scenic overlooks incorporated into this narrow, winding roadway. Only at Cleetwood Cove on the northern shore does a trail lead down to the water. The **Cleetwood Trail** drops 700 feet in a mile past large hemlock, fir, and

192

ABOVE: *Excursion boats stop at Wizard Island, which is shaped like a sorcerer's hat. Visitors can climb the 760-foot peak, actually the top of a volcanic cone that now rises a half mile from the caldera floor.*

pine trees to the lakeside, where boat tours depart regularly, and one can look up at the cliffs, some of which rise 2,000 feet above the lake.

The boat tour gives visitors close looks at huge lava dikes and the cinder cone volcano at the western end of the lake known as **Wizard Island** because it resembles a sorcerer's hat. The boat stops briefly at Wizard Island; passengers who want to explore can disembark and take a later boat back. The island rises 760 feet above the water, and the crater at its summit measures 300 feet wide and 90 feet deep. The cinder cone was formed after Mount Mazama's collapse, when a new volcanic vent in the caldera spewed out a pile of hot lava fragments that accumulated in a circle, piling higher with each eruption. Vegetation and wildlife have colonized the island over the years. Puffy white pasqueflower seedpods remain in the fall. Mountain hemlock and red fir forest grow on the lower slopes, and garter snakes and ground squirrels inhabit the island.

Crater Lake is a closed ecosystem; no streams or rivers feed or drain it. Until humans stocked the waters, the lake contained no fish. Seven fish species were introduced from 1888 to 1941; only two remain: the kokanee salmon and rainbow trout. However, more than 600 plant species have crept into the area since the great eruption blasted life from

193

thousands of surrounding square miles. The gray blanket of ash and pumice gradually gave way to shrubby red elderberry, smooth-barked manzanita, and the golden yellow flowers of rabbitbrush. Today meadows of pink alpine phlox and spiky blue lupines cover the drier areas; magenta cliff penstemon, purplish blue larkspur, and pink and yellow varieties of monkeyflowers carpet the moister ones. Where the soil is richer and less ash remains, trees can grow. Mountain hemlocks have drooping crowns that shed heavy loads of winter snow; twisted and gnarled by the wind, pines cling tenaciously to high elevations.

To get away from the crowds, climb 8,926-foot **Mount Scott,** the highest point in the park. The summit provides a view of the lake's sheer south-shore cliffs, as well as (in the distance) much of southern Oregon, including Diamond Peak and the Klamath Basin, and Mount Shasta in California. The park also includes a number of short nature trails (two miles long or less) leading to canyons and forested glens. Wildflower meadows harbor moisture-loving species such as violets, shooting stars, and monkeyflowers, as well as phlox, gilia, and pussy paws, which thrive in drier locations.

North of the lake, the forest gives way to the flat, stark pumice desert, where low, extremely fragile vegetation sinks shallow roots into 50 feet of pumice deposited by Mount Mazama. Pumice pinnacles rise in the southeastern corner of the park, in the canyon of Sand Creek. In the otherwise dry northwestern corner, some of the Rogue River's headwaters rise from Boundary Springs, among moss and water-loving plants. Not far away, in a sphagnum bog, grow four species of insectivorous plants—two kinds of bladderworts and two sundews.

SOUTHERN CASCADES: WILDERNESS AREAS

National forests surround Crater Lake National Park, and many wilderness areas preserve the Cascade wildlife and vegetation. At the southern end of Crater Lake, the south entrance road leads to Route 62 and the northern part of the **Sky Lakes Wilderness❖**, which protects the crest of the Cascades around the high point of 9,495-foot Mount McLoughlin (more accessible from Route 140 to the south). Ponds, streams, and springs are scattered through Sky Lakes, and the middle fork of the Rogue River rises here.

From the north entrance of the park, head west on Route 138 to enter the wilderness areas of the **Umpqua National Forest❖.** North of the park, trails into the **Mount Thielsen Wilderness❖** start right at the road. Near the intersection of the northern Crater Lake entrance road and Route 138, the **Pacific Crest National Scenic Trail❖** also leads north into the Mount Thielsen Wilderness. To reach the **Rogue-Umpqua Divide Wilderness❖,** detour south from Route 138 on Route 230, from which forest roads lead to trailheads. The Rogue-Umpqua Divide contains lakes, unusual rock formations, heavily forested valleys, and high meadows. North of the Rogue-Umpqua Divide, waters drain into the Umpqua River; south of the divide, everything drains into the Rogue. Back on Route 138, head west again past Toketee Falls to reach the **Boulder Creek Wilderness❖,** which touches the far bank of the North Umpqua River, flowing beside the road. Trails start right across the river. Within the wilderness, Boulder Creek, with its rapids and small waterfalls, flows through an area of rock monoliths and old-growth forest.

Wilderness areas located on the mountain crest south of the Three Sisters Wilderness and farther north from Crater Lake National Park are more easily reached via Route 58 to the north. **Waldo Lake Wilderness❖,** the northernmost, adjoins the southern boundary of Three Sisters; the southernmost, **Diamond Peak Wilderness❖,** contains perhaps the most conspicuous landmark in this part of Oregon, glacier-carved 8,744-foot Diamond Peak. (Both are part of the **Willamette National Forest❖.**) Diamond Peak, visible for miles, is surrounded by small lakes. There are no major peaks in the Waldo Lake Wilderness, but there are plenty of lakes; on the eastern boundary of the wilderness, Waldo Lake holds some of the purest water in the world.

To reach Waldo Lake or Diamond Peak, take forest roads north and south of Route 58. Forest Road 19, running north from Route 58 just past the town of Oakridge and ending at Route 126, is a national forest scenic byway. Also known as **Robert Aufderheide Memorial Drive,** it is named for a former Willamette National Forest official. The drive offers access to Waldo Lake Wilderness and follows a lovely river canyon

---

OVERLEAF: *A part of the high Cascades' jagged spine and often hidden by clouds, volcanic Mount Thielsen rises above Diamond Lake, which was created by glaciers. Huge ponderosa pines line the lake's shores.*

past shady forests with fern understories, wildflower meadows, water-falls, and numerous campgrounds. The Pacific Crest Trail, which crosses Route 58 near the crest of the mountains, passes through the Diamond Peak Wilderness and connects it with Mount Thielsen, Crater Lake National Park, and the Rogue River National Forest, all to the south. To continue investigating the eastern Cascades, follow Route 58 east to Route 97 north; Route 58 west leads to the Willamette Valley and I-5.

THE BEND AREA

The resort town of Bend makes a good base for exploring the wilderness forests, lava flows, and peaks of the central Cascades, as well as the volcanic craters and lakes to the east.

East off Route 97, reachable by a road that begins six miles beyond the community of La Pine, lie the volcanic landforms of **Newberry National Volcanic Monument❖.** The Bend area is known not only for its winter skiing and resorts and easy access to the Three Sisters Wilderness, but also for its striking volcanic terrain. The Newberry region was first considered for national park or national monument status in 1903, but Crater Lake was chosen instead. The idea cropped up several more times, but nothing happened until the 1980s, when a group of private citizens in the Bend area formed a committee, forged a consensus among environmental, recreational, and industry groups, and started lobbying Congress. The 50,000-acre Newberry National Volcanic Monument was established at the end of 1990.

The entire monument occupies the slopes of Newberry Volcano, which covers some 500 square miles pocked with more than 400 cinder and spatter cones. Calderas seem to have been formed there more than once, starting at least a million years ago. The **Big Obsidian Flow,** a square mile of volcanic glass up to 300 feet thick, was created by an eruption only 1,300 years ago. The two lakes in the caldera of Newberry Volcano are surrounded by lava fields, obsidian flows, cinder cones, hot springs, and caves, plus 8,000-foot Paulina Peak. An archaeological site beside Paulina Lake, in the caldera, has been dated at 10,000 years, making it one of the oldest documented sites in the Pacific Northwest. To learn more about the human and natural history of this central Oregon area, continue north on Route 97 to the excellent **High Desert Museum❖.** Outdoor trails lead past a trout stream;

others, past raptors and porcupines. One can see an old steam sawmill and replicas of a covered wagon and a settler's cabin. Lizards, owls, and other dry-country wildlife inhabit the Desertarium. Other exhibits explain the workings of various eastern Oregon habitats and illustrate the lives of Native Americans and early nonnative settlers.

MOUNT JEFFERSON AND THE THREE SISTERS

To approach the southern half of the dramatic **Three Sisters Wilderness❖,** follow the Cascades Lakes Highway (Route 46) west from Bend past the Mount Bachelor Ski Area (open for year-round activities) to trailheads for the wilderness. The highway traverses the **Deschutes National Forest❖** and forms part of the **Cascades Lakes Highway National Forest Scenic Byway,** passing lakes, wildflowers, peaks, and campsites and opportunities for boating, fishing, swimming, picnicking, and hiking.

The Three Sisters Wilderness, part of the **Willamette National Forest❖,** is heavily used, and the Forest Service prohibits entering the area without a permit. Trailheads into the wilderness leave the road from several spots. The Three Sisters landscape does not look like the Cascades farther north, and the wilderness feels different underfoot. On one steep route, a hiker can leave a little glacier-melt lake 9,000 feet far below. A pumice plain with its clusters of mountain hemlocks lies even farther down, along with the huge rock pile left by a vanished glacier and lava from volcanic eruptions long ago. To the south, the dark slopes of the southern Cascades roll away toward the California border, and lakes break the sweep of forest. About 50 miles off, the pyramid of Diamond Peak rises above the rolling slopes. Underfoot lies a thick layer of volcanic ash, loose as sand, which makes the scramble up the mountainside feel like climbing an enormous sand dune. The loose, ashy footing is a constant reminder that this mountain is a dormant volcano surrounded by other volcanoes, craters, calderas, and lava flows.

Look north from the summit over a pumice plain dotted with small lakes to a string of 10,000-foot volcanoes stretching to the horizon: Middle Sister, North Sister, Mount Jefferson, and finally, in the distance, Mount Hood. Mount Washington is there too, and a bit to the east, the 9,175-foot summit of aptly named Broken Top. The lineup is like hav-

ing the planets in conjunction: A single view encompasses four 10,000-foot volcanoes, the Oregon Cascades' volcanic spine. Farther along Cascades Lakes Highway, about 18 miles after it turns south near Sparks Lake, stop at **Crane Prairie Reservoir**❖ to see bald eagles and ospreys fishing and building nests. The rare Cascade spotted frog shares the waters of the reservoir with good-sized rainbow trout. Green-winged teal, goldeneyes, and wood ducks, unmistakable in their showy plumage, frequent the reservoir waters as well, while deer and elk graze in nearby meadows. Continue east on the scenic byway, then head back to Bend via Route 242, passing through old-growth ponderosa pines, more camping and fishing areas, and experimental forest plantings, to Route 97 to the city of Bend.

To reach other Cascade wilderness areas take Route 20 northwest from Bend. About 10 miles past Sisters (where the route becomes 20/126), a short detour north on Route 14 leads to the head of the **Metolius River.** Old-growth ponderosa pines and a variety of wildlife live here, but the big attraction is the river itself: Water simply gushes up out of the ground from hidden springs. At Camp Sherman, a few miles beyond, an observation platform at the **Metolius Fish Overlook** allows

200

RIGHT: *Common throughout the western mountains, mule deer avoid the summer heat by climbing to the timberline; they descend to lower, warmer elevations for the winter.*

LEFT: *Part of a trio once called Faith, Hope, and Charity, 10,358-foot South Sister, tallest of the Three Sisters volcanoes, rises over Sparks Lake.*

visitors to see rainbow trout year-round, and in the fall, spawning kokanee salmon.

Routes 20/126 and steep, twisting Highway 242 form the **McKenzie–Santiam Pass Loop,** another national forest scenic byway that passes lakes, waterfalls, lava flows, beaver ponds, and the Cascades. The area has been developed with abundant campsites and features many recreational opportunities—and, in the summer, numerous Oregonians taking advantage of them.

Route 20 extends past the junction where Route 126 turns south; just beyond, more than 200 species of wildflowers bloom every July and August at **Tombstone Prairie** and **Iron Mountain**. South of Route 20 lies the **Mount Washington Wilderness❖,** reached by traveling south from Route 20 to the Big Lake Campground on Forest Road 2690 and following other forest roads to the trailheads. Or take the scenic byway on Route 242 to find trailheads for both the Three Sisters and Mount Washington wildernesses.

This area has seen more recent volcanic activity than anywhere else in the Oregon Cascades, which is obvious to anyone who crosses the mountains on Route 242. At mile-high **McKenzie Pass,** on the border between the Three Sisters and Mount Washington wildernesses, lava fields stretch to the mountains north and south. The lava here is not a thin, bubbly crust like dried taffy; it is a jumble of dark boulders extending for miles.

The road actually crosses the southern slope of Belknap Volcano, an unprepossessing cone that has spewed out much of the lava in the area, some as recently as 1,400 years ago. Newer lava flows poured from the even less impressive cones of South Belknap and Little Belknap. The newest lava of all, the rock upon which the little observatory north of the

highway stands, flowed from Yapoah Cone, south of the road, which erupted perhaps a thousand years ago. North beyond the field of black boulders rise the distant, snaggletoothed peaks of Mount Washington and the taller Mount Jefferson. To the south, glacier-covered North Sister and Middle Sister are visible. The landscape of dark, rock-covered lava plains and distant peaks is, otherworldly, surreal.

At McKenzie Pass, the **Pacific Crest National Scenic Trail❖** leads north from Route 242 into the relatively small Mount Washington Wilderness, which like the Three Sisters Wilderness requires a Forest Service permit to enter. Known as the "black wilderness" for its miles of dark lava, it surrounds the 7,794-foot volcano of Mount Washington. It also contains lodgepole-pine forests and 28 lakes. From the same point on Route 242 at McKenzie Pass, the Pacific Crest Trail leads south into the 286,708-acre **Three Sisters Wilderness❖.**

The Three Sisters, volcanic peaks more than 10,000 feet high, are the main but not the only attractions in more than a quarter-million acres of wilderness. **Collier Glacier,** which lies between North Sister and Middle Sister at an altitude of 7,400 to 9,000 feet, is the largest in Oregon, and there are many other glaciers, waterfalls, and lava fields. **Broken Top,** a 9,175-foot mountain that looks as if its top has been shattered by a huge explosion, was actually shaped by glaciers and is considered the Northwest's best example of what advanced glaciation can do. Trails worn into loose volcanic ash wind among widely spaced trees and clumps of bear grass in parklike pine forests near the Cascade crest. The stands of pine and fir provide habitat for elk, deer, bears, and bobcats, and the pumice soils found here and elsewhere in central Oregon support plants found nowhere else in the world.

West of Santiam Pass, Route 22 intersects Route 20. To sample two more very small wilderness areas in the Willamette National Forest, Menagerie and Middle Santiam, head toward Corvallis and I-5, following Route 20 west to Albany. Trails into the **Menagerie Wilderness❖** leave Route 20 at the Trout Creek and Fernview campgrounds. To reach trails into the **Middle Santiam Wilderness❖,** turn before Sweet

---

LEFT: *Looking north from McKenzie Pass, miles of dark lava, some only 400 years old, form a surreal foreground for Mount Washington. Early astronauts used this otherworldly terrain to practice for lunar landings.*

Home at the Foster Reservoir onto Quartzville Drive and take it past Sunnyside County Park to Forest Road 1142. Climbers visit the Menagerie Wilderness for its rock pinnacles. In the Middle Santiam Wilderness, attractions include the Middle Santiam River, Donaca Lake, and a dense forest of old-growth Douglas fir.

To reach difficult parts of the central Cascades, take Route 22 through the mountains to the town of Detroit. (The road is scenic but should be driven with some care. One local bumper sticker reads, "Pray for me. I drive Highway 22.") Turn north on Breitenbush Road (Forest Road 46). Forest Roads 46 and 2209 provide access to trails into the **Bull of the Woods Wilderness❖** from the south and west. The steep terrain in Bull of the Woods is broken by lakes, streams, and the headwaters of the Breitenbush, Collawash, and Little North Fork Santiam rivers.

Other roads lead from Forest Road 46 to the much larger **Mount Jefferson Wilderness❖,** which straddles the Cascade crest. (Entering the area requires a Forest Service permit.) Farther east along Route 22 before Detroit, more forest roads run to the edge of this wilderness, where it is possible to climb through miles of parklike old-growth forest to a square mile of flower meadows at Jefferson Park. In spring and early summer, the reds, blues, purples, yellows, and whites of paintbrush, lupine, heather, and other flowers turn the meadows into a kind of giant Impressionist canvas. In good weather, 10,497-foot Mount Jefferson forms a striking backdrop. (When clouds roll in, a hiker standing in the meadows would never know the mountain was there.) Besides its spectacular flowers, the Mount Jefferson Wilderness includes 150 lakes. Climbers can tackle Mount Jefferson, and hikers can take a variety of routes through the mountains. The Pacific Crest National Scenic Trail crosses the wilderness from north to south.

Head west toward the Willamette Valley on Route 22, which follows the North Santiam River. A few miles before reaching the city of Salem and I-5, a detour back east on Route 214 leads to **Silver Falls State Park❖,** Oregon's largest, which offers some highly developed picnic and camping areas, patches of dense forest, scattered old-

---

RIGHT: *A wooded trail climbs through mixed conifers in the Mount Jefferson Wilderness. Some of the highest country in the Cascades, there hikers find wildflower meadows, summer snow, and solitude.*

growth trees, and a string of waterfalls.

Five of the falls are more than a hundred feet high. A single 4.3-mile trail leads past all ten of them. At **South Falls,** a ribbon of water pours over the lip of a curved rock wall stippled with green ferns and drops 177 feet into a plunge pool. The gray rock with green plants sprouting from every cleft gives the falls a Hawaiian look; other big falls in the park share the almost tropical feel. Because caverns have eroded into the rock behind several of the falls, the trail sometimes runs behind falling water. Kids love it. At the **Middle North Falls,** a tall fir and a smaller tree dripping with moss are visible through the cascade, and the water in the pool below is acutely blue.

WILLAMETTE VALLEY REFUGES

Most of the wetland refuges of the Willamette Valley are located just west of I-5 between Eugene and Salem. At Eugene, turn west onto Route 126 and proceed six miles to the Willow Creek wetlands and the three-part **Fern Ridge Wildlife Area❖** surrounding the Fern Ridge Reservoir. From footpaths or canoes or kayaks, visitors can see the waterfowl, including geese, swans, ducks, and a variety of shorebirds, that frequent Fern Ridge from October to March, and the ospreys and bald eagles that arrive in the summer. Noisy yellow-headed blackbirds inhabit the tall marsh grasses. Fern Ridge may be just a wetland in western Oregon, but to visitors surrounded by tall rushes and egrets, it can feel distinctly exotic.

The three national wildlife refuges in the Willamette Valley form one complex, all administered from the **William Finley National Wildlife Refuge❖,** the southernmost. To reach the refuge take Route 20 west from I-5 to the city of Corvallis, about 40 miles north of Eugene, then proceed south of the city on Route 99W and follow the signs. Although various species of ducks, grouse, pheasant, quail, elk, and deer use the refuge's hardwoods, fields, and marshes, the main goal is to provide wintering habitat for dusky Canada geese, a subspecies of Canada geese. Individual "duskies" are slightly smaller than their Canada geese relatives, and their breast feathers are noticeably darker. Access to the refuge is limited when the geese are around, from November through mid-April. The **Willamette Flood Plain Research Natural Area,** within the refuge, contains about 400 acres of original Willamette Valley prairie plant communities. It is one of the few remaining high-quality wetland habitats in the entire Willamette Valley.

The **Ankeny National Wildlife Refuge❖,** about 20 miles north, can be reached by taking the Ankeny Hill exit from I-5 and following Ankeny Hill Road. The refuge consists of agricultural land broken by hedgerows and clumps of trees. A hiking trail traverses grasslands, hardwood forests, and wetlands, providing some of the best birding opportunities in the mid-Willamette Valley. Like the other refuges in the complex, Ankeny was set up primarily to supply winter habitat for dusky Canada geese, but the refuge also shelters herons, hawks, woodpeckers, and songbirds, as well as red foxes and black-tailed deer.

West of Salem from I-5, on Route 22, is the **Baskett Slough National Wildlife Refuge❖.** None of the Willamette Valley refuges is entirely natural, but Baskett Slough provides a major source of food and shelter for birds. Its raison d'être is also to maintain winter habitat for dusky Canada geese. Herons, hawks, and many other species feed on Baskett Slough's farmland, too.

Continue north on I-5 to Portland to explore the northernmost part of Oregon's central section, the Columbia River Gorge, and the Mount Hood area.

COLUMBIA RIVER GORGE

To reach the cliffs and waterfalls of the **Columbia River Gorge,** drive east from Portland on Interstate 84. The gorge stretches roughly between the outskirts of Portland and The Dalles. At Troutdale, a detour south along the west bank of the Sandy River leads to thousand-acre **Oxbow Park❖,** which encompasses old-growth forest and osprey nesting sites along the river, where American dippers, common mergansers, and great blue herons can be spotted. The noisy, crow-sized pileated woodpecker, with its unmistakable red crest, feeds in old-growth forest areas. A festival takes place here every year in mid-October, when the salmon return to spawn.

Beyond the Sandy River, the **Columbia River Gorge National**

OVERLEAF: *The Columbia River Gorge, here winding east some 700 feet below Crown Point, is a basalt-walled passageway through the Cascade Mountains. The Columbia River flowed here long before the mountains arose.*

Scenic Area❖ begins. The old free-flowing river, which once charged through this section in forbidding runs of cascades and rapids, disappeared when the Bonneville Dam was built in the 1930s. The wind still blows freely, however, making the gorge the wind-surfing capital of the mainland United States. Hood River, toward the upstream end of the gorge, is the wind surfers' center, and on a good day—a windy one—the whole width of the river is flecked with the colors of moving sails.

The new, broad river flows beneath towering basalt cliffs where waterfalls, some of them hundreds of feet high, plunge over the rock. Among the cliffs and waterfalls are towns and farms, highways and railroad tracks, sawmills and a huge federal dam; but a large percentage of the land remains undeveloped, saved from future development by the creation of the national scenic area. Not that everyone favored a scenic area. Many people in economically struggling small towns on the Washington side wanted to be free to pursue any economic development opportunities that came their way, and as a result preserving the gorge involved a bitter political feud.

It is possible—but not recommended—to see the Columbia River Gorge at 65 miles an hour from I-84, a straight-shot freeway that follows the Oregon riverbank. To reach most of the parks, waterfalls, and trailheads along the gorge—and to appreciate the scenery at a more congenial pace—detour onto the winding old scenic highway built by a lumber baron in the early years of this century. The Columbia River Highway (Route 30) separates from and rejoins I-84 at a number of points along the freeway.

The first stop probably should be **Vista House** near Crown Point. A domed octagonal structure built in the same era as the old highway, this building provides a panoramic view of the gorge. The 700-foot bluffs and cliffs here have a mass, a verticality—and by late summer a tawniness—reminiscent of the Southwest, not unlike a desert canyon with a broad river flowing through it. With its planes and masses, its diffused brightness on water and rock, it is a landscape worthy of Cézanne.

The view from Vista House one evening inspired Nancy Russell to

---

LEFT: *Western rhododendrons bloom unrestrainedly every spring at Multnomah Falls, which is by far the highest waterfall and the greatest single magnet for visitors in the Columbia River Gorge National Scenic Area.*

launch the citizens' campaign that led to creation of the Columbia River Gorge National Scenic Area in the 1980s. Although many others worked for years on the campaign, which won the support of the governors and congressional delegations of both Oregon and Washington, Russell played a crucial role. She loved the gorge and knew that half a century of efforts to save it from piecemeal development had led nowhere. "I can remember standing at Vista House that evening and thinking someone should do something," Russell remembered several years later. "I decided I couldn't not be the one to do it."

ABOVE: *In the damp, generally temperate forests along the Columbia River Gorge, a chipmunk will probably be able to get through the entire winter without hibernating.*

RIGHT: *To visit Oneonta Falls, hikers wade up an icy stream-bed between the sheer, mossy walls of Oneonta Gorge and watch the cascade plunge 100 feet into the blue green world below.*

Beyond Vista House, Route 30 passes close to a whole string of waterfalls. At **Bridal Veil Falls State Park❖,** a one-mile trail leads to the graceful falls. From April to June, the park showcases the largest field of camas lilies in this part of the gorge; they bloom alongside a variety of other wildflowers.

At 620-foot **Multnomah Falls,** the nation's second-highest waterfall, a great ribbon of water cascades down the rock, glances off the cliff face, plunges into a stone pool, and then spills over the lip of the pool into a second, lower falls, where American dippers, favorites of naturalist John Muir, congregate. The paths here are all paved, which is probably a good idea given the busloads of tourists that swarm toward the scenic overlooks each year.

Horsetail Falls, farther up the river, may be a lesser attraction, but a visitor will find less company and less pavement. The lower falls are near the road; to reach the upper falls, climb the trail that twists among maples and Douglas firs clinging to the shallow soil of the steep slope. At the top, the trail enters a cavern behind the falls.

Beyond the falls, the trail, bordered with springtime wildflowers, offers a distant view of the **Oneonta Gorge.** For a closer look, drive a bit farther west and walk in from the parking area. Whole families do just that; dressed in shorts and protective wading shoes or old sneakers, they step from rock to rock or plunge through the cold water as they head upstream between sheer rock walls toward a waterfall at the other end. The rock walls are so close together that looking upstream is almost like looking through a tunnel. Sunshine filters through the leaves of trees above and reflects from plants on the rock below, creating for the waders a world bathed in green light.

Farther up the river, **Bonneville Lock and Dam❖** is worth a stop. Construction of the dam in 1938 was the first big step toward converting the Columbia from a wild river into a series of lakes that provide water for the largest integrated hydroelectric system in the world. Before it was tamed the Columbia became a torrent of melted mountain snow every spring, and 15 million wild salmon, some weighing more than a hundred pounds, crowded up it every year on their journey to spawning grounds as remote as interior British Columbia, 1,200 miles from the sea. A few million salmon, most raised in hatcheries, still enter the Columbia every year, struggling up the fish ladders at the gauntlet of dams. Fish-viewing windows at the Bonneville visitor center give visitors a chance to watch them.

When Lewis and Clark reached the upstream end of the Columbia River Gorge on their way to the Pacific in 1805, Clark was struck by "the horrid appearance of this agitated gut swelling, boiling & whorling in every direction." **The Dalles,** where Clark found the water so intimidating (although he and the other members of the expedition did run the river there), was one of the great Indian fishing and trading sites; archaeologists have found salmon bones here dating back nearly 8,000 years. Just upstream, at Celilo Falls, Indians speared fish from platforms built over white water until the 1950s. "The Celilos [Indians] stood on shaky wooden platforms extended over the churning water, holding the long dipnets steady by bracing the pole handles against their chests and shoulders," remembers a character in Craig Lesley's 1986 novel *Winterkill.* "They wore rubber boots and raingear to keep from getting soaked by the mists rising above the falls, and they smoked their pipes upside down to prevent the mists from putting out the tobacco. Some wore floppy hats, and all had safety ropes tied to their waists and hooked to support posts on the platforms. . . . If the men fell, they most likely would drown in the churning whitewater before their friends could pull them to safety, but the ropes made them feel better anyway." Celilo Falls was flooded by The Dalles dam in 1957. To get some sense of the untamed Columbia, stand at the foot of Bonneville when the floodgates are open and watch a wall of water boil into the riverbed while the crests of churning waves whip spray into the air.

MOUNT HOOD

Near the exits from I-84 for Bonneville Dam and Cascade Locks are trailheads for the **Columbia Wilderness❖,** part of the **Mount Hood National Forest❖,** an area of cliffs, rock outcroppings, lakes, and waterfalls. From Cascade Locks, one route into the wilderness is the **Pacific Crest National Scenic Trail❖;** another, about 2.5 miles east, is the Eagle Creek Trail.

The Columbia is one of four small wilderness areas that lie in the vicinity of 11,235-foot **Mount Hood.** Not only is Hood Oregon's highest peak, it is also Oregon's totemic high volcano, just as Mount Rainier is Washington's. Lying partly inside the **Mount Hood Wilderness❖** and surrounded by a 40-mile hiking trail and famous flower meadows, the mountain attracts hikers and climbers as well as skiers and sightseers. Less than two hours from Portland, near the Columbia River Gorge, the wilderness offers many miles of hiking trails with views both of and from the mountain. To reach the northeastern section, follow I-84 to the community of Hood River and turn south on Route 35. Before the Mount Hood Ranger Station, the Hood River Highway leads to the Cooper Spur and Clear Creek roads, which give access to wilderness trails. Other approaches branch west from Route 35.

From Bennett Pass, Forest Road 3550 leads to roads and trails that penetrate the **Badger Creek Wilderness❖,** to the southeast. The steep, glacier-formed landscape of the wilderness is marked by basalt outcrops and covered by vegetation ranging from mountain hemlock to ponderosa pine to white oak and grasslands.

Route 35 intersects Route 26, which runs west toward the road to **Timberline Lodge.** Built by the federal Works Progress Administration (WPA) during the Great Depression, the lodge is filled with textiles and

LEFT: *Early each spring, western trillium, also known as wake robin, blooms on streambanks and forest floors.*

RIGHT: *Even in late summer, snow gleams on the volcanic summit of 11,235-foot Mount Hood, which is Oregon's tallest peak.*

stone-, metal-, and woodwork fashioned by WPA artisans. Many designs incorporate stylized renditions of native flora and fauna. From Timberline, it is possible to take the Timberline Trail around the mountain much of the distance through the Mount Hood Wilderness. It forms part of a whole trail network that leads to views of glaciers, Mount Jefferson to the south, and Mount Hood to the north. Timberline is also a starting point for climbing Mount Hood. Not considered a particularly difficult climb, Hood can nevertheless be a dangerous one. Many consider it safe to ascend only in May, June, and the first half of July; even then, it's a good idea for novices to go with an experienced climber who knows how to avoid avalanches, and it is a good idea to carry enough cold-weather gear. In one well-publicized incident, students from a nearby private high school died on the mountain during a school-sponsored outing. Caught in a surprise blizzard without adequate equipment, they froze before rescuers could find them.

Mount Hood is an active volcano that last gave a few intermittent puffs during the nineteenth century. Geologists label it an andesite volcano, built up by accumulations of lava, ash, and combined flows of water and ash that formed heated, fast-moving mud.

West of Timberline, at the town of Zigzag, Salmon River Road runs south to the **Salmon Huckleberry Wilderness❖,** which encompasses the waterfalls of the Salmon River Gorge and the high ground of Huckleberry Mountain and Salmon Butte. The Salmon River, which flows from the wilderness to the Sandy River, is federally classified as a national wild and scenic river for nearly half its 33-mile length. Its wilderness gorge is paralleled by the **Salmon River National Recreational Trail.** The cliffs and pinnacles of the Salmon Huckleberry Wilderness all lie a very short drive from Portland.

EASTERN OREGON

astern Oregon differs substantially from the Pacific coast
and the forested Cascades, but like both those areas, its
landscape reflects the slow collisions of the earth's plates
and the violent volcanic activity they unleash. As described
in this chapter, the area covers a wide range of habitat and terrain: the
great gorge of Hells Canyon along the Idaho border, the peaks and
lakes of the high Wallowas, the almost southwestern landscape around
John Day Fossil Beds National Monument, Succor Creek and Leslie
Gulch, and the nationally significant Malheur National Wildlife Refuge,
which protects a great variety of birds.

Eastern Oregon stretches from the dry side of the Cascades, the rain
shadow of the range, to the Idaho border. The northeast is occupied
by the Blue Mountains, and the southeast by the Owyhee Upland; the
northwest is part of the Columbia River Basin. Extending east from
Bend, the high lava plains were formed by the floods of basalt that
covered the area 17 to 12 million years ago. The southwestern and
south-central portions of eastern Oregon are typical basin-and-range
country, where basins—broad, flat plains—are separated by ranges of
sharply rising fault-block mountains.

Although many alpine lakes dot the Wallowas, and several rivers

LEFT: *Streaked red and yellow in the morning light, the arid Painted Hills
unit of John Day Fossil Beds harbors fossils of plants and such animals
as the extinct sheeplike oreodonts that lived some 30 million years ago.*

wind through the landscape, much of eastern Oregon is very dry country where pine trees dominate the highlands and sagebrush covers the rest. In arid basin-and-range areas, snow collects on high fault-block mountains every winter. When it melts in the spring, the resulting runoff is trapped in lakes and wetlands, creating watery oases in the desert—such as the one at Malheur National Wildlife Refuge, south of Burns—that become magnets for great numbers and varieties of birds. Where water is scarce, however, wildlife and ranchers compete for both the water and the right to use the land around it. Livestock have destroyed native grasses all over Oregon's high desert country. Early in this century an estimated three million sheep roamed the state, devouring whatever had not been destroyed by the great cattle herds of the late nineteenth century. Today, ranching continues to be an important source of income in the area.

Ranching and wildlife have coexisted on the Malheur refuge ever since it was established in 1908, only five years after the first national wildlife refuge was founded on a tiny Florida island to protect egrets, herons, and other plumed birds from hunters supplying feathers to milliners. For decades, almost any level of grazing on the Oregon refuge was considered compatible with wildlife. Cattle proliferated into the 1970s, eating some plants, trampling others, destroying streamside vegetation, breaking down stream banks, and probably driving some species from the refuge altogether. In the mid-1970s, refuge management decided to protect habitat by limiting grazing, keeping cattle away from stream banks, and restoring the damaged streamside vegetation. An early sign that the efforts were paying off was the discovery beside streams of black-headed grosbeaks, birds that had not been seen nesting on the refuge before.

This chapter travels through a varied landscape, beginning west of The Dalles beyond the Columbia River Gorge and continuing through the Blue Mountains to Hells Canyon and the Eagle Cap Wilderness, near the Idaho border. (If Hells Canyon and the high Wallowas were combined into a single national park—as they may be—they would be

---

OVERLEAF: *A rich wetland set in arid basin-and-range country, the Malheur National Wildlife Refuge attracts hundreds of bird species: trumpeter swans, white-faced ibis, American white pelicans, and sandhill cranes.*

one of the region's top attractions.) The route then turns south, passing through the striking rock formations of the state's arid eastern edge before swinging around into southeastern Oregon to visit the Malheur National Wildlife Refuge and heading north to the John Day Fossil Beds. Along the way, the route touches a number of high, rugged wilderness areas that remain unfamiliar even to most northwesterners. (In the difficult mountain country, remember that many forest roads are unpaved and closed in winter; always call ahead for information.)

NORTHEASTERN OREGON

East of Portland and south of the Columbia River Gorge, I-84 enters high desert country, now largely devoted to cattle and wheat, creating the usual uneasy compromise between ranching and nature. East of The Dalles, the **Lower Deschutes National Backcountry Byway❖**, managed by the Bureau of Land Management, provides a chance to see native flora and fauna as it winds 36 miles along paved and gravel roads next to the river. To the south, in the 12-mile-long **Lower Deschutes State Wildlife Management Area,** many species of birds and mammals live in the steep terrain marked by basalt rimrock. In the wildlife management area, where some riverbanks had been badly overgrazed, streamside vegetation is slowly being restored. Damming the water and planting crops on the land do not necessarily make an area unsuitable for wildlife; such measures can, in fact, produce an unnatural concentration of food that attracts wildlife, particularly birds, in great numbers.

To visit a case in point, continue on I-84 to just east of Boardman, then take Route 730 northeast about four miles toward Irrigon to the **Umatilla National Wildlife Refuge❖** complex. The sheer numbers of wintering waterfowl in the refuge's sloughs, farmland, and sage-covered hills are astonishing. North America's most plentiful duck, the mallard, shares the refuge with at least ten other duck species, including the blue-winged and cinnamon teal, along with the Canada goose, American white pelican, double-crested cormorant, and others. Long-billed curlews, geese, and other birds nest here, as do burrowing owls, which raise their young in uninhabited badger burrows. Deer, coyotes, and other mammals use the uplands, and beavers and otters join salmon, sturgeon, and other fish in the water. But the appearance of hundreds of thousands of migratory birds during the fall migration is the main event.

ABOVE: *Mallards (left)—both the flashy male and his more subtle mate—prefer marshes, although they glean grain from harvested fields. A male ruddy duck (top right) in breeding plumage sports a pale blue bill, with which it forages on pond and lake bottoms. Colorful and distinctive, wood ducks (bottom right) nest in tree cavities and winter in large flocks.*

Nearly half a million ducks have been seen here on a single day.

The Umatilla refuge administers other refuges in the region, including the Cold Springs and McKay Creek area. At the **Cold Springs National Wildlife Refuge❖,** south of the town of Umatilla on Route 395 and east on the Stanfield loop, the marsh, grasslands, and sage around a Bureau of Reclamation reservoir make up a winter resting and feeding area for large numbers of ducks and Canada geese. In the winter, the ducks can include mallard, green-winged and cinnamon teal, and pintail; songbirds and shorebirds use the area in the fall. At the **McKay Creek National Wildlife Refuge❖** south of Pendleton, off I-84 on Route 395, the marshes and open water of another Bureau of Reclamation reservoir provide an additional fall resting and feeding area for Canada geese and ducks.

East of Pendleton, the freeway climbs steeply into the Blue Mountains. This northeastern corner of Oregon is generally mountainous, and the slopes that are not simply arid grazing land are dark with pon-

225

derosa pines and a mixture of other conifers. Cutting through the mountains are swift rivers, flowing eventually to the Columbia. Northeast of Pendleton, the North Fork Umatilla River is the focus of its own **North Fork Umatilla Wilderness,** part of the **Umatilla National Forest❖,** reached by the roads that follow the river from Pendleton. Here the bunchgrass-covered plateaus are sliced by steep, forested canyons, and the river is an important salmon spawning stream.

A detour southeast of Pendleton on I-84 leads to La Grande, a Blue Mountain town between Pendleton and Baker. South of La Grande, adjacent to the freeway, the **Ladd Marsh Wildlife Area❖** includes the only original wetland left in the Grande Ronde Valley and the largest bulrush marsh anywhere in northeastern Oregon. Thousands of waterfowl use it all year.

Wilder habitat is found farther south, along the **North Fork John Day River❖.** Classified as wild for 28 miles and scenic and recreational for 26 more, this significant salmon river arises northwest of Baker in a wilderness named for it. Forty miles of spawning streams for chinook salmon and steelhead trout, and nearly a hundred miles of other streams, flow through the old mining area now preserved as the **North Fork John Day Wilderness❖.** Elk and mule deer roam the rolling benchlands. The terrain rises from the gorge of the North Fork John Day River to the granite of the Greenhorn Mountains. To reach the wilderness, take forest roads that branch from Route 244, which intersects I-84 a little west of La Grande. At the town of Ukiah, Route 244 meets Forest Road 52, part of the **Blue Mountain Scenic Byway,** administered by the national forest. The byway leads past the Bridge Creek Wildlife Area, where Rocky Mountain elk may be seen, and to the **Elkhorn Drive Scenic Byway,** a 106-mile paved loop road through the mountains. Elkhorn Drive passes old mining sites and alpine lakes; wildlife can be seen at Crane Flats, especially north of Granite on Forest Road 73.

East of Pendleton is the town of Elgin, reachable via Route 11 north and Route 204 east. East of Elgin on Route 82 is the town of Minam. From here, rafters can float ten miles down the Wallowa River to the remote, federally designated wild and scenic segment of the Grande Ronde River. The Wenaha River flows through basalt outcroppings up to 1,600 feet high and has been designated wild for nearly 19 miles.

Both the Wenaha and Grande Ronde rivers flow through the **Wenaha**

Wildlife Management Area❖ near Troy, where steep canyons and heavy timber supply winter habitat for 750 mule deer and 1,000 Rocky Mountain elk; the wildlife area is also home to bighorn sheep, dozens of other species of small mammals such as ground squirrels and chipmunks, and bald eagles and wild turkeys. Route 82 through Elgin passes through Wallowa, due south of Troy, reachable either by the Troy road or via Route 3 north from the town of Enterprise. Beyond the wildlife management area, the Wenaha also flows through the **Wenaha-Tucannon Wilderness❖,** which encompasses rugged country on both sides of the Oregon-Washington border in the Umatilla National Forest.

THE HIGH WALLOWAS AND HELLS CANYON

South of the wilderness, near the ranching and logging towns of Enterprise and Joseph on Route 82, Oregon's largest wilderness area, the 361,000-acre **Eagle Cap Wilderness** in the **Wallowa-Whitman National Forest❖,** preserves the heart of the Wallowa Mountains. Rising steeply from the high plains west of the Snake River, the Wallowas are a bit reminiscent of the Pyrenees. Only one peak reaches 10,000 feet, but 31 peaks rise above 8,000 feet and 17 above 9,000. Forested to high elevations, the Wallowas are dotted with high-country lakes, 41 of which lie at altitudes above 7,000 feet. These are classic alpine lakes: cirques scooped out by glaciers and dammed by glacial moraines, the rubble dropped by retreating glaciers. The lakes that are deep enough not to freeze solid in the winter sustain natural fish populations; others are stocked with fish. The wild Minam and Imnaha rivers flow from the mountains to the Snake, through a landscape marked by big ponderosa pines, waterfalls, and wildflowers and populated by a variety of wildlife, including mule deer, elk, and eagles.

Climb to a high lake. Gray granite stippled with dark trees rises behind the water, and the high cliffs are bare of trees, bare of soil, bare of anything but wind-scoured rock. Climbing through meadows of paintbrush and lupine, among columns of ponderosa pine, a hiker hears the lake water cascading down the mountainside and roaring through the valleys, looks through the trees, and sees waterfalls plunging over rocks and logs. Deer startled on the trail are long gone. The predator—was it a bobcat? a cougar?—that left its scat on the trail stayed out of sight. One is alone with the lake. The clear water lies

227

nearly 8,000 feet above sea level; the granite peaks behind it rise to almost 10,000 feet. On the return trip, beyond the waterfall, below the richest flower meadows—but not yet to the river that foams over jackstraw tangles of huge gray logs—an eagle soars above the peaks.

Historically, this was Nez Percé country, high meadows where the Nez Percé took their horses to graze every summer until the U.S. Army drove them away in 1877. Their leader, Chief Joseph, took the tribe on a thousand-mile odyssey pursued by soldiers all the way, following the Imnaha River to the Snake, fording the Snake, winding through Montana, and almost reaching the safety of the Canadian border, only to be trapped and defeated just 30 miles from safety. Joseph's father, old Chief Joseph, is buried overlooking Wallowa Lake, near the edge of the wilderness, just south of the town of Joseph. At the other end of the lake lies **Wallowa Lake State Park❖** and just beyond it, trailheads for the Eagle Cap Wilderness. Other trails can be reached near Enterprise.

Today, parts of the Minam, Imnaha, and Snake rivers are all classified as wild: the **Minam River** for 39 miles in the Eagle Cap Wilderness, the **Imnaha River** for 15 miles in the same wilderness, and the **Snake River** for nearly 32 miles in nearby Hells Canyon. (Sixty-seven miles of the Snake and 77 miles of the Imnaha have been included in the national wild and scenic river system, but only the portions that have no roads or railroads alongside and no logging or agriculture nearby can be classified as wild.) Thirty-six miles of the Snake and the last 4 miles of the Imnaha have received the less-restrictive scenic classification, and another 58 miles of the Imnaha are classified as recreational (a category that allows adjacent logging and agriculture as long as the activities do not cause erosion along the banks).

Within Hells Canyon, both the Oregon and Idaho banks of the Snake River lie in the **Hells Canyon Wilderness❖,** the center of the much larger **Hells Canyon National Recreation Area❖,** which is administered by the Wallowa-Whitman National Forest. Together they cover the open country and pine forests, the mountains and steep ravines above the rim. The Eagle Cap Wilderness and the Hells Canyon

---

Right: *A hiking path winds around glacially formed Moccasin Lake in the Eagle Cap Wilderness. At more than 7,000 feet, this high-country area supports populations of elk, bighorn sheep, bears, cougars, and bobcats.*

ABOVE: *Near the western rim of Hells Canyon, the vivid yellow flowers of arrowleaf balsamroot create a golden carpet around the scattered ponderosa pines, brightening the rangeland near the Idaho border.*

National Recreation Area overlap southeast of Joseph, in an area accessible from Forest Road 39. There, a hiker can follow the Imnaha River into the mountains, pass through parklike stands of big ponderosa pine, climb over rocks, smell mock orange growing wild beside the trail, and look across the Imnaha at rock benches dark with pine; upstream, past huge boulders, the gorge winds through the rocks. The landscape could have been painted by an artist of the nineteenth-century Hudson River School transported to the northwestern wilderness.

Most of this country is dry, and the Snake River, like the larger Columbia and Colorado, creates one of those paradoxical western landscapes where large volumes of water pour through a desert. Just a little east of the Eagle Cap Wilderness, across dramatically broken country veined by steep ravines, the Snake flows through Hells Canyon. East of Enterprise, Forest Roads 39, 3960, 3965, 46, 4260, and 315 lead to a variety of campsites and scenic overlooks. Remote and arid, nearly eight thousand feet deep, Hells Canyon is the deepest gorge in North America, the deepest river-cut gorge in the world.

At **Granite Creek,** the tallest of the nearby mountains reaches nearly 9,400 feet, about 8,000 vertical feet or almost 1.5 miles above the river. Although the mountains on top are stepped back so far that there is no way to stand at water level and see the full vertical sweep, the view from the bottom, as the eye follows the cliffs and brushy benches from the water's edge to the final meeting of rock and sky, is impressive. From the river, where nearby boulders have been polished smooth by rushing water, one can look up along battlements of rock spiked with isolated pines.

Because the range of elevation creates a wide variety of distinct habitats, an estimated 350 species use the area as a seasonal or full-time home. Mule deer, mountain goats, Rocky Mountain elk, and bighorn sheep (reintroduced after domestic sheep grazing decimated the original population) roam the canyon; cougars and bobcats look for prey; Cascade golden-mantled ground squirrels and yellow-pine chipmunks provide food for raptors such as sharp-shinned and Cooper's hawks and golden and bald eagles. Cougars prowling in winter and hungry bobcats play their predatory roles in the food chain. In side canyons, songbirds nest in the spring while river otters play in nearby streams. And yes, there are rattlesnakes.

The rock at higher elevations is all basalt, which flowed here—and into central Washington too—from vents some 30 miles north of Enterprise, where geologists assume there used to be a large volcano. As the basalt erodes away along the canyon, weight is removed from the ground below, and the earth rebounds upward, so that the canyon rim is now the highest part of the plateau. The dark basement rock below the basalt resembles nothing else in this region because it was part of a continent or island arc that moved through here 150 million years ago, when the coastline bent much farther east than it does today. Some of the rock from the passing land mass was scraped off and has been here ever since. The rest kept drifting northwestward, where it is now part of Alaska's Wrangell Mountains.

Under the cliffs are excavations, petroglyphs, and pictographs made by Native Americans who wintered here centuries ago. Because snow is rare at the bottom of Hells Canyon—the temperature at river level usually stays above freezing—the tribes used it as a winter home. At first they preferred narrow, easily defended side canyons; once they started raising horses, though, they found winter quarters in parts of the canyon that offered more room and easier access for large animals.

Archaeologists working in Hells Canyon have identified Native American sites dating back 8,000 years that lie below the layer of ash from Mount Mazama's cataclysmic eruption. Beside the banks where Indians camped, the Snake River plunges through the canyon in a series of rapids with big standing waves. These are often negotiated by rafts and jetboats, but they can be formidable; two class IV rapids guard the upstream end of the wild river.

Commercial jetboats will pick up or drop off hikers who want to make the steep, hot journey between river and rim a one-way trip. Visitors can also get part or all of the way into the canyon on either horseback or foot. A few roads lead to overlooks and trails from the town of Imnaha, northeast of Joseph. To reach the river launch sites, follow Forest Road 39 south to Route 86, then cross the river and drive north along the Idaho shore, crossing back to Oregon over the **Hells Canyon Dam.** At the end of the road are the boat launch and the jetboats. Once on the Snake, it is possible to raft for five days seeing no signs of civilization—none of the fences or jeep roads of the area above.

Above: Because snow virtually never falls at the bottom of Hells Canyon, Native American groups long wintered there, covering the steep walls with petroglyphs.

LEFT: *A mile and a half beneath the peak of He Devil Mountain on the east rim, the Snake River flows through Hells Canyon, the deepest gorge in North America.*

In the 1970s, dams were completed above and below Hells Canyon. Even earlier, a private power company and a consortium of public utilities had developed competing plans to build dams in the canyon. Hells Canyon would be flooded and the wild Snake River turned into a long lake; the lower cliffs, with their polished rock and Indian petroglyphs, would be submerged. In 1967, the conflict between the would-be dam builders reached the U.S. Supreme Court, where then Justice William O. Douglas—who grew up near Yakima, Washington, and returned often to hike the landscape of the Northwest—suggested that the key question was not who got to construct the dam, but whether a dam should be built at all. Douglas's decision opened the issue up, and local environmentalists waged a successful campaign to preserve a free-flowing river in the canyon. Congress created the Hells Canyon Wilderness in 1975, and today rafters can still float for days on a free-flowing river.

ARID SOUTHEASTERN OREGON

To enter a part of the state with striking scenery and very few people, begin at the eastern border of Oregon, where I-84 crosses into Idaho, and head south on Route 95 from Ontario before turning west to enter the Owyhee uplands. (Although the area will not remind anyone of the tropical Pacific, the name Owyhee is a nineteenth-century spelling of Hawai'i. Hudson's Bay Company ships called regularly at Hawai'i, and islanders worked for the company in the Northwest. In 1826, explorer Peter Skene Odgen named this area for two Hawaiians who had been killed there seven years earlier.) South of the town of Nyssa, off the beaten track and miles off the pavement, lies **Succor Creek State Park❖**. A section of unpaved road that leads to the park has been designated and marked as part of the **Leslie Gulch–Succor Creek Scenic Byway,** a national backcountry byway. It is definitely scenic—and definitely a byway. The gravel and graded dirt roads provide 52 miles of opportunity to observe Three Fingers Rock and the Leslie Gulch tuff formations, part of eastern Oregon's volcanic legacy. The approach from Nyssa is the short way to Succor Creek, the long way to Leslie Gulch. Those who just want to visit Leslie Gulch will find it quicker to cross the Idaho border and drive down Route 95 to the southern end of the byway.

This is distinctive country. Aesthetically, the looming rock walls and deeply colored rock formations of Succor Creek have less in common with the coastal rain forests or even the sage-covered high desert of Oregon and Washington than with similar landscapes in Utah and other southwestern states. Despite the desolate appearance, rare plants, nesting golden eagles, and occasional bighorn sheep live in this terrain. In the rock, two big rhyolite flows and the rim of a caldera can be seen.

South of Succor Creek, follow the Leslie Gulch Road and various dirt roads from rock walls to rock labyrinths. Stone spires with twists, hollows, and honeycombs, spires with bands of deep colors, spires that seem to

ABOVE: *Catching the slanted sunlight, the pillars of Rome cast fluted shadows over Oregon's high desert near the remote Owyhee River, a stream favored by river rafters and designated wild for more than 100 miles.*

have reached an uneasy truce with gravity—all rise from the desert in the **Leslie Gulch–Honeycombs** area. It is not surprising that such a landscape was shaped by an unimaginably violent volcanic event. Leslie Gulch lies in the Mahogany Mountain caldera, which was created by a great blast some 15.5 million years ago. The area was not recognized as a caldera until 1984; in an unusual process, it has been eroded down so that the remnants of the volcano are not visible, as they are at Newberry Crater, just southeast of Bend, or Crater Lake, in the Cascades. One geologist speculates that the Leslie Gulch area looks like Yellowstone might if the Wyoming park had been worn down for the last 15 million years. The comparison is not so far-fetched because some geologists theorize that Leslie Gulch was formed by the same hot spot beneath the earth's crust that currently produces all the hot springs activity at Yellowstone. Whatever the source of the energy, the caldera was formed by an explosion so vast that one geologist says nothing comparable "has been seen in human lifetimes." The Mahogany Mountain explosion was 100 to 200 times as powerful as the eruption of Mount St. Helens.

This enormous blast spewed out an estimated 225 cubic miles of tuff, a volcanic rock composed of small volcanic particles fused together during the heat of the explosion. Over the millennia, minerals appeared at the surface of some of the tuff, creating a hard shell. When pieces of this shell wore away, erosion scooped out the softer rock beneath, creating the unlikely hollows and honeycombs at Leslie Gulch. Three-hundred-year-old curlleaf cercocarpus, or mountain mahogany, grows in part of the Leslie Gulch region, along with the only stand of ponderosa pine in this part of Oregon. Ten different plant species here, including types of clover, buckwheat, and blazing star, are candidates for listing as threatened, rare, or endangered.

Leslie Gulch might make an unbeatable backdrop for a western movie, but this harsh country would be a terrible place to get lost. It seems appropriate that the pioneer for whom the area is named was killed by lightning here. (An electrical storm in this country is truly an event. Bolts and chains of lightning fill the sky like the trails of skyrockets on the Fourth of July.)

Just west of Leslie Gulch lies Lake Owyhee, which is popular with powerboaters, and **Lake Owyhee State Park❖,** where layered rock walls rise above the lake, and waterfowl, pronghorn, wild horses, and small mammals such as rabbits can be seen. Farther south, upstream from Lake Owyhee, the **Owyhee River** winds through the empty southeastern corner of the state. Designated wild for 120 miles, the Owyhee has cut steep canyons in a desert area with few roads or people. Mountain lions, bobcats, bighorn sheep, and hawks inhabit the canyons. A tributary, the **West Little Owyhee River,** is designated as wild for 57 miles more. The West Little Owyhee also flows through the high plateau of extreme southeastern Oregon, joining the main stem of the Owyhee far from any paved roads and less than 10 miles from the Idaho border. Rafters can reach the river at Rome and float it all the way north to Lake Owyhee. Rome was named for the nearby cliffs of weathered volcanic ash that reminded settlers of Roman columns.

RIGHT: *Surrounded by high desert, the Malheur National Wildlife Refuge is a vital oasis for a number of bird species. Varying amounts of snowmelt on Steens Mountain provide seasonal water for the Buena Vista Ponds.*

THE MALHEUR REFUGE

Route 95 crosses the Owyhee River near the town of Rome. Take Route 95 west and then Route 78 north to reach the **Malheur National Wildlife Refuge❖,** probably the best-known refuge in the Northwest. (Alternately, head west from Ontario on Route 20 to Burns, then east on Route 78 and south on Route 205.) A regional official of the U.S. Fish and Wildlife Service aptly calls the Malheur refuge "one of our jewels." Partly natural lakes and marshes, partly artificial ponds and farmland where people still graze cattle and cut hay, all surrounded by high desert, Malheur provides habitat for a staggering variety of migrating and nesting birds. More than 325 species have been seen in the refuge.

ABOVE: *A yellow-beaded blackbird alights on a cattail frond. Living in colonies, these birds are also partial to fence-wire perches.* RIGHT: *An adaptable Asian native, the multicolored ring-necked pheasant is plentiful at the Malheur refuge year-round.* LEFT: *A great egret demonstrates its eye-catching courtship display. Egrets were among the species that the Malheur refuge was formed to protect in 1908.*

Trumpeter swans live here year-round. Sandhill cranes and egrets nest here. Hawks swoop low over the wetlands. Flocks of yellow-headed blackbirds rest on fence wire along the roads. A great horned owl and a couple of fuzzy owlets often perch on tree branches right by the refuge headquarters. (A pair of owls virtually always nest near here. Malheur may have the greatest concentration of great horned owls in the country.) Knowledgeable birders can see a hundred species in a day.

A marsh in the desert is obviously something of a rarity. In this vast, arid portion of the inland basin and range, it is unique. "There are parts of it that are even startling to me," says one refuge official. He notes that approaching Malheur from the west, "you would feel like a very parched early traveler going through Death Valley, and then you overtop that hill and see a sparkling marsh before you." The wetlands of Malheur and neighboring Mud and Harney lakes, which are all within the refuge, form a kind of oasis that attracts migrating songbirds as well as waterfowl, giving the refuge its great biological diversity.

Bird species come and go with the seasons, although the only truly slow time for birders is midwinter. The early spring months of February and March mark the melting of winter ice. By late March, ducks such as pintail, cinnamon teal, gadwalls, mallards, and redheads, and snow, Canada, and white-fronted geese arrive in droves. Two months later, migrating songbirds—including bobolinks, mountain bluebirds, many warbler species, tanagers, and phoebes—fill the area, while the gadwalls, teal, and ruddy ducks, among others, nest here, raising their broods in June and July. Herons and egrets roam the flats in late summer; by September and October, the mallard ducks and Canada geese are back to feed, preparing for the long migration southward. Flocks of snow geese and tundra (formerly known as whistling) swans flood into the area as well, only to leave by mid-November. Trumpeter swans stay all year, searching out open water in the ice of December and January.

Malheur and Harney lakes are calderas into which volcanoes collapsed millions of years ago. The Silvies River and Silver Creek flow into the depression of Malheur Lake from the northwest and north. A much larger volume of water, which starts as snowmelt in the Steens Mountain area, is carried from the south by the **Donner und Blitzen River.** (The Donner und Blitzen and its tributaries are wild for more than 72 miles from their headwaters to the edge of the wildlife refuge. The name means "thunder and lightning" in German.) Water once flowed out of the lake to the Snake River and from there to the Columbia and the Pacific. A lava flow blocked that outlet, though, and now the only water loss is through evaporation. Normally, centuries of evaporation would leave the lake saline; but in years of high precipitation, water overflows into Mud Lake and then into Harney Lake, carrying the salts with it and keeping Malheur fresh. Depending primarily on the amount of water flowing north through the Donner und Blitzen River, Harney is sometimes salty and sometimes not.

In high water years, Harney Lake may hold more water than Malheur; after a long dry period, it may contain none at all. During the early 1990s, when Harney still held a lot of water from the heavy rainfalls of a decade before and Malheur had been shrunk by years of drought, Harney had both more water and higher salinity than Malheur. The higher salinity has made it attractive to different kinds of birds, including grebes, phalaropes, and snowy plovers, which are considered threatened on the coast.

In the first half of the 1980s, when heavy runoff from melting snow turned Mud, Harney, and Malheur lakes into a single liquid expanse, fish and wildlife officials noted that the diving duck population dropped while the ibis, cormorant, and egret populations grew tremendously. White pelicans began to nest at the refuge for the first time in decades. By 1990, the roadbed here had to be raised ten feet, and the local rail line was wiped out. Four years later, Mud Lake had vanished again. The area underwater went from approximately 100,000 acres in 1990 to 60 acres by 1995. Wildlife watchers are strongly advised to call ahead before visiting, as conditions change rapidly.

Harney Lake is currently a research natural area that can be visited only by people with special-use permits. It was closed to general use first because people disturbed archaeological sites—the area was a winter home for the northern Paiutes for 6,000 years—and rode off-road vehicles through the dunes, and second because snowy plover nests and eggs are so hard to see that people might inadvertently step on them.

In summer, the area offers another attraction. From Frenchglen, at the southern end of the refuge—named for an early rancher, not a Gallic colony—visitors can drive, weather permitting, around the 66-mile gravel road of **Steens Mountain❖** loop, a national backcountry byway. At 9,733 feet, rising a mile above the flat, bone-white hallucinatory playa of the Alvord Desert to the east, Steens Mountain is the largest fault-block mountain in North America. Its high rock and glacier-carved canyons are managed as a recreation area by the Bureau of Land Management. Pronghorn, mule deer, bighorn sheep, and Rocky Mountain elk are all seen there. Flowers bloom among the desert sage while the top of the mountain is still covered with snow. Many consider Steens Mountain the most spectacular single site in eastern Oregon. To the east, at the north end of the Alvord Desert, **Mickey Hot Springs** contains bubbling mud pots. Feral horses roam the area.

The Steens Mountain loop adjoins a backcountry byway that continues on paved and gravel roads to the town of Lakeview, passing in the

vicinity of the **Hart Mountain National Antelope Refuge❖** (see Chapter 5). To continue this route through eastern Oregon, take Route 205 north to Burns, then Route 395 north to Route 26.

JOHN DAY FOSSIL BEDS

At the town of John Day, where Routes 26 and 395 intersect, head east on 26 to visit several wilderness areas in the **Malheur National Forest❖**. South of Route 26, accessible from roads that start at Unity and Prairie City, the **Monument Rock Wilderness❖** occupies high, forested country along the Little Malheur River. The low point is the river itself at 5,120 feet. Ponderosa pine, lodgepole pine, quaking aspen, and Douglas fir all grow here. In addition to Rocky Mountain elk, mule deer, and bears, badgers and wolverines live in the area.

ABOVE: *Considered one of the strongest mammals for its size in the world, the rarely seen wolverine weighs less than 50 pounds but has been known to kill animals as large as elk and moose*

LEFT: *Burnished with the golden colors of autumn, the immense fault block of Steens Mountain divides the rich wetlands of Malheur from the stark, lunar Alvord Desert stretching to the east.*

Closer to the town of John Day, the **Strawberry Mountain Wilderness❖**, south of Prairie City, is easily accessible from Route 26. The centerpiece is 9,038-foot Strawberry Mountain, but the wilderness contains five of the seven major life zones in North America, the headwaters of nine creeks, and the **Canyon Creek Research Natural Area.** A six-mile trail leads from Strawberry Campground to the top of the mountain.

Continuing west on Route 26, head north on Route 19 beyond Dayville to enter the **Sheep Rock Unit,** one of three units that make up the **John Day Fossil Beds National Monument❖.** The **Painted Hills**

Unit lies 45 miles west, near Mitchell, and the **Clarno Unit** requires a drive north from Mitchell, then 25 miles west from the appropriately named town of Fossil. (Clarno is just east of Antelope, the little town that became notorious in the 1980s when it was taken over by red-clad followers of the Bhagwan Sri Rajneesh, who had established themselves on a nearby ranch.) The visitor center and its museum, which displays more recent fossils found by the National Park Service, are located in the Sheep Rock Unit.

ABOVE: *The most common wildcat in North America, the bobcat preys on cottontail rabbits and snowshoe hares as well as squirrels, mice, and porcupines.*

RIGHT: *In spring, new green vegetation softens the austere, basalt-ribbed landscape along the John Day River between the town of Antelope and the Painted Hills.*

OVERLEAF: *Erosion and climate reacting on volcanic ash have produced the striking shapes and colors—red, pink, bronze, tan, and black—of the Painted Hills at the John Day Fossil Beds.*

Fossil collecting by visitors is expressly prohibited at all three sites (individuals may collect on the slope behind the high school in Fossil), but the fossils that others have dug here since the nineteenth century—now in the permanent collections of major natural history museums around the country—provide an unbroken evolutionary record of 40 million years. The Clarno Unit is rich in fossils from the period 50 to 35 million years ago, while the Painted Hills and Sheep Rock units contain fossils from 37 to 6 million years old. The fossils are buried in layered volcanic deposits that make them easy to date. Two trails at the Clarno Unit wind through areas where plant fossils are embedded in the rock. The sites also offer a variety of striking desert landscapes: the looming forms of Cathedral Rock, the bright layers of the Painted Hills, the surreal colors of the Blue Basin.

The well-exposed and mappable layers that form over time are

called formations: The Clarno formation was laid down 50 to 35 million years ago, when the hot, wet climate nourished tropical and subtropical forests. The John Day formation, created about 30 to 20 million
years ago, is the result of enormous clouds of volcanic ash that blew
here from the southern mountains of the western Cascades. The rhyolite ash and tuff deposits separate a succession of fossil beds. Tracing
the ash deposits of the John Day formation is like following a time
line. Floods of basalt spread across the relatively flat area, only to
weather into soil a few million years later. This soil provided the basis
for a new kind of habitat, which is reflected in the plant and animal
fossils from the Mascall formation of 16 to 14 million years ago. In the
past five or six million years, erosion has revealed strikingly colorful
bands of rock in the area.

Rather than capturing a single point in time 40 or 25 million years
ago, the John Day Fossil Beds contain the long evolutionary records of
many species. The rock holds a wide range of fossil mammals (including sabertooths and many species of long-extinct browsing sheeplike
animals called oreodonts) and literally hundreds of fossil plant species,
many of them as yet unidentified. The greatest variety of plant species
has been found in the Clarno Nut Beds, named for the large fossil wal-
nuts found there. The fossils include early varieties of tree species that
are found in Oregon today, among them oak, alder, and Oregon-myr-
tle, and tropical plants such as palms, figs, and bananas. Forty-five million years ago, when the ocean was much closer and the earth's climate
warmer, this part of central Oregon had near-tropical forests.

To the west between the towns of John Day and Prineville, Route 26
passes three little-known wildernesses in the **Ochoco National
Forest❖:** Mill Creek, Bridge Creek, and Black Canyon. All three are relatively small, with elevations higher than 6,000 feet, shallow volcanic soil,
and forests of pine and other conifers. The steep, broken, forested terrain of the **Mill Creek Wilderness❖,** northeast of Prineville and accessible from Forest Road 33, includes trout streams and streamside habitat
for wildlife. In the 5,000-acre **Bridge Creek Wilderness❖,** accessible
from roads off Forest Road 22 south of Mitchell and east of Prineville,
two forested 6,000-foot plateaus provide nesting sites for goshawks and
prairie falcons and habitat for elk. The **Black Canyon Wilderness❖,**
south of Dayville, is dominated by steep canyons and sharp

ABOVE: *The yellow John Day chaenachtis, a rare plant that blooms in mid-June, covers the hummocks of the Painted Hills, which encase an unusual variety of plant and animal fossils that span millions of years.*

ridges—Black Canyon itself is the main landform—but old-growth ponderosa pines rise from its soil, steelhead spawn in its streams, and many species of wildlife, especially elk and deer, live here.

This dry country is laced with rivers that people drive long distances to float and paddle. The main stem of the **John Day River❖,** which can be rafted from Service Creek (accessible off Route 207 north of Route 26) to Tumwater Falls, contributes nearly 150 miles of free-flowing water to the wild and scenic river system. Although none of the main stem of the John Day is classified as wild, the river flows through rugged canyons and seldom runs close to roads or towns. It churns in class IV rapids shortly below the Clarno bridge and class III rapids farther downstream. The river flows much of the way through sheer basalt canyons, although the landscape is not all rock. In the John Day valley volcanic soils support a number of unusual plants, including the John Day cinquefoil.

The **South Fork John Day River National Backcountry Byway**

runs along the river for 50 miles south of Dayville. From paved, gravel, and dirt roads, seasonally maintained by the Bureau of Land Management, visitors equipped for backcountry travel can see mule deer, Rocky Mountain elk, waterfowl, and chukar partridge among the juniper, bunchgrass, and sage. Moisture-loving willows arch over the river, and dark stands of ponderosa pine provide a little shade. About a hundred wild horses inhabit the area of Murderer's Creek, which is managed for their use.

West of the John Day River, 100 miles of the **Lower Deschutes River** are part of the national wild and scenic river system. Starting in central Oregon's high desert at Pelton Regulating Dam, the river flows north into the Columbia River. People often float the Deschutes from Maupin, off Route 197. Rainbow trout, steelhead, and chinook salmon also make the river popular with fly-fishers.

A short drive east of Route 97 north of Redmond leads to the striking rock formations of **Smith Rock State Park❖,** which attract climbers from all over the world. The Crooked River flows below rose- and cream-colored pinnacles. Eagles soar overhead. A steep trail leads to views of the rocks, the Cascades, and the sagebrush and juniper of the high desert. One admirer calls the hike "beyond aerobic" but adds, "the view is truly awesome—even spiritual."

Farther south on Route 97, just beyond **Fort Rock State Park❖** (see Chapter 5), is an ancient Ice Age cave that once lay at lake level. Here archaeologists have found stone points and fragments that have been carbon-dated at an astonishing 13,200 years. Although that date is controversial, a pair of sagebrush-bark sandals from the cave has been more definitively dated at 9,050 years, and scientists believe that people inhabited the basin-and-range region at least 12,500 years ago. If someone really did live in it 13,200 years ago, the Fort Rock cave is the oldest archaeological site in the Northwest.

People have never been very plentiful in this landscape, but they have been part of it for a long time.

LEFT: *Cathedral Rock towers over an arid landscape where archaeologists have found fossil evidence of a damp subtropical environment.*
OVERLEAF: *Ripe for a Georgia O'Keeffe painting, brilliant reds and yellows splash themselves across the badlands at John Day's Painted Hills.*